American Elections
The Rules Matter

Robert L. Dudley
George Mason University

Alan R. Gitelson
Loyola University—Chicago

New York • Boston • San Francisco
London • Toronto • Sydney • Tokyo • Singapore • Madrid
Mexico City • Munich • Paris • Cape Town • Hong Kong • Montreal

Vice President/Publisher: Priscilla McGeehon
Senior Acquisitions Editor: Eric Stano
Senior Marketing Manager: Megan Galvin-Fak
Supplements Editor: Kelly Villella
Senior Production Manager: Eric Jorgensen
Project Coordination, Text Design, and Electronic Page Makeup:
         UG/GGS Information Services, Inc.
Cover Designer/Manager: Nancy Danahy
Cover Photos: Butterfly ballot © AP/Wide World Photos; President Harry Truman ©
         AP/Wide World Photos; Vice President Richard Nixon and Senator John F. Kennedy
         © AP/Wide World Photos; Candidates George Bush and Ronald Regan with former
         President Gerald Ford © AP/Wide World Photos; Ronald Regan © CORBIS;
         Candidate Bill Clinton and President George Bush © AP/Wide World Photos;
         Governor George W. Bush © Liaison Agency, Inc.
Manufacturing Buyer: Roy Pickering
Printer and Binder: The Maple-Vail Book Manufacturing Group
Cover Printer: Phoenix Color Corp.

Library of Congress Cataloging-in-Publication Data

Dudley, Robert L.
   American elections : the rules matter / Robert L. Dudley, Alan R. Gitelson.
      p. cm.
   Includes bibliographical references and index.
   ISBN 0-321-08684-8 (alk. paper)
      1. Elections—United States. 2. Campaign funds—United States.   I. Gitelson, Alan R. II.
Title.

JK 1976 .D83 2002
324.6'3'0973 dc21

                                                                    2001038522

Please visit our website at *http://www.ablongman.com*

ISBN 0-321-08684-8

1 2 3 4 5 6 7 8 9 10—MA—04 03 02 01

Contents

Chapter 3 ·· 61

The Money Constituency

Chapter 4 ·· 87

Campaigning to Election Day

Introduction

The Rules of Game and the 2000 Election

On the evening of November 7, 2000, millions of Americans turned on their televisions to watch the drama of another presidential election unfold. In an era of exit polling and computerized projections Americans have become used to learning the winner early in the evening. However, the 2000 election turned out to be (with apologies to Jerry Garcia) a long strange trip.

Initially, television reports conformed to the pattern: a winner declared before all the votes were counted. As the networks projected the winner in state after state, lighting up their big maps in alternating colors to signify the victor in each state, everything looked normal. On CBS, Dan Rather, referring to their projections, assured viewers that, "If we say somebody's carried the state, you can take that to the bank. Book it!" Thus, when just a few minutes before 8 P.M. Eastern time, the networks projected Al Gore the winner in Florida, he seemed on his way to winning a close election. As the evening wore on, however, network analysts began to worry about the Florida projection. Two hours after that first projection, one by one the network anchors announced that they were no longer projecting Gore as the winner in Florida. Instead, and with great fanfare, the color of Florida was changed and the anchors breathlessly announced that the state was "too close to call." Then, just after 2 A.M. Eastern time, the networks reversed even that call and projected George W. Bush the winner in Florida and in the electoral college vote.

Disheartened by the projection, Gore phoned Bush and offered his congratulations. An hour later, however, convinced by his advisors that the thousands of uncounted Florida votes would swing the state and thus the Electoral College his way, Gore called Bush again and retracted his concession. As strange as the evening was, Americans soon learned that the election was far from over. Since the fall, the candidates had battled each other across the country, state by state. On November 8, an entirely new campaign began, however. For the next 36 days the candidates and their organizations fought each other in the press and the courts. Between them, the candidates and their supporters filed more than 50 lawsuits, held countless press conferences, and deployed armies of workers to Florida to both protest and oversee vote recounts.

It wasn't until December 12, 2001, when the United States Supreme Court ordered an end to manual recounts of Florida votes, that Americans finally had a decision. The day after the Supreme Court announcement, Gore conceded and Bush called for national unity.

Throughout these 36 days, Americans learned more than they perhaps wanted to know about the way our elections are run. Indeed our vocabulary was enriched with terms such as undervote, overvote, chad (dimpled, pregnant, and swinging), and butterfly ballots. More importantly, however, the 2000 election demonstrated that there is no such thing as a national election. There are national candidates, but elections are primarily state and local affairs. The fact that a candidate could be elected without winning the popular vote brought home to many Americans the importance of winning states rather than popular votes. However, the focus on Florida also demonstrated the great variability across the country in the way Americans cast and count votes.

Disputes over counts and recounts also documented the fact that in addition to campaign activities and voters' decision-making processes, the rules matter. Elections are governed, at every stage, by a myriad of rules set by national political institutions, state laws, and even local ordinances.

Our interest here is the impact the rules have on not just the way campaigns are run, but on the choices offered voters. We argue that understanding elections requires more than knowledge of voting behavior and campaign tactics. Over the last several decades, political scientists have become extraordinarily adroit at understanding and explaining how voters make up their minds. Concepts such as partisan identification, issue space, and retrospective voting have become the coin of the realm in discussing electoral politics. Aided by vast improvements in polling technology, political scientists and political operatives have become very skillful at anticipating voter responses to issues and candidate characteristics. Flipped the other way, political scientists and practitioners have also become adept at using this information to make strategic choices in shaping campaigns. We contend, however, that this is only part of the story. To understand elections it is necessary to appreciate the variability and importance of the rules of the game. These complex sets of rules, which are applicable to any election campaign, determine who runs, how candidates campaign, what resources they can deploy, and which votes count. The choices that voters and candidates make are not simply exercises in selecting their preferences but responses to the rules of the game.

Plan of the Book

In Chapter 1 we begin by discussing the growth of the American electorate. Originally, states decided who voted. The states, and often local jurisdictions within the states, defined the extent of the franchise. Although suffrage was initially linked to some form of property requirement, by the late 1820s such restrictions on suffrage largely disappeared. Breaking the connection between voting and property was done state by state.

Other expansions of suffrage did not follow this model, however. The battles to enfranchise African Americans and women were resolved by actions of the national government—through the 15th and 19th Amendments respectively. State resistance to enfranchising African Americans also prompted the Voting Rights Act of 1965, which set severe limitations on the states' power to limit the franchise. Similarly, despite the traditional assumption of state power over suffrage, the national government, through the 26th Amendment, lowered the voting age to 18.

Each of these efforts represents a trend toward the nationalization of the electorate. But as we show in the chapter, the nationalization was far from complete. Even as the national government was expanding the franchise, most states were implementing registration systems that often served to deny suffrage to particular races or classes of people. As state registration requirements proliferated so too did the burdens placed on potential voters. Whether one could vote or not depended on meeting a series of registration requirements that varied dramatically from state to state. Although the people disadvantaged by registration requirements varied across the states, the often complicated process effectively reduced the pool of voters. In 1993, however, Congress passed the National voter Registration Act (NVRA) that made voter registration easier and, more importantly, uniform across the states.

The passage of the National Voter Registration Act would appear to have nationalized the franchise, but as we point out it is still incomplete. Voter registration is still administered by the states: there is no national voter registration, only procedures that all states must follow. The importance of this point was illustrated frequently by the 2000 election, which was ripe with reports of states ineffectively running the system. Individuals may, as the statute requires, be able to register when they acquire a drivers license but supervision of that process is still a state matter. Moreover, as we show there is still some variability in the breadth of the franchise across the states. For many people, it still holds true that whether they can vote depends upon where they live.

The second half of Chapter 1 concentrates on the construction of electoral districts. How many districts does a jurisdiction have? How large are the constituencies in these districts and how many representatives are elected from each district are decisions left to state and local governments. Although often wrapped in highly technical language these decisions define how much power individual voters have. The decision to rely on single-member districts using "first past the post" as opposed to multimember districts has, for instance, serious consequences for voters and candidates alike. Under the single-member system the seats-to-votes ratio problem becomes particularly acute. This multitude of decisions regarding apportionment and reapportionment in the final analysis define how voters' decisions are linked to representation.

In Chapter 2 we discuss the various ways in which candidates secure nomination for office. This chapter traces the evolution of nomination procedures as defined by state laws. We then discuss the use of primaries, caucuses, and conventions at the national, state, and local levels. Chapter 2 also discusses the nomination rules governing third parties and independent candidates. As is clear, the state laws controlling access to the general election ballot habitually place sizeable barriers to third parties and independent candidates. Obviously, the nomination stage determines who the candidates will be. However, nominations also set the tone for general elections and directly influence the issues discussed in the campaign. How states regulate this early stage of elections determines the choices available to voters.

It is often said that money is the mother's milk of politics. This may be an exaggeration, but it is true that campaigns are an increasingly expensive activity. Money does not guarantee victory, but a significant shortfall makes winning all but impossible. Chapter 3 analyzes the laws, rules, and regulations that govern the funding of campaigns at the national, state, and local levels. As we note, concerns about money in campaigns is not a recent phenomenon. To the contrary, campaign finance reform is an ongoing process, not a recent development. The difficulty with reform efforts is that they always have real consequences for candidates and interests. No system of campaign financing is neutral. The question to ask of reform efforts is: Who will be advantaged, or, conversely, who will be hurt by changes?

Chapter 4 takes us into the campaigning process itself. Although the goal of all political campaigns is the same—to win—the available strategies differ according to several factors. Many of these are defined by the candidate, but all campaigns take place against a complex set of laws and regulations that shape the strategic options available to the candidates. Candidates and potential candidates must, for instance, factor into their calculations the electoral calendar. Whether a potential candidate runs or not may be dictated by the other offices up for grabs that year. Crowded electoral calendars also limit the ability of some candidates to raise campaign funds and attract voters. As we also demonstrate, candidates must build into their strategies the national, state, and local laws that limit the reporting and spending of campaign money. The various laws limiting spending may, as is often the case, be avoided by legal maneuvers, but candidates must take these rules into account. Because some candidates are better positioned under the spending limits than others are, the regulation of campaign spending is not a neutral activity. We take a similar view of the interaction between candidates and the media. Modern campaigning is largely a media affair. These interactions are, however, regulated activities. Whether candidates receive sufficient exposure to be viable often depends on government regulations controlling media behavior.

Chapter 5 takes up the subject of casting and counting the votes. For most Americans, at least until 2000, this probably seemed an automatic process. We tended not to think about the structure of ballots and the operation of polling places. However, the various decisions that define the voting experience have consequences. The design of ballots and the medium used are, for instance, far from inconsequential in determining electoral outcomes. Candidates must adapt their campaigns to take into account voting mechanisms and even counting procedures. As we demonstrate, these choices effect voter turnout and the definition of a valid vote.

Finally, in Chapter 6 we discuss the special case of the electoral college. In and of itself, the electoral college is worthy of study, but we argue that it makes for an interesting case study. All of the elements discussed in the previous chapters come together in this unique selection system.

Acknowledgments

All authors incur debts to an uncountable number of people. We are no exception. Unfortunately we cannot express, in print, our gratitude to all of those who have, over the years, contributed to our understanding and sensibilities. Kevin Fullam, Alan's very able research assistant throughout the project, has been more help to us than he will ever know. For Bob Dudley, three great teachers, Craig Ducat, L. Douglas Dobson, and Kevin McKeough, made this book possible. Bob Dudley also owes a special gratitude, not to mention his life, to Dr. Stephen Boyce. We dedicate this book to Judith, Patrick, and Michael Dudley and Idy, Laura, and Rachel Gitelson. Your tolerance is amazing.

We would also like to thank the reviewers who provided valuable feedback on the manuscript in its various stages of development:

Amy E. Black—Wheaton College
Andrew E. Busch—University of Denver
Christian Goergen—College of DuPage
Susan Johnson—University of Wisconsin at Whitewater
John J. Klemanski—Oakland University
William J. Kubik—Hanover College
Russell A. Dondero—Pacific University
Shad Satterthwaite—University of Oklahoma
Todd M. Schaefer—Central Washington University
David J. Hadley—Wabash College
Jon R. Taylor—University of St. Thomas

Chapter 1
Defining the Electorate

entral to the design of any electoral system is the definition of the electorate. Who, among a nation's inhabitants, is to be enfranchised? What
are the requirements for voting? Traditionally, these questions were
decided by the states, with little involvement by the national government,
due to the American preference for a decentralized electoral system. Gradually, in fits and starts this has changed. Where once the balance of authority
in defining voters belonged with the states, it has now shifted. Replying to
calls for voting rights, the national government has extended the franchise.
In the process, the national government has extended its own power. So
great has been its reach that, with some minor exceptions, the 1990s marked
the completion of the construction of a national electorate. Yet different def-
initions of those eligible to vote remain and these differences have an impact
on elections.

Likewise, how those enfranchised individuals are to be apportioned for
representational purposes has long been a matter of state concern. Once
again, demands by aggrieved groups in American society have been heard and
responded to by the national government—often, although not exclusively,
by the U.S. Supreme Court. Supreme Court decisions and congressional
enactments have changed the landscape in this vital area also. But while the
national government has come to play a greater role in the apportionment
process, much remains in state hands. These state-level decisions regarding
the construction of voting districts and apportioning seats in state legislatures
as well Congress may appear purely technical, but they do much to define the
choices available to voters. They also determine the weight of individual
votes.

Expanding the Franchise

For most of our history, who could vote was decided by the individual states. There were no national standards, instead the right to vote was secured by state laws and each state developed its own prerequisites for voting. When the Constitution was drafted, the states were so reluctant to give a national government power to control elections that any attempt to enforce uniformity in voting requirements among states would have severely imperiled ratification.[1] Thus Article 1, Section 2 of the U.S. Constitution recognized the preeminent role of the states, even in congressional elections, by providing that, "The House of Representatives shall be composed of Members chosen every second Year by the People of the several States, and the Electors in each State shall have the Qualifications requisite for Electors of the most numerous Branch of the State Legislature."

Property and the Vote

The best known prerequisite for voting in early America was property ownership. Ten of the original thirteen states restricted the franchise to those who owned property. The remaining three states—New Hampshire, Pennsylvania, and Georgia—had no formal property requirement, but limited voting to taxpayers. (Of course, because taxes were assessed on property, limiting the vote to taxpayers was an indirect property requirement.) Limiting the franchise to men of property reflected a deep distrust of the people; a distrust typified by John Jay's observation that "the mass of men are neither wise nor good—those who own the country ought to govern it."[2] This distrust of the masses was not, however, universal. Benjamin Franklin, for instance, mocked the property requirements by noting:

> Today a man owns a jackass worth fifty dollars and he is entitled to vote; but before the next election the jackass dies. The man in the meantime has become more experienced, his knowledge of the principles of government, and his acquaintance with mankind, are more extensive, and he is therefore better qualified to make a proper selection of rulers—but the jackass is dead and the man cannot vote. Now gentlemen, pray inform me, in whom is the right of suffrage? In the man or in the jackass?[3]

Moreover, there is some evidence that property requirements may have been more apparent than real, because they were often ignored. Occasionally, the qualifications of voters were challenged, but colonials were often "ignorant or indifferent to the suffrage laws."[4]

Enforced or not, property qualifications for voting in state and national elections did not develop beyond the original thirteen states. Vermont, the fourteenth state admitted to the Union, was the first state to separate formally property and taxpaying from the right to vote and no subsequent state embraced a property qualification. Pressure from propertyless veterans and the egalitarian forces of the emerging western states produced an expanded electorate.

By the late 1820s, property and taxpaying qualifications for voting in national and statewide elections had largely disappeared. Universal white male suffrage had become the norm. (North Carolina, the last state to abandon property qualifications, did so in 1859.) Nevertheless, property qualifications in certain kinds of local elections remained common well into the mid-twentieth century.

For example, until 1969 when the U.S. Supreme Court declared the law unconstitutional, New York State specified that residents who were otherwise eligible to vote in state and federal elections could vote in school district elections only if they owned or leased taxable real property in the district or were the parents of children enrolled in the public schools.[5] The Supreme Court further curtailed property qualifications, in 1969 and 1970, when the justices ruled that Louisiana and Arizona laws restricting voting in municipal bond elections to property taxpayers violated the Fourteenth Amendment's guarantee of equal protection of the laws.[6]

Race and the Vote

Eliminating property requirements did not, of course, mean the establishment of universal suffrage or even universal male suffrage. Black males were still denied the right to vote, even in states that never permitted slavery. Indeed, as property requirements were lifted, several states rewrote their laws to deny the vote to blacks specifically. In the pre-Civil War era, only Massachusetts, New Hampshire, Vermont, Maine, Rhode Island, and New York allowed blacks to vote. (New York, while allowing blacks to vote, placed special property requirements on them; requirements not applied to white males.) Eventually, the legal barriers came down, but unlike the elimination of property requirements, enfranchisement of blacks required action by the national government. The traditional deference to state control over voter qualifications was supplanted by a series of national efforts.

First among these national endeavors was the Military Reconstruction Act of 1867. Congress, under the control of the Radical Republicans, used the Reconstruction Act to dictate suffrage requirements in the southern states. The act, for instance, barred Confederate leaders from holding office and coerced ratification of the Fourteenth Amendment by the rebellious states. Furthermore, each Confederate state was required to draft and ratify a new constitution, one approved by Congress and one which guaranteed the right to vote to all freedmen—including the recently freed slaves. Because these mandates applied only to the Confederate states, they did not comprise a national standard. Indeed, at the end of the Civil War eighteen northern and western states denied black citizens the right to vote.[7] The Reconstruction Act was only a prelude, however. A year later, the states ratified the Fourteenth Amendment which, in Section 2, empowered Congress to reduce congressional representation of states that denied the franchise to *any* male citizen twenty-one years of age. Then in 1870 the states ratified the Fifteenth Amendment, which guarantees that "the right of citizens of the United States to vote shall not be denied or abridged by the United States or by any state on account of race, color, or previous condition of servitude." With this amendment, Congress, at least in a limited sphere, clearly established a national power to fashion voting qualifications. Moreover, for a short period it seemed to work.

From the end of the Civil War to the turn of the century, black males were, in most jurisdictions, broadly enfranchised. The turn of the century appearance of "Jim Crow" laws stripped black males of their voting rights, however.[8] Throughout the South, state governments established a wide array of legal devices aimed at keeping blacks out of the voting booth. Typically, states required the passage of some highly subjective literacy test or some version of a constitutional-understanding examination. Applicants might, for example, be asked to demonstrate that they were literate by reading and then explaining the meaning of some provision of the Constitution. Election officials were given complete discretion in determining the level of difficulty presented by the passage selected, as well the authority to proclaim the "correct" interpretation of the constitutional clause unilaterally. Moreover, the election officials were generally barred from explaining why the applicant failed, because this could be viewed as helping the applicant. Under these conditions rejecting an applicant was an easy matter, as the U.S. Civil Rights Commission documented in 1959 when it noted that in one Mississippi city where no whites had ever failed the literacy exam, five black teachers, three of whom had master's degrees, were declared illiterate.[9] Many states also used a "good character" requirement. This meant that the would-be-voter had to provide a registered voter who would vouch for the applicant's good moral character. Additionally, several states instituted poll taxes in an effort to disenfranchise poor blacks.

As daunting as these requirements were, they were often supplemented by an absolute ban on black participation in primaries. Under the theory that political parties were private clubs and that their primaries were not part of any official election process, several states adopted all-white primaries. In the one-party states of the South, barring blacks from participation in the Democratic party primary was tantamount to a denial of the right to vote.

In the final analysis these inventive efforts to purge black voters, combined, at times, with intimidation and violence, were incredibly effective. In 1896, for example, there were 130,334 registered black voters in Louisiana; eight years later only 1,342 remained on the rolls.[10] Similarly, in 1961, the Civil Rights Commission pointed out that in seventeen representative counties in the South where blacks constituted a majority of the population, registration rates for blacks ran about 3 percent.

Giving reality to the promise of the Fifteenth Amendment was slow in coming for disenfranchised blacks. It took over twenty-five years of legal struggle before the U.S. Supreme Court finally outlawed the white primaries.[11] Likewise, efforts to ban the poll tax began in the early 1940s but did not prove fruitful until 1962 when the Twenty-fourth Amendment was finally ratified.[12] In both 1957 and 1960 Congress passed sweeping but ineffectual civil rights acts aimed primarily at enfranchising blacks. Finally, Congress passed the Voting Rights Act of 1965.

This momentous effort to curb electoral discrimination constitutes an extraordinary nationalization of the electoral process. Through the Voting Rights Act of 1965 Congress clearly proclaimed that "no voting qualification or prerequisite to voting" was permissible if it worked to deny or abridge the right to vote on account of race or color. Thus, the use of devices such as literacy tests, constitutional-interpretation requirements, and "good character" tests was singled out by the act as potentially discriminatory. The remedial aspects of the act applied to any state or subdivision found by the Department of Justice to have maintained a test or device as a prerequisite to voting on November 1, 1964 and which was determined by the Director of the Census to have less than 50 percent of its voting-age population registered or voting in the 1964 election. Six southern states were covered by the act: Alabama, Georgia, Louisiana, Mississippi, South Carolina, and Virginia. Additionally, the state of Alaska and twenty-six counties in North Carolina were targeted by the act. On the other hand, because they did not use any of the suspect devices as qualifications for voting, Arkansas, Texas, and Florida escaped coverage even though they exhibited voter turnout below 50 percent.

In those states and subdivisions covered by the act, all suspect tests and devices for voter qualification were automatically suspended and the national government was empowered to appoint voting registrars to conduct registration drives. Moreover, under Section 5 of the act, the identified states and subdivisions are required to secure permission from the Attorney General of the United States or the U.S. District Court for the District of Columbia before making any changes to their electoral laws.

Clearly the Voting Rights Act of 1965 redefined the national government's role in setting voter qualifications. In the cause of combatting racial discrimination, the national government exerted significant powers traditionally belonging to the states and thereby significantly nationalized the electoral process. But the act did have a dramatic impact on the makeup of the electorate. Following passage of the Voting Rights Act the black electorate grew by 11 percent in 1966 and another 8 percent was added over the next two years.[13] Between 1965 and 1972 the proportion of blacks registered to vote in states covered by the act increased from 29.3 percent to 56.6 percent. Even more notable was the declining gap between the proportion of white and black voting-age residents registered to vote which, during these years, fell from 41.1 percent to 11.2 percent.[14]

Initially the Voting Rights Act was to have a five-year life span, but in 1970 it was extended for another five years. The 1970 extension revised the formula for coverage, thereby bringing more states under its provisions and making the suspension of literacy tests nationwide. In 1975 the act was again renewed, this time for seven years. The 1975 extension permanently banned literacy tests in all states. More consequential, however, were the changes in the act that expanded coverage to states where Spanish, Asian, Indian, and Alaska languages and dialects were spoken by significant numbers of people. The new act required the distribution of bilingual voting information and provided for federal registrars in states and subdivisions where less than 50 percent of the language minorities registered to vote in 1972. Finally, in 1982 the act was extended for twenty-five years, with the stipulation that states and subdivisions previously covered could "bail out." Any state or subdivision that can prove that it has not discriminated for ten years and can further document positive steps that it has taken to promote minority voting can be released from the preclearance procedures of Section 5.

Women and the Vote

Originally the colonies did not specifically exclude women from voting because it seemed, at least to men, implausible that they would even want the franchise. It is true, however, that in the eighteenth century various local governments tolerated voting by prominent women in the community, much the way property requirements were often ignored. Nevertheless, by the end of the first decade of the nineteenth century every state had expressly outlawed women's suffrage.

Although a women's suffrage movement predated the Civil War, indeed it was strongly tied to the abolitionist effort, women did not benefit from the national government's postwar interest in voting rights. Prior to the war, several prominent abolitionists pledged their support to the cause of women's suffrage, but in the end these same abolitionists abandoned the women's cause. Fearing that the issue of women's suffrage would jeopardize support for black enfranchisement, abolitionist leaders such as Horace Greeley, Frederick Douglass, and Wendell Phillips cautioned restraint in seeking voting rights for women. It was, they often said, the "Negro's hour."[15] Much to the dismay of many of the suffrage movement's leaders, neither the Fourteenth nor the Fifteenth Amendments addressed the voting status of women. Still the post–Civil War era offered some hope for women in the form of the western territories.

The Wyoming territory first granted women the right to vote in 1869.[16] When, in 1890, Wyoming's petition for statehood was attacked in Congress for what some called its "petticoat provision," the territory's legislature is reported to have responded that it would stay out of the Union a hundred years rather than enter without women's suffrage.[17] Whether this story of legislative defiance is true or apocryphal is inconsequential, the fact that Wyoming was the first of what was to be a string of western states enfranchising women is of great import. Indeed, led by the western states, more than one-half of the states in the Union had granted women the right to vote by the end of World War I. Of course, these were for the most part sparsely populated states. As of 1915, only 17 percent of the population lived in states granting women the right to vote and there was little indication that the older states intended to embrace women's suffrage. Clearly, the right of women to vote was not going to be achieved state by state. National action was needed, but this meant overcoming powerfully entrenched opposition. Arrayed against women's voting rights were the southern states, where women's suffrage was still equated with abolitionist sentiments. America's corporate interests also lined up against granting women the right to vote fearing the enfranchisement of huge numbers of working-class women. Finally, the close association of women with the temperance movement provoked strong opposition from the nation's breweries.

Overcoming these powerful interests required great political skill and courage; for in the end the cause was won by a combination of political maneuvering and civil disobedience. But success did come. In 1920 Tennessee, by one vote, ensured ratification of the Nineteenth Amendment, which stated simply, "The right of citizens of the United States to vote shall not be denied or abridged by the United States or by any State on account of sex." Once again, Congress amended the Constitution to nationalize voter qualifications.

A Uniform Voting Age

The long struggles to win voting rights for blacks and women contrast starkly with the swift and only moderately controversial action enfranchising eighteen year olds. Until 1943, when Georgia lowered its voting age to eighteen, all states set the minimum voting age as twenty-one. Later Kentucky followed suit, and at the time of their admission to statehood, Alaska and Hawaii allowed voting at nineteen and twenty, respectively. This all changed in 1970 when Congress, apparently persuaded by the argument that if young men were old enough to fight a war in Vietnam they were old enough to vote, included provisions in the Voting Rights Act granting eighteen year olds the vote in all federal and state elections.[18] That same year, however, the U.S. Supreme Court struck down that portion of the law that applied to state elections. The badly divided Court argued that Congress could legislate with regard to presidential and congressional elections, but not in elections for state offices.[19] Consequently, Congress immediately proposed the Twenty-sixth Amendment to overrule the Supreme Court with regard to state elections. In the well-practiced language of the Nineteenth and before that the Fifteenth Amendment, the Twenty-sixth Amendment states simply, "The right of citizens of the United States, who are eighteen years of age or older, to vote shall not be denied or abridged by the United States or by any State on account of age." Two months and seven days after it was proposed, the amendment was ratified by the requisite number of states and some 11 million young people in fifty states were enfranchised by order of the U.S. Constitution.

Registration

During the twentieth century the most important factor in defining the electorate has been the existence of voter registration systems. Each state created its own system with its own registration requirements, so that even as portions of the population were seemingly enfranchised by constitutional amendments, they were still left to the vagaries of the state registration laws. In 1800 Massachusetts became the first state to require personal registration prior to voting, but until the late nineteenth century, few states adopted the innovation. Then at the end of the century, during the so-called Gilded Age, personal voter registration requirements became a favorite reform of the Progressive movement. The Gilded Age has long been characterized as a period of rampant electoral corruption, coercion, bribery, and fraud.[20] Reform groups of the period pushed for detailed registration qualifications as a means of cleaning up elections and making it "more difficult for the few and easier for the many" to control government.[21] That political machines dominated the political landscape was for the Progressives proof that democracy was imperiled. For the most militant reformers, democracy was threatened by "an ignorant proletariat" led by a "half-taught plutocracy."[22] Personal registration by eliminating the unfit, the ignorant, and the easily corrupted voters would, the Progressives argued, break the back of the political machines and return power to the people. In the North, registration schemes were generally aimed at lessening the impact of recently arrived immigrants.

It was, however, southern states, desirous of disenfranchising blacks, that were among the first to implement voter registration qualifications—qualifications that the overwhelming number of black citizens were unable to meet. By using stringent but seemingly neutral registration qualifications (e.g., literacy tests, good character requirements), southern states deprived blacks of their right to vote while appearing to comply with the Fifteenth Amendment.[23] The effects of voter registration laws were not limited to the South, however. Throughout the nation evolving complex registration requirements constricted the electorate and—intentionally or unintentionally—undermined universal male suffrage across the nation.[24] This spread of personal registration requirements, many believe, explains the marked decline in voter participation that began about the same time.[25]

As state registration requirements proliferated, the American electoral system increasingly placed substantial burdens on many otherwise eligible voters. In most democratic nations the government assumes the responsibility for registering voters, but the American system placed the obligation on the individual.

Putting the burden of registering on the individual, rather than government, has long been considered a leading cause of low voting rates in the United States. Indeed, this view dates at least to 1930 when Harold Gosnell concluded a comparative study of European and American voting systems by noting:

> In the European countries studied, a citizen who is entitled to vote does not, as a rule, have to make any effort to see that his name is on the list of eligible voters. The inconvenience of registering for voting in this country has caused many citizens to become non-voters.[26]

But there is more to it than simply shifting the burden. Although all registration laws are burdensome, some are more so than others. Residency requirements, for instance, have, depending on length, the potential to disenfranchise millions every election. In a society as mobile as ours, a residency requirement of even a few weeks will always disenfranchise some otherwise qualified people. But a residency requirement of a few months greatly reduces the size of the electorate. As late as the 1960s, thirty-eight states required at least a year's residence in the state before one could register—a few states required two years' residence. In the 1970 renewal of the Voting Rights Act, Congress imposed a maximum thirty-day residency requirement for voting in presidential elections. Furthermore, the act permitted those recently relocated to a new state to vote (in the presidential election) in their former state—either in person or by absentee ballot. Longer residency requirements also came under scrutiny in the Supreme Court's decision in *Dunn v. Blumstein*.[27] Here the Court concluded that excessive residency requirements unconstitutionally impeded the constitutionally protected rights to vote and to travel. Although the Court did not define excessive, Justice Thurgood Marshall opined, "30 days appears to be an ample period for the state to complete whatever administrative tasks are necessary to prevent fraud."[28]

State laws can also dampen voting rates by making the registration process exceedingly inconvenient. For example, statutes limiting registration activities to the county seat and then only during normal business hours created a substantial obstacle to those who could not afford to miss work. Some states remedied this problem by deputizing volunteers to conduct voter registration drives, establishing satellite sites for registration, or extending office hours into the evening and on weekends. But these voter registration outreach efforts were generally the exception, not the rule. Moreover, most states left these options open to the discretion of local governments. Thus broad differences in registration systems were characteristic not just across states, but within states. Similarly, state laws with early closing dates—that is, the last day one can register before an election—have an obvious effect on turnout. Early closing dates force people to decide if they are going to vote before the election campaign peaks. At the other end of the process, state policies on purging the rolls of nonvoters discourage those who are not habitual voters by forcing them to re-register.

The consequence of these complex registration systems, most political scientists agreed, was lower voter participation. Raymond Wolfinger and Steven Rosenstone, for instance, estimated that "If every state had had registration laws in 1972 as permissive as those in the most permissive states, turnout would have been about 9 percentage point higher in the presidential election."[29] Likewise, Ruy Teixeira argued that significant registration reform could increase voter turnout by about 8 percent.[30] Moreover, the highly decentralized nature of registration was said to be the cause of regional differences in voter turnout, because as the authors of a major study examining voting in 104 U.S. cities concluded, "Local differences in the turnout for elections are to a large extent related to local differences in rates of registration, and these in turn reflect to a considerable degree local differences in the rules governing, and arrangements for handling, the registering of voters."[31]

In 1971, 1973, 1975, and 1976, bills calling for a national postcard registration system were introduced in Congress only to be blocked by a coalition of Republicans and southern Democrats who feared an increase in liberal voters. President Jimmy Carter's 1976 legislation proposing universal election day registration met a similar fate. Interestingly, among political scientists the consensus was that registration reform, while increasing the number of voters, would not significantly alter the ideological or partisan predisposition of the electorate. Thus Ruy Teixeira confidently predicted that "registration reform, under virtually any conceivable scenario, will have negligible partisan impact. The Democrats will not be significantly helped, and the Republicans will not be significantly hurt."[32] Nevertheless, reform continued to generate substantial partisan opposition—as President George Bush's veto of the 1992 "motor voter" law demonstrated. The opposition failed in 1993, however, leading to the passage of the National Voter Registration Act (NVRA). Calling the previous registration systems unfair and discriminatory, Congress in the NVRA declared that "it is the duty of the Federal, State and local governments to promote the exercise" of the right to vote. To this end the act requires states to adopt uniform voter registration procedures for the election of all federal officers.[33] (Federal officers are defined in the statute as senators, representatives, the president, and the vice-president.) States must take all necessary steps, including amending their constitutions, to implement the law's provisions. Although supposedly applicable only to federal elections, NVRA, in practice, dictates the procedures for all elections because no states separate registration for federal elections from state and local contests. (Both Mississippi and Illinois tried this for a short time, but they have acceded to the spirit of NVRA and now have only the single registration process.)

Under the NVRA, states must allow citizens to register to vote by mail and must accept a universal mail-in form, The National Mail Voter Registration Form, designed by the Federal Election Commission (FEC). Still as Table 1.1 shows, the states do not have a uniform deadline for voter registration, as the act does not require it.

That portion of the act known as the "motor voter" provision requires states to incorporate voter registration into the process of applying for or renewing a driver's license. An application for or a renewal of a driver's license serves as an application for voter registration unless the applicant fails to sign the voter registration portion of the form. But it is not just offices of motor vehicles that must provide the opportunity to register; any office dispensing public assistance (e.g., Food Stamps or Medicaid) must make registration forms available.

NVRA provides detailed regulations governing the purging of voter rolls by states, but the most important limitation on the states is the prohibition against removing individuals from the voting list simply for not voting. Finally, the act specifies that the cut-off date for voter registration can be no longer than thirty days before the election.

TABLE 1.1   Deadlines for Voter Registration, State by State

State	Registration Deadline	State	Registration Deadline
Alabama	10 days prior to election	Missouri	by the 4th Wednesday prior to election
Alaska	30 days prior to election	Montana	30 days prior to election
Arizona	29 days prior to election	Nebraska	30 days prior to election by mail or by the second Friday prior to election in person
Arkansas	30 days prior to election	Nevada	by the 5th Saturday prior to primary or general election; by the 3rd Saturday prior to recall or special election
California	29 days prior to election	New Hampshire	10 days prior to election
Colorado	29 days prior to election	New Jersey	29 days prior to election
Connecticut	14 days prior to election	New Mexico	28 days prior to election
Delaware	20 days prior to election	New York	25 days prior to election
District of Columbia	postmarked 30 days prior to election	North Carolina	25 days prior to election
Florida	29 days prior to election	North Dakota	no registration requirement
Georgia	30 days prior to election	Ohio	30 days prior to election
Hawaii	30 days prior to election	Oklahoma	25 days prior to election
Idaho	30 days prior to election by mail or 15 days prior to election if in person	Oregon	21 days prior to election
Illinois	28 days prior to election	Pennsylvania	30 days prior to election
Indiana	30 days prior to election	Rhode Island	30 days prior to election
Iowa	10 days prior to election	South Carolina	30 days prior to election
Kansas	14 days prior to election	South Dakota	15 days prior to election
Kentucky	28 days prior to election	Tennessee	30 days prior to election
Louisiana	24 days prior to election	Texas	30 days prior to election
Maine	15 days prior to election by mail or application can be delivered in person up to and including election day	Utah	20 days prior to election
Maryland	30 days prior to election	Vermont	second Saturday prior to election
Massachusetts	20 days prior to election	Virginia	29 days prior to general or primary election; 13 days prior to special election
Michigan	30 days prior to election	Washington	30 days by mail prior to election; 15 days prior to election if delivered by hand
Minnesota	20 days prior to election or at polling place the day of election	West Virginia	30 days prior to election
Mississippi	30 days prior to election	Wisconsin	election day, there is no registration in communities under 5,000
		Wyoming	30 days prior to election

The sweep of the NVRA is, given the long struggle for voting rights, stagger-ing. In ten admittedly complex sections the act managed, for all intents and pur-poses, to define a national electorate. What was once almost purely a state mat-ter has become nationalized. If, however, the goal was to register more people, the act worked. According to the FEC, states reported for 1996 (the first election following full implementation of the act) a total of 142,995,856 registered voters. This means that 72.77 percent of the voting age population was registered to vote in 1996; the highest percentage of voter registration since reliable records began in 1960. The percent of voters registered since 1996 has declined slightly.

If, however, the goal of NVRA was to increase voter turnout, the results are less encouraging. Again, according to the FEC, the percentage of Americans vot-ing in 1996 declined by more than 5 percent from 1992. This was the first time since 1972—the first election in which eighteen year olds were enfranchised—that voter registration rose and turnout declined. This tracks with a handful of studies that have cast doubt on motor voter laws as an effective means of increasing turnout.[34] Still there is some evidence that the procedures inherent in the NVRA may over the long term increase not just registration, but turnout. Looking at states that had adopted motor voter procedures prior to the passage of NVRA, Stephen Knack argues that turnout increases substantially but only over the course of time. According to Knack, motor voter's effect on turnout is substantial but builds to a peak at about the fifth election following the proce-dure's implementation.[35]

An alternative to NVRA some states utilize is election day registration (EDR). Would-be voters may register prior to the election or they may do so the day of the election. Although NVRA's impact on turnout remains in doubt, scholars generally agree that election day registration increases turnout. The latest esti-mates, which include those states that instituted EDR in 1994 as a way to opt out of NVRA, project as much as a 6 percent increase in turnout as a result of election day registration.[36]

Whether NVRA or EDR will have long-term consequences for turnout nation-wide remains to be seen. Careful studies of the 2000 election should answer many questions. Still, anecdotal evidence shows that easier registration proce-dures can have an impact on particular elections. Illustrative of this is the 1998 election of Jesse (The Body) Ventura to the Minnesota governorship. Through-out the campaign, Ventura trailed his opponents substantially. The last polls before election day showed him well behind, but gaining. Ventura's surprising victory was, at least in part, the result of an increased voter turnout particularly among first-time voters. Thousands of unregistered voters marched to the polls on election day, registered, and cast their ballots for Ventura. This late surge of support for Ventura would have been considerably weaker had Minnesota not provided for EDR. Those unregistered Ventura supporters who decided late in the campaign would have been barred from voting under, say, a thirty-day cut-off rule common in most states. Jesse (the Body) became Jesse (the Mind), at least in part because of EDR.

Remaining Differences

As encompassing as the NVRA's nationalization of the registration process is, dif-ferences among the states remain. States certainly play a diminished role, but they have not become irrelevant to the process of defining voters. It is, for example, still a matter of state law whether a convicted criminal can register to vote (see Table 1.2 on page 14). Although disenfranchising criminals has a long history dating back to Greek and Roman traditions and carried to the United States in common law, historically states have implemented the ban differently.

Like the registration process itself, the practice of banning criminals from the voting booth was honed by southern states in the latter half of the nineteenth century as a way to disenfranchise blacks. Following the example set by Mississippi, southern states tailored the criminal disenfranchisement provisions to crimes that legislators thought blacks more likely than whites to commit—or more truly, crimes that blacks were more likely to be convicted of committing.[37] This often meant that criminal disenfranchisement attached only to cases of petty crimes; crimes for which false, malicious, and selective prosecutions could easily occur. Thus while conviction for vagrancy might result in a permanent ban on voting, a conviction for murder, in the same state, often carried no such disability. Not until 1985, in *Hunter v. Underwood*[38] did the U.S. Supreme Court rule that such blatant practices, if adopted with racially discriminatory intent, violate the Constitution. The plaintiffs in this suit had been prohibited from registering to vote in Alabama because they had been convicted of presenting a worthless check, a misdemeanor. Here the Court was able to cite ample evidence of intent to discriminate on the basis of race. Indeed one delegate to the Alabama Constitutional Convention that framed the criminal disenfranchisement provision noted that "everybody knows that this Convention has done its best to disenfranchise the Negro in Alabama."[39]

In general the Supreme Court has been supportive of criminal disenfranchisement rules, questioning them only if they appear to be racially motivated. Rather than violating the Fourteenth Amendment's equal protection clause, Chief Justice William Rehnquist has written that criminal disenfranchisement is permissible under the little used Section 2 of that Amendment. Section 2, the Chief Justice argued, implies that states possess the prerogative to deny the right to vote "for participation in rebellion or other crime."[40] It is, the Court ruled, up to the states to define "other crime."

Currently only three states—Maine, New Hampshire, and Vermont—allow prison inmates to vote. In the remaining states and the District of Columbia, felons are prohibited from voting while in prison. Further, thirty-two states prohibit offenders from voting while on parole and twenty-nine states bar voting by those on probation. More drastic still are those fourteen states that impose a permanent ban on convicted felons. Whether or not a convicted criminal votes depends less on the nature of the crime—disenfranchisement is now largely confined to felony offences—than on the state of residence.

In the nation at large, criminal disenfranchisement makes only a small difference in the number of eligible voters. It is estimated that a mere 2 percent of all adults are ineligible to vote in any given election because of their criminal status. Nevertheless, changing criminal disenfranchisement laws has become a priority of several groups—particularly civil rights organizations. Owing largely to the crackdown on drug possession that began in the 1980s, the American prison population has been soaring for two decades. Moreover, the proportion of black men incarcerated has, during this period, increased ten times faster than for whites. Nationally, approximately 13 percent of African-American men are ineligible to vote because of criminal conviction, but in some states the number barred from voting is considerably higher. In Florida, where a felony conviction results in a lifetime ban on voting, it is estimated that 31 percent of the state's black men are barred from voting. Similarly in Texas, an estimated 4.5 percent of the adult population and a full 21 percent of the African-American male population are disenfranchised because of a criminal conviction. It is these rising numbers that have given birth to several reform efforts. Bills restoring voting rights to criminals have, in recent years, been introduced in several states, but they face an uphill battle. Legislators do not want to appear soft on crime, and Republicans have little incentive to enfranchise a group of voters they believe more likely to vote Democratic.

Another group of citizens denied the right to vote by some states are those judged mentally disabled. Until recently, nearly every state prohibited what were often referred to as "mental incompetents" from voting. Either in constitutional provisions or statutory language, almost all states banned voting by people who were variously labeled insane or of unsound mind. Currently, eight states have no provisions disenfranchising those with a mental disability of any kind. The remaining states and the District of Columbia ban voting by people who have been placed under court-ordered guardianship or been judged to be mentally incompetent.

A final difference in registration procedures that is still practiced entails the selection of a party affiliation. Twenty-eight states and the District of Columbia utilize some form of partisan system, whereby individuals are asked to state a partisan choice when they register. Of course, it is always possible in these states to register as unaffiliated or as an independent. There may be costs in doing so, however. Either through state law or party rules, participation in a party's primary or caucus may be limited to those who are registered as members of the party. But even here there is a great deal of variability across the states.

The majority of states with partisan registration systems restrict participation in the primaries and caucuses to party members, but there are several alternative formulations of the rules. In Colorado, Kansas, Maine, New Hampshire, and Rhode Island, those registered as independents may participate in a party primary, but they are then automatically registered as members of the party in which they cast a primary ballot. On the other hand, in Oklahoma and Oregon, either party may, if it chooses, open its primary to independents. In North Carolina and West Virginia, the Democratic primary is open only to registered Democrats, while the Republican primary is open to those registered as unaffiliated as well as Republicans. Iowa limits participation in the caucuses to registered party members, but registration can take place as late as caucus night. Under the statutes of Massachusetts, a nonenrolled voter (one who has registered as unaffiliated) may, on primary election day, show up at the polling place, formally declare a party affiliation, vote, and then lawfully change affiliation back to nonenrollment. Most unusual in the party registration states is perhaps Ohio, which allows any registered voter to vote in either the Democratic or Republican primary, but which keeps local lists of individuals and their voting history and requires crossover voters to sign a form. States without a party registration system allow voters to participate in the primary of their choice. All that is, except Hawaii. There is no formal partisan registration in Hawaii, but there are procedures for becoming what are called "card-carrying" members of the two major parties. Only "card- carrying" members may participate in the precinct caucuses. Because the two major parties combined have only about

	Disenfranchised While in Prison	Disenfranchised While on Probation	Disenfranchised While on Parole	Disenfranchises All Ex-Felons
TABLE 1.2 Felony Disenfranchisement Laws of the States				
State				
Alabama	X	X	X	X
Alaska	X	X	X	
Arizona	X	X	X	X (after 2nd felony conviction)
Arkansas	X	X	X	
California	X		X	
Colorado	X		X	
Connecticut	X	X	X	
Delaware	X	X	X	X
District of Columbia	X			
Florida	X	X	X	X
Georgia	X	X	X	
Hawaii	X			
Idaho	X			
Illinois	X			
Indiana	X			
Iowa	X	X	X	X
Kansas	X			
Kentucky	X	X	X	X
Louisiana	X			
Maine				
Maryland	X	X	X	X (after 2nd felony conviction)
Massachusetts	X			
Michigan	X			
Minnesota	X	X	X	
Mississippi	X	X	X	
Missouri	X	X	X	

SOURCE: "Losing the Vote: The Impact of Felony Disenfranchisement Laws in the United States," The Sentencing Project. 1998. Updated by authors.

43,000 "card-carrying" members, just over 8 percent of Hawaii's registered voters are eligible to participate in the precinct caucuses.

Apportionment and Districting

A second set of vital functions performed by electoral laws is to define the electoral districts of a political system. Electoral districts are those political units that translate voting returns into legislative seats. (These should not be confused with voting districts, like the local precinct, where votes are tabulated and tallied but no allocation of seats takes place.)[41] Most often, electoral districts are,

	Disenfranchised While in Prison	Disenfranchised While on Probation	Disenfranchised While on Parole	Disenfranchises All Ex-Felons
State				

TABLE 1.2   Continued

State	Disenfranchised While in Prison	Disenfranchised While on Probation	Disenfranchised While on Parole	Disenfranchises All Ex-Felons
Montana	X			
Nebraska	X	X	X	
Nevada	X	X	X	X
New Hampshire	X			
New Jersey	X	X	X	
New Mexico	X	X	X	X
New York	X		X	
North Carolina	X	X	X	
North Dakota	X			
Ohio	X			
Oklahoma	X	X	X	
Oregon	X			
Pennsylvania	X			
Rhode Island	X	X	X	
South Carolina	X	X	X	
South Dakota	X			
Tennessee	X	X	X	X (pre-1986)
Texas	X	X	X	X (for two years after completion of sentence, probation, or parole)
Utah				
Vermont				
Virginia	X	X	X	X
Washington	X	X	X	X (pre-1984)
West Virginia	X	X	X	
Wisconsin	X	X	X	
Wyoming	X	X	X	X

as in the United States, geographically based, but that need not be the case. Electoral districts may defined by other characteristics, such as ethnicity. New Zealand, for instance, utilizes districts that are both geographically and ethnically defined.[42] Again what delineates an electoral district is that the vote totals are converted into seats.

Electoral districts may also be distinguished by their magnitude; that is, by the number of seats in a district. Depending on their magnitude districts may be "single-member districts" or "multimember districts." The criterion is simply the number of seats assigned to the district; anything greater than one is a "multimember district." Additionally, seats may be awarded to plurality winners, a system sometimes known as first-past-the-post, or by the utilization of some version of proportional representation—whereby seats are assigned to party candidates in proportion to the percentage of the vote that the party received in the election. Most, indeed the substantial majority, of elections in the United States occur in single-member electoral districts using the first-past-the-post requirement, but several other alternatives are or have been used.

Considerations as to the size, form, and characteristics of electoral districts are the result of deliberate decisions made by national, state, and local governments. Most of these decisions rest with state governments, but there are some national government constraints on the process of formulating electoral districts.

Apportioning Seats

If we consider the issue of electoral districts in the context of filling legislative seats, the initial question is: How many electoral districts should a jurisdiction (e.g., nation, state) have? Unfortunately, there is no easy answer. Many people assume that small (in population) electoral districts are best. After all, the smaller the district, the closer the link between constituents and legislators. The problem is that, in heavily populated jurisdictions, small electoral districts can be accomplished only by creating a larger number of legislative seats. Increasing the size of a legislative body lessens its ability to act, however. At some point a legislative body can become so large that it no longer fulfills its policy-making function. The question then turns on the balancing of competing values—representation versus institutional capacity.

For the U.S. House of Representative, the question of size was not resolved until 1910. Article I, Section 2, Clause 3 of the Constitution apportioned the first House of Representatives. Following the 1790 census Congress set the membership of the House at 105, with each state allocated one for every 33,000 inhabitants. After this initial apportioning, the size of the House continued to grow with each decennial census. As new states were added and populations shifted, Congress avoided the politically charged task of reducing any state's representation by simply adding new seats. Eventually the growth of the House threatened to overwhelm its capacity to act, and in 1910, Congress set the maximum size of the House at 435.

Setting a ceiling for House membership did not, however, resolve the question of how many seats to allocate to each state. Apportioning the 435 seats among the states is far from straightforward. Always a controversial point, Congress has, over the years, used five different methods of calculating each state's share. The problem is what to do with the fractions. Dividing the nation's total population by 435 produces the optimal district size, but unfortunately state populations do not come in multiples of this number. Since 1950, Congress has used a complex method known as the Huntingdon system. This complicated system starts by awarding each state one representative. The remaining 385 seats are assigned based on a priority value computed by multiplying the population of a state by a multiplier. The multiplier is calculated by using the formula for the reciprocal geometric mean: 1 divided by the square root of $n(n-1)$, where n is the number of seats a state would have if it gained a seat. Thus the multiplier for the 51st seat is 1 divided by the square root of $2(2-1)$, or .707. This number is then multiplied by each state's population, and the state with the highest product (priority value) is assigned the seat. The procedure is then repeated for the each seat until all 435 seats have been assigned.[43]

Although most seem content with the system, it does appear to have a slight bias toward the small states. Reverting to other previously used methods gives, in each case, slightly different results that generally favor the larger states.[44] The Huntingdon system is also very sensitive to small population changes. Following the 2000 census, for instance, a seat in the U.S. House of Representatives turned on a Census Bureau decision not to count some 14,000 U.S. citizens temporarily abroad serving as missionaries for the Church of the Latter Day Saints. Utah officials protested the failure to count those on mission, noting that including them would entitle the state to another representative. Instead the seat went to North Carolina.

In the final analysis there is no single way of apportioning the seats, and none would change the fact that in recent years each reapportionment has shifted congressional seats and thus electoral votes to the South and West (see Table 1.3). These so-called Sunbelt states have been gaining population and thus seats, while the northeastern and midwestern states have suffered losses.

No matter what system is used to apportion seats it cannot eliminate across-state variations. As long as state boundaries are to be respected and as long as each state is guaranteed at least one representative, inequality across states will

TABLE 1.3   States Gaining or Losing U.S. House Seats as Result of 2000 Census

State	Number of House Seats, 1990	Number of House Seats, after 2000 CENSUS	Change
States Gaining Seats			
Arizona	6	8	+2
California	52	53	+1
Colorado	6	7	+1
Florida	23	25	+2
Georgia	11	13	+2
Nevada	2	3	+1
North Carolina	12	13	+1
Texas	30	32	+2

State	Number of House Seats, 1990	Number of House Seats, after 2000 CENSUS	Change
States Losing Seats			
Connecticut	6	5	−1
Illinois	20	19	−1
Indiana	10	9	−1
Michigan	16	15	−1
Minnesota	5	4	−1
New York	31	29	−2
Ohio	19	18	−1
Oklahoma	6	5	−1
Pennsylvania	21	19	−2
Wisconsin	9	8	−1

TABLE 1.4	State Legislative Seats and Average Constituency Size			

	House		Senate	
State	Total Seats	Average Constituency Size	Total Seats	Average Constituency Size
Alabama	105	42,353	35	127,060
Alaska	40	15,673	20	31,346
Arizona	60	85,510	30	171,021
Arkansas	100	26,734	35	76,382
California	80	423,395	40	846,791
Colorado	65	66,173	35	122,893
Connecticut	151	22,553	36	94,599
Delaware	41	19,112	21	37,314
Florida	120	133,186	40	399,559
Georgia	180	45,480	56	146,186
Hawaii	51	23,755	25	48,461
Idaho	70	18,485	35	36,970
Illinois	118	105,248	59	210,496
Indiana	100	60,804	50	121,609
Iowa	100	29,263	50	58,526
Kansas	125	21,507	40	67,210
Kentucky	100	40,417	38	106,362
Louisiana	105	42,561	39	114,589
Maine	151	8,443	35	36,426
Maryland	141	37,563	47	112,691
Massachusetts	160	39,681	40	158,727
Michigan	110	90,349	38	261,538
Minnesota	134	36,712	67	73,425
Mississippi	122	23,316	52	54,704
Missouri	163	34,326	34	164,565
Montana	100	9,021	50	18,043
Nebraska	n/a	n/a	49	34,923
Nevada	42	47,577	21	95,155
New Hampshire	400	3,089	24	51,491
New Jersey	80	105,179	40	210,358
New Mexico	70	25,986	42	43,310
New York	150	126,509	61	311,089
North Carolina	120	67,077	50	160,986
North Dakota	98	6,553	49	13,106
Ohio	99	114,678	33	344,034
Oklahoma	101	34,164	48	71,888
Oregon	60	57,023	30	114,046
Pennsylvania	203	60,497	50	245,621
Rode Island	100	10,483	50	20,966
South Carolina	124	32,354	46	87,217
South Dakota	70	10,783	35	21,566
Tennessee	99	57,467	33	172,402
Texas	150	139,012	31	672,639
Utah	75	29,775	29	77,005
Vermont	150	4,058	30	20,294
Virginia	100	70,785	40	176,962
Washington	98	60,144	49	120,288
West Virginia	100	18,083	34	53,186
Wisconsin	99	54,178	33	162,535
Wyoming	60	8,229	30	16,459

occur. Thus in the first decade of the twenty-first century, congressional districts had an average population of 600,000, but there was substantial variation across the states. Montana, for instance, failed to qualify for a second congressional seat and as a result has one representative for 902,195 people. Wyoming's single House member, on the other hand, represents less than 500,000 people.

When it comes to apportioning their legislatures, the states have very different traditions and practices. Even a cursory glance at Table 1.4 demonstrates the variability across state legislatures. California, for example, allocates eighty seats in its lower house, that is, 1 state representative for every 423,000 Californians. New Hampshire, on the other hand, continues the colonial tradition of basing representation on communities, not on aggregates of people. In order to represent all the communities and abide by the U.S. Supreme Court decisions demanding that districts within a state be of approximately equal size, New Hampshire has a lower house with 400 members—1 representative per 3,000 persons. Similarly, Vermont has 150 members in its lower house, to serve just over 600,000 people.

Magnitude

A majority of electoral districts in the United States are single-member districts utilizing first-past-the-post criteria. This is not to say, however, that multimember districts are alien to American politics. As late as the 1840s some states elected their congressional delegations in multimember groupings. Congress put an end to this practice when, in 1842, it required the election of representatives from "contiguous territories" with the added prohibition against any "district electing more than one representative." Nevertheless, multimember districts have long been part of the makeup of state legislatures. In the 1950s only nine states elected all of their legislators from single-member districts. The extensive use of multimember legislative districts has been obscured by the rapid decline in their use after the U.S. Supreme Court's reapportionment decisions of the 1960s. Although the Supreme Court has never declared multimember districts unconstitutional, as long as the populations represented are equal, it has, on occasion, concluded that particular multimember districts unconstitutionally discriminated against minorities. Because there is in multimember districts a strong possibility that the majority population will win all the seats, racial minorities, particularly in the South and Southwest, have generally opposed their use. The willingness of minority groups to attack multimember districts as racially discriminatory and the Supreme Court's preference for single-member districts has accelerated their decline. As recently as 1990 seventeen states made use in one or both legislative chambers of multimember districts; by 1999, however, only thirteen states used multimember districts for either house.

The vote choices offered in single-member and multimember districts differ greatly. In single-member districts the voters have a single vote to cast for each office. In some of the states still using multimember districts, voters may cast as many votes as there are seats to be filled, and the candidates with the highest number of votes win. Alternatively, in a few states using multimember districts, candidates declare for a specific seat, voters cast a single vote for each seat, and the top vote getter for each seat wins.

Does it matter whether the districts are single-member or multimember? There is, unfortunately, no clear answer to the question. Illustrative of the issue is the debate over what is known as "Duverger's law." According to Duverger, single-member districts combined with the first-past-the-post system foster two-party political systems as opposed to multiple-party systems. As Duverger said, "An almost complete correlation is observable between the simple-majority single-ballot system (single-member, first-past-the-post) and the two-party system: dualist countries use the simple-majority vote and simple-majority vote countries are dualist."[45] Intuitively, Duverger's law makes sense.[46] Because voters are wary of wasting their votes on candidates who cannot win, they tend, even when faced with multiple candidates, to gravitate toward the two major parties. Similarly, potential third-party candidates will be reluctant to enter races they cannot win.[47] As a result, the two major parties try hard to appeal to the median voter and build broad-based ideologically blunted coalitions.[48] Although widely accepted, Duverger's law does have its detractors. Giovanni Sartori in particular has argued that a single-member, first-past-the-post system "cannot provide by itself a nationwide two-party format, but . . . it will help maintain an already existing one."[49]

Multimember districts without proportional representation systems, on the other hand, are often presumed to disadvantage minority interests. It is, for instance, commonly asserted that multimember districts harm the minority party in a district. The assumption is that members of the majority party will vote for their party's entire slate, denying the minority party any victories. Even if the minority party gets, say, 45 percent of the vote, it might fail to win a single seat. Alternatively, the argument goes, if the district were divided up, it is more likely that the minority party supporters would constitute a majority in at least one of the districts. The most complete accounting of the states' experience with multimember districts refutes this argument, however. Contrary to expectations the authors of the study could find no evidence that minority political parties were routinely shut out of power in multimember districts. Instead, the authors found two-party multimember districts to be more common than supposed. Furthermore, the authors could find no evidence that minority parties were generally underrepresented in state legislative elections.[50]

There is, however, a second sense in which multimember districts are assumed to disadvantage minority interests, with minority interests meaning racial and ethnic minority groups. As Niemi, Hill, and Grofman note:

> The logic behind this argument is simple. If a cue such as race . . . predominates, as is likely to be the case in many state legislative elections, then the majority will sweep a multimember district; yet if that district were divided into single-member districts, the minority might predominate in some of them.[51]

Of course, there are several other factors to consider. Majority domination will depend on the degree to which the minority is geographically concentrated as well as the propensity of both the majority and minority interests to vote homogeneously. Still the assumption that multimember districts disadvantage racial and ethnic minorities has, as previously discussed, fueled frequent litigation before the federal courts. For the most part, multimember districts have not fared well before the U.S. Supreme Court. In 1971, for instance, the Court forced Mississippi to divide Hinds County into single-member districts.[52] Two years later the Court ordered Texas to create single-member districts out of two multimember districts.[53] Through it all, the Court has maintained that multi-member districts are not *per se* unconstitutional, but it has exhibited a strong distrust of such arrangements. And well it should. Distrust is warranted, because the empirical evidence strongly supports the notion that racial minorities are underrepresented in multimember state legislative districts. The outcomes of state legislative elections in multimember districts significantly underrepresent racial minorities, suggesting that they may serve unconstitutional goals.[54]

Designing the Districts

Just as defining the electorate was, for some time, left exclusively to the states, so too were the issues of districting and redistricting. Congress, in an 1842 statute, required that congressional representatives be "elected by districts of contiguous territory equal in number," rather than in at-large elections (without districts) as had been the case in a few states. In 1872, Congress also decreed that districts should contain "as nearly as possible an equal number of inhabitants." Finally, in 1901, Congress specified that these districts be constructed of "compact territory." None of these statutes, however, constituted a profound nationalization of the congressional districting process. Again the construction of district boundaries was, for most of our history, a matter almost wholly of state concern. With each decennial census, legislatures or their designated agents in states with changing populations redrew their congressional districts and sometimes their legislative districts, with little direction from the national government.

In most states today, redistricting is done by the state legislature, but some states rely on commissions or boards to do the work (see Table 1.5). Only five states use commissions or boards to design congressional districts, but eleven states use some type of nonlegislative body to redistrict one or both of their houses. (Two states use advisory commissions, leaving the final authority to the legislature, while five other states provide for the use of backup commissions.) In those states in which the legislature takes on the redistricting, the process resembles any other piece of legislation. Bills are voted out of committee to the floor of their respective house, debated, voted upon, and if necessary different versions of the two houses are reconciled. Then, like general legislation, the redistricting bill is sent to the governor. The governor can sign or veto the bill. Generally, the governor's veto can be overridden by a two-thirds vote, but there are important differences in gubernatorial authority. In Illinois, for instance, there is a slight modification in normal procedures; state law requires a three-fifths majority to override a veto of a redistricting bill. In New York, on the other hand, the governor cannot veto redistricting plans. Three states, Idaho, Tennessee, and West Virginia, limit the governor's ability to impede partisan redistricting by requiring a simple majority for a veto override.

When it comes to redrawing congressional districts then, incumbent members of Congress have no direct role. They obviously have a great interest in the outcome and may prevail upon friends and political backers for advantageous districting. Incumbent members of Congress may be invited, by legislators, to submit informal plans and suggestions. Nevertheless, their role in the process is limited. This may explain that while historically most congressional districts exhibited some deviation from the statutory requirement that they contain "as

| TABLE 1.5 | Primary Redistricting Authority in the States | | | | |

State	U.S. House Districts	State Legislative Districts	State	U.S. House Districts	State Legislative Districts
Alabama	Legislature	Legislature	Montana	Commission	Commission
Alaska	Legislature	Commission	Nebraska	Legislature	Legislature
Arizona	Legislature	Legislature	Nevada	Legislature	Legislature
Arkansas	Legislature	Board	New Hampshire	Legislature	Legislature
California	Legislature	Legislature	New Jersey	Commission	Commission
Colorado	Legislature	Commission	New Mexico	Legislature	Legislature
Connecticut	Legislature	Legislature (Commission if legislature misses deadline.)	New York	Legislature	Legislature
Delaware	Legislature	Legislature	North Carolina	Legislature	Legislature
Florida	Legislature	Legislature	North Dakota	Legislature	Legislature
Georgia	Legislature	Legislature	Ohio	Legislature	Board
Hawaii	Commission	Commission	Oklahoma	Legislature	Legislature (Commission if legislature misses deadline.)
Idaho	Commission	Commission	Oregon	Legislature	Legislature
Illinois	Legislature	Legislature (Commission if legislature misses deadline.)	Pennsylvania	Legislature	Commission
Indiana	Legislature	Legislature	Rode Island	Legislature	Legislature
Iowa	Legislature	Legislature	South Carolina	Legislature	Legislature
Kansas	Legislature	Legislature	South Dakota	Legislature	Legislature
Kentucky	Legislature	Legislature	Tennessee	Legislature	Legislature
Louisiana	Legislature	Legislature	Texas	Legislature	Legislature (Commission if legislature misses deadline.)
Maine	Legislature	Legislature	Utah	Legislature	Legislature
Maryland	Legislature	Governor/	Vermont	Legislature	Legislature
Massachusetts	Legislature	Legislature	Virginia	Legislature	Legislature
Michigan	Legislature	Legislature	Washington	Commission	Commission
Minnesota	Legislature	Legislature	West Virginia	Legislature	Legislature
Mississippi	Legislature	Legislature (Commission if legislature misses deadline.)	Wisconsin	Legislature	Legislature
Missouri	Legislature	Commission	Wyoming	Legislature	Legislature

nearly as possible an equal number of inhabitants," the deviations were not great and they were lower than those found in other democratic nations. The extreme illustrations of malapportionment were to be found in the state legislative districts, where incumbents were deciding their own political fate. Despite the fact that a majority of state constitutions long required equal population sizes among legislative districts, malapportionment was rampant until the 1960s. The problem was that as populations shifted, many states simply ignored these provisions and failed to undertake the redistricting necessary to equalize populations. State legislators found ignoring malapportionment easier than redistricting themselves out of the legislature. Alabama, Tennessee, and Delaware were illustrative of this phenomenon, having failed to redistrict for the first sixty years of the twentieth century.[55] Not surprisingly these years of neglect produced extraordinarily wide divergences in these and several other states. In some states there were legislative districts containing up to 100 times the population of others. The resulting malapportionment (sometimes referred to as the silent gerrymandering) was neglected for decades by the Supreme Court, which declared the issue a political question not subject to adjudication.

In 1962, however, the Supreme Court sparked an electoral revolution, ruling in *Baker v. Carr* that because malapportionment constituted a threat to the equal protection of the laws as guaranteed by the Fourteenth Amendment the issue was appropriately brought before the federal courts.[56] The *Baker* majority did not mandate any particular standard or scheme of reapportionment, it simply stated that these questions could be litigated. The standard came in 1964, when in *Reynolds v. Sims* Chief Justice Earl Warren demanded that legislative districts be apportioned solely on the basis of population.[57] Furthermore, the Chief Justice proclaimed, " . . . the Equal Protection Clause requires that a State make an honest and good faith effort to construct districts, in both houses of its legislature, as nearly of equal population as is practicable." Subsequently, the Court applied this so-called "one-person, one-vote" standard to reapportioning congressional districts[58] and all local governments exercising general jurisdiction.[59]

What happened then is that much of the power over districting shifted from the state legislatures to the courts, and most particularly, the federal courts. Redistricting, even if done by the legislature, is carried out against the backdrop of court decisions limiting the alternatives and with the almost certain knowledge that everything will be reviewed by the courts. More subtly but no less importantly, the discussion of apportionment shifted the focus from the right to vote to the right to have the vote counted equally. Since the *Reynolds* decision the Supreme Court has habitually grappled with just how much deviation from perfect equality is acceptable. Proclaiming that there are no fixed standards, the Court has on a case-by-case basis reviewed the work of states and accepted or rejected their plans with little by way of clear guidance. It is true that the Court will tolerate less deviation from perfect equality among congressional than state legislative districts, but it is not clear in either case precisely how much deviation is acceptable. Lacking clear standards, states can only be assured that courts will continue to play a role in redistricting.

Having districts of equal size does not mean that discriminatory and distorted districts have been expelled from the political landscape, however. One person–one vote does not prohibit gerrymandering—"intentional manipulation of district lines for political purpose."[60] Nor do additional court-imposed standards such as requiring districts to be compact and contiguous (all parts of the district must be connected to the rest of the district) eliminate gerrymandering. With a little care and inventiveness legislators can still disarm their opponents by cracking—dispersing the members of a group into several districts—and packing—compacting the members of a group into a single district.

Since the 1980s concerns about gerrymandering have increased. Indeed these concerns represent another fundamental shift in the understanding of voting rights. It is no longer enough for many analysts that individuals have the right to vote and that they have the right to have that vote weighed equally, increasingly the argument is made that individuals have the right to an undiluted vote.[61] According to this argument, district lines drawn to weaken the voting power of one group in order to enhance that of another violate the Constitution. Talk of dilution is common in two divergent types of gerrymanders: (1) the political gerrymander and (2) the racial or ethnic gerrymander.

That political gerrymandering exists is unquestionable. After all, the term gerrymandering comes from a blatant effort by Massachusetts Governor Elbridge Gerry to maneuver his partisan opponents out of power. But identifying a political gerrymander is difficult. Unlike Gerry's salamander-shaped district that has become a textbook icon, modern gerrymanders are seldom obvious. As Bernard Grofman has observed, "One cannot recognize a gerrymander by its shape. Gerrymandering may take place even though districts are perfectly regular in appearance."[62] A lack of compactness creates a suspicion of gerrymandering, but it is not proof. Nor is it true that a compact district cannot be a gerrymandered district.[63]

One popular approach to identifying a political gerrymander is to compare the percent of votes that a party gets in an election to the percent of seats that it wins. Logically it would seem that if the party gets a smaller percentage of seats than votes then it must be the victim of gerrymandering. Alas, the logic does not hold. To the contrary, in a single-member, first-past-the-post electoral system, parties, except under very special conditions, will not win the same percentage of votes and seats.[64] The relationship between votes and seats is not linear. Instead, the translation of votes into seats in this type of electoral system is such that a small majority in the electorate often creates a sizeable legislative majority. Conversely, large electoral minorities are likely to be underrepresented in legislative seats. To see how this works, imagine an electoral system with two highly competitive parties. Party A claims 50.1 percent of the citizens as adherents, while party B commands the loyalty of 49.9 percent of the citizens. Now if each of the districts contained the same proportions of party supporters as exists in the larger system, party A would win all of the seats. Conversely, party B would win no seats, despite its near majority status. Of course the real world is never this simple and party supporters are never evenly distributed across the districts. Some districts have large concentrations of one or the other party, but there are always some districts where the parties are highly competitive. Indeed, in countries using the single-member, first-past-the-post system there are many such districts. This means that small vote changes in these districts produce large shifts in seats. These distortions in the relationship between votes and seats won are not constant and can be affected by political factors such as incumbency. Nevertheless, the distortions are often remarkably stable. The minority party is regularly disadvantaged by the single-member, first-past-the-post system.

No single-member, first-past-the-post electoral system is likely to produce seats in direct proportion to the votes that a party receives. Talk of vote dilution sometimes misses the simple point that single-member, first-past-the-post electoral systems are not proportional representation systems and they are unlikely to achieve proportional representation.

There are a variety of ways to measure the bias of the electoral system and thereby isolate distortions that may be attributed to political gerrymandering. Most commonly political scientists talk about the swing ratio—the percentage change in legislative seats associated with a 1 percent change in votes. But the rub is, there are several methods and little agreement on the best technique for calculating the swing ratio. This is indicative of the broader problem. As one group of authors note, political gerrymandering may be like Justice Potter Stewart's characterization of hard-core pornography, "hard to define, but one knows it when one sees it."[65] Moreover, successful political gerrymandering may be less significant than assumed. As one student of Congress has noted, "Despite its nefarious reputation, gerrymandering has had surprisingly little systematic impact on congressional elections in the postwar period."[66] Of course, particular districts may be shaped by political gerrymandering, even though the overall effect is small. Philip Burton's effort in 1982 to secure a seat for his brother by redrawing the 6th congressional district in California is a classic example. As constructed, the 6th district was composed of three segments connected only by the waters of the San Francisco Bay and two sections linked by a narrow strip of land running through railroad yards. Ironically, Burton's brother retired from Congress before he could reap the benefits. Nevertheless, Burton's plan probably cost California Republicans three or four seats in the 1980s. These were, however, counterbalanced by artful districting in Indiana which wiped out the Democratic seat advantage. Even in these cases, however, the advantages tended to be short-lived.

A second kind of problem, the racial or ethnic gerrymander, although based on the assumption that individuals have the right to an undiluted vote, presents a different set of questions. An early version of the racial gerrymander occurred in 1957 when the Alabama legislature redefined the borders of Tuskegee; changing it from a square-shaped city to one with twenty-eight sides. Ingenuously, the statute managed to exclude nearly every African-American voter (over 400), while leaving all of the white voters in the newly drawn city. Noting that the Fifteenth Amendment "nullifies sophisticated as well as simpleminded modes of discrimination," the Supreme Court in *Gomillion v. Lightfoot* (1960) ruled the Alabama statute unconstitutional.[67] Later the Voting Rights Act of 1975 outlawed gerrymandering that sought to dilute the political strength of racial and ethnic minorities.

More recently, states have used racial gerrymandering for the opposite reasons. Racial gerrymandering has in the last couple of decades been justified as a means of remedying past discrimination. To do this, states have constructed so-called majority-minority districts—districts in which the majority of voters are from a racial minority. Prior to 1982, redistricting arrangements could be found unconstitutional only if they were shown to intentionally dilute the votes of minority interests—as was the case in *Gomillion*.[68] But the 1982 amendments to the Voting Rights Act removed the need to prove an intent to discriminate and outlawed districting plans that had the *effect* of diluting minority strength. Many states, and to some extent the Department of Justice, interpreted this

amendment as requiring the creation of majority-minority districts. Thus following the 1990 census several states took affirmative action and created majority-
minority districts.

The constitutionality of these racial gerrymanders first came before the
Supreme Court in *Shaw v. Reno* (1993).[69] Following the 1990 census, North
Carolina, which gained a seat, added at the insistence of the U.S. Assistant Attorney General for Civil Rights, a second majority black district. (Because North
Carolina falls under the coverage of the Voting Rights Act of 1965, its redistricting plans must be cleared by the Department of Justice or the U.S. District Court
for the District of Columbia.) This newly formed district—the 12th—was 165
miles long, winding snake-like through tobacco country, financial centers, and
manufacturing areas. The district was so narrow that one candidate for the seat
quipped, "I can drive down Interstate 85 with both car doors open and hit every
person in the district." Justice Sandra Day O'Connor, writing for the Court,
remanded the case back to the district court for reconsideration. In doing so,
Justice O'Connor ruled that even "benign" racial gerrymandering could violate
the Equal Protection Clause of the Fourteenth Amendment. Racial gerrymandering, whatever the motive, is constitutionally suspect and may be justified
only by proof of compelling state interest.

On remand the district court once again upheld the North Carolina plan,
arguing that it was narrowly tailored to serve a compelling state interest—remedying past racial discrimination. The Supreme Court considered the case again
in *Shaw II*,[70] and this time Chief Justice William Rehnquist declared the redistricting plan unconstitutional. "Racial classifications," the Chief Justice wrote,
"are antithetical to the Fourteenth Amendment, whose 'central purpose' was 'to
eliminate racial discrimination emanating from official sources in the States.'"
Taking race into account while drawing district boundaries is not, the Chief Justice claimed, unconstitutional. The constitutional violation occurs, Rehnquist
said, when "race becomes the dominant and controlling consideration for
assigning voters to districts." Just how much evidence is needed to determine
that race was the "predominate," and therefore unconstitutional, factor in drawing a district or merely a factor in the decision-making process is unclear. Nor
was this issue clarified in 1999 when the 12th district of North Carolina came
before the Supreme Court once again (*Hunt v. Cromartie*). This time the state
justified the majority-minority district by arguing that it was drawn for political
reasons. North Carolina wanted to keep the 12th district Democratic and to help
guarantee the reelection of the incumbent Representative Melvin Watt. The
lower court invalidated the plan as an impermissible racial gerrymand, but the
Supreme Court unanimously overturned that decision. Writing for the Court,
Justice Clarence Thomas announced that judges must look carefully at the evidence before concluding that lawmakers had unconstitutionally used race to
draw the lines. Although he conceded the difficulty of proving that state lawmakers looked "predominately" at race in drawing district lines, the Justice
made it clear that more than circumstantial evidence is required before a state's
plan can be invalidated. Where other justifications, such as party balance or
incumbent protection, exist, courts may not intervene unless they are convinced that race was the most important basis for the districting.

In the end, the status of majority-minority districts is unclear. As we approach
the next redistricting, the quarrels over majority-minority districts will intensify.
Indeed the Court's inability to provide any clear guidance guarantees that this

issue will bedevil state lawmakers. The problem, as one wag put it, is that the Supreme Court's decision tells state legislators, "You must pay attention to race, but not too much."

At-Large Elections: The Local Alternative

For many local governments districting and redistricting are not prominent issues, because about 60 percent of American cities elect their council members at-large—elected from the entire city rather than districts or wards. Another 30 percent of the cities use some mixed electoral system that combines ward or district elections and some seats at-large. Only about 10 percent of American cities elect members from districts or wards.

At-large municipal elections have their origins in the Progressive era when they were touted as a means of cleaning up corrupt and inefficient city governments. Enthusiasm for businesslike principles of management and a disdain for foreign-born and lower-class voters motivated reformers to adopt at-large elections, often in conjunction with the commission and council-manager forms of government.[71] In the South, many cities switched to at-large elections in response to a growing African-American electorate.[72] The at-large option was said to be superior because it forced council members to be responsible to the entire city, not merely their wards. Ward elections, on the other hand, were said to encourage the representation of parochial viewpoints and give neighborhood and ethnic leaders far too much power.

Whatever the motives for the institution of at-large elections, political scientists have long suspected that their major effect was to dilute the votes of the poor and ethnic minorities in favor of business interests. Robert Lane made the point over fifty years ago when he argued that:

> By doing away with "peanut politics" (which apparently got its name from a political row over an Italian peanut vendor's stand), abolishing the small constituencies, and making election of councilmen citywide, ethnic solidarity is weakened.[73]

Lane was not alone in making this point. That at-large local elections diluted minority votes quickly became accepted wisdom.[74] Logically the conclusion seemed inescapable because at-large elections make it difficult for people of limited resources to run a competitive campaign. Moreover, there is the possibility of a "sweep effect," whereby a majority, even a small one, can win all or most of the seats, allowing, as Justice William O. Douglas said, "the majority to defeat the minority on all fronts."[75] Conversely, some have theorized that at-large local elections advantage women seeking office. It has been suggested that "voters would be more prone to support women in multimember [at-large] than in single member districts" because many will be reluctant to have a female as their only representative.[76] Whereas, in an at-large election voters could select candidates of each sex, thus increasing the number of women winning seats.

Intriguing as these arguments are, there is no longer agreement on these issues. In the 1980s it was generally agreed that at-large local elections disadvantaged racial minorities. Indeed, based on an impressive number of studies Richard Engstrom and Michael McDonald argued in 1986 that the proposition that blacks will be represented more proportionally on councils using district-based rather than at-large elections "is among the best verified empirical generalizations in political science."[77] More recent research has called this conclusion into question, however. A new wave of research, using more contemporary data, argues that there is scant evidence that the type of electoral system is significantly related to the number of African Americans or Hispanics elected to council seats.[78] Nor does there seem to be much evidence of a relationship between election type and the presence of women on city councils. Contrary to expectations, women do not do better in at-large elections than district contests.[79]

Whatever the empirical evidence, the fate of at-large elections is at best uncertain. Although neither the Congress nor the U.S. Supreme Court has ever declared at-large elections illegal, it is becoming increasingly difficult for local governments to rely exclusively on these electoral arrangements. Because the 1982 amendments to the Voting Rights Act made the test for discrimination effects and not intent, federal courts have increasingly disallowed at-large elections, whenever the percentage of seats held by minorities is significantly lower than their proportion of the population. The likelihood that at-large elections will be held unconstitutional is also increased if the jurisdiction has a history of racial discrimination and a record of racial polarization in voting.[80] As a result of adverse court decisions, local governments appear to be shifting away from at-large elections and toward mixed systems—election of some council members from districts and others at-large. In contrast to the purely at-large arrangements, these mixed electoral systems receive favorable review by federal courts.

Conclusions

Initially our national commitment to federalism and state power meant that the electoral system was highly decentralized. It was the states, not the national government, that possessed responsibility for allocating voting rights and regulating the electoral process. The original Constitution provides for a limited national role in this process. Indeed, Article I, Section 2 of the Constitution concedes the balance of power over these issues to the states, by allowing the states the power to define the electorate for elections to the U.S. House of Representatives.

Much has changed since the Constitution's ratification, however. Although initially most states attached property requirements to voting, these constraints had largely disappeared by the 1820s. Elimination of property requirements was the product of state reform. The states themselves, often bowing to internal pressures, shied away from the property requirements—although it took Supreme Court decisions to end the practice entirely. The states cannot be said to be the originators of the more conflictual expansions of the electorate, however. Although some states were quick to grant women the right to vote, in the final analysis it took action at the national level to truly enfranchise women. A similar conclusion can be reached regarding the enfranchisement of African Americans. The difference is that in the case of African Americans, it took more than a Constitutional amendment. It also required positive and sweeping legislative actions on the part of the U.S. Congress. Decades of efforts also finally overcame many of the dampening effects that registration requirements placed on the citizenry.

Two points clearly emerge from the historical broadening of the American electorate. The electorate was not expanded in an evolutionary fashion. Instead the expansion of the electorate has been highly conflictual and efforts to restrict the electorate have been common. Even as the vote was being extended to a group of people, policies were adopted to disenfranchise whole classes of people. The other point to be learned is that the enlargement of the electorate has come about through national government action. Except for the elimination of property requirements and the early promotion in some states of women's right to vote, the electorate has been expanded at national government direction.

That there has been a substantial nationalization of the electorate is not debatable. It is true that the states still possess some leeway in defining who votes, but it is in very restricted areas. In balancing the desirability of a decentralized voting system administered by the states against a commitment to universal suffrage, the latter has won. This broad-based suffrage has come about as a result of a nearly complete nationalization of the process

Guaranteeing the right to vote and assuring that votes count equally are, however, different questions. The sometimes arcane and technical questions of apportionment and reapportionment provide the bridge between voting and representation. How districts are constructed and seats apportioned defines the power of an individual's vote.

On these questions, there has been some nationalization. U.S. Supreme Court decisions have by requiring "one person, one vote" decreased the extent of malapportionment in the country. Nevertheless, within these broad guidelines, the states have great freedom and responsibility. The decisions that states and, to a lesser extent, local governments make on these questions define voting power.

Single-member, first-past-the-post districts are the most common in American elections, but multimember districts flourish at the state and local level. The vote choices offered vary greatly across these systems and have significant consequences for connecting voting to representation. Single-member districts disadvantage minority parties and promote a two-party political system. The experience of the states legislatures with multimember districts, on the other hand, suggests that they disadvantage racial minorities.

Drawing geographical districts creates other problems for democratic theory and the voter's link to representation. Although blatant political gerrymandering is relatively rare, more subtle versions are common and very difficult to identify. The problem is that a single-member, first-past-the-post electoral system does not produce seats in direct proportion to the votes a party receives. Attempts to identify political gerrymanders by use of the swing ratio are instructive, but unfortunately there are several methods and little agreement on the best way to calculate the swing ratio. The simple fact is, single-member, first-past-the-post electoral systems are not proportional representation systems.

Emphasis on the weight accorded a vote has, in recent years, spawned a new apportionment issue. On the theory that people have not just the right to vote, but the right to an undiluted vote, the construction of so-called majority-minority districts has become a significant challenge to the system. Although the Supreme Court has ruled that race cannot be the predominate factor in the drawing of districts, it can be one of the factors taken into consideration. Because it is unclear what proves that race is the predominate factor, the status of majority-minority districts remains uncertain. Nevertheless, the debate over majority-minority districts demonstrates the importance of these arcane and technical decisions underlying apportionment and reapportionment.

Endnotes

1. Indeed many at the Constitutional Convention were greatly concerned by Article I Section 4—the times and places clause of the Constitution. To many, particularly anti-federalists, the possibility that the national government would abuse even this limited authority was high. For a general discussion of this debate, see Kevin Green, "A Vote Properly Cast? The Constitutionality of the National Voter Registration Act of 1993," *Journal of Legislation* 22 (1996): 45-84.

2. Marchette Chute, *The First Liberty: A History of the Right to Vote in America, 1619-1850* (New York: Dutton, 1969), 253. Some of the colonies also supplemented these property requirements with religious qualifications. Catholics were not allowed to vote in colonial Maryland and non-Christians (specifically Jews) were barred from voting in Maryland, New York, Rhode Island, and South Carolina. After the Revolution, only South Carolina retained a religious qualification requiring would-be voters to acknowledge the existence of God.

3. Quoted in Alexander Keyssar, *The Right to Vote: The Contested History of Democracy in the United States* (New York: Basic Books, 2000), 3.

4. Chilton Williamson, *American Suffrage: From Property to Democracy 1760-1860* (Princeton: Princeton University Press, 1960), 50.

5. *Kramer v. Union Free School District No. 15*, 395 U.S. 621 (1969).

6. *Cipriano v. City of Houma*, 395 U.S. 701 (1969) and *City of Phoenix v. Kolodziejski*, 399 U.S. 204 (1970).

7. On this point, see Forrest G. Wood, *Black Scare: The Racist Response to Emancipation and Reconstruction* (Berkeley: University of California Press, 1968), 85-86.

8. For an important history of the period that documents the rise of "Jim Crow," in voting and all other aspects of southern life, see C. Vann Woodward, *The Strange Career of Jim Crow* (New York: Oxford Press, 1955).

9. *Report of the United States Commission on Civil Rights, 1959* (Washington: Government Printing Office, 1959), 80.

10. Harrell R. Rogers, Jr., and Charles S. Bullock, III, *Law and Social Change: Civil Rights Laws and Their Consequences* (New York: McGraw-Hill, 1972), 17.

11. See *Smith v. Allwright*, 321 U.S. 649 (1944) and *Terry v. Adams*, 345 U.S. 461 (1953).

12. Technically, the amendment applied only to elections (primary and general) involving the president or members of Congress. Thus four states—Alabama, Mississippi, Texas, and Virginia— maintained a poll tax requirement for state elections until 1966 when the U.S. Supreme Court declared the poll tax an invidious discrimination in violation of the Fourteenth Amendment. See *Harper v. Virginia State Board of Elections*, 383 U.S. 663 (1996).

13. Rogers and Bullock, *Law and Social Change*, 30.

14. Cited in C. Herman Pritchett, *Constitutional Civil Liberties* (Englewood Cliffs: Prentice-Hall, 1984), 345.

15. Rogers M. Smith, *Civic Ideals: Conflicting Visions of Citizenship in U.S. History* (New Haven: Yale University, 1997), 311-312.

16. In a more limited sense, Kentucky was actually the first state to grant women the right to vote. In 1838, Kentucky granted widows with children the right to vote in school elections.

17. Cited in Henry J. Abraham, *Freedom and the Court: Civil Rights and Liberties in the United States*, 5th ed. (New York: Oxford, 1988), 502.

18. This is, of course, a simplified explanation of the congressional action. Assuming that most young people supported liberal causes, Democrats were eager to enfranchise the youth. Republicans were at first reluctant, but when it became clear that young people were not as ideologically distinct as the presence of radical protestors would suggest, they too supported the issue.

19. *Oregon v. Mitchell*, 400 U.S. 112 (1970).

20. For arguments as to the general corruption of the electoral system during this period, see Samuel T. McSeveney, *The Politics of Depression: Political Behavior in the Northeast, 1893-1896* (New York: Oxford University Press, 1972); Phillip E. Converse, "Change in the American Electorate," in Angus Campbell and Phillip E. Converse, eds., *The Human Meaning of Social Change* (New York: Russell Sage, 1972); and Peter H. Argersinger, "New Perspectives on Election Fraud in the Gilded Age," *Political Science Quarterly* 100 (Winter, 1985-1986), 669-687.

21. The phrase is from Robert La Follette and quoted in James A. Morone, *The Democratic Wish: Popular Participation and the Limits of American Government*, rev. ed. (New Haven: Yale University, 1998), 108.

22. Morone, *The Democratic Wish*, 109.

23. For a general discussion of the rise of registration laws, see Kevin Phillips and Paul Blackman, *Electoral Reform and Voter Participation* (Washington, DC: the American Enterprise Institute, 1975), and Joseph P. Harris, *Registration of Voters in the United States*, (Washington, DC: Brookings Institution, 1929).

24. There are many historians who view the registration laws as part of the Progressives' effort to roll back universal male suffrage and purge the electorate of working-class voters. Not surprisingly, these authors point out, demands for registration laws tended to first appear in urban centers—particularly those with strong party organizations. From this perspective the claim that the Gilded Age was rife with political corruption is a fabrication of the Mugwumps to incite action limiting the franchise. For this viewpoint, see Paul Kleppner and Stephen C. Baker, "The Impact of Voter Registration Requirements on Electoral Turnout, 1900-16," *Journal of Political and Military Sociology* 8 (Fall, 1980): 205-226; Walter Dean Burnham, "Theory and Voting Research: Some Reflections on Converse's Change in the American Electorate," *American Political Science Review* 68 (September 1974): 1002-1023; and Howard Allen and Kay Warren Allen, "Vote Fraud and Data Validity," in Jerome M. Chubb, William H. Flanigan, and Nancy H. Zingale, eds., *Analyzing Electoral History: A Guide to the Study of American Voting Behavior* (Beverly Hills: Sage, 1981).

25. Bingham G. Powell, Jr., "Voting Turnout in Thirty Democracies: Partisan, Legal, and Socioeconomic Influences," in Richard Rose, ed., *Electoral Participation: A Comparative Analysis* (Beverly Hills: Sage, 1980), 5-34.

26. Harold F. Gosnell, *Why Europe Votes* (Chicago: University of Chicago, 1930), 185. See also Seymour Martin Lipset, *Political Man* (New York: Doubleday Press, 1960), 205.

27. 405 U.S. 330 (1972).

28. The following year, the Court accepted residency requirements as long as fifty days. See *Martson v. Lewis*, 410 U.S. 679 (1973) and *Burns v. Fortson*, 410 U.S. 686 (1973).

29. Raymond E. Wolfinger and Steven J. Rosenstone, *Who Votes?* (New Haven: Yale University, 1980), 88.

30. Ruy A. Teixeira, *The Disappearing American Voter* (Washington, DC: The Brookings Institution, 1992), 146.

31. Stanley Kelley, Jr., Richard E. Ayres, and William G. Bowen, "Registration and Voting: Putting First Things First," *The American Political Science Review* 61 (June 1967): 373.
32. Teixeira, *The Disappearing American Voter*, 143.
33. The act exempts Minnesota, North Dakota, Wyoming, and Wisconsin from its provisions. North Dakota is exempt because it has no registration requirements. Minnesota, Wyoming, and Wisconsin are excluded because they have election day registration.
34. See Royce Crocker, *Voter Registration and Turnout in States with Mail and Motor-Voter Registration Systems* (Washington, DC: Congressional Research Services, Library of Congress, 1990); and Jerry W. Calvert and Jack Gilchrist, "Suppose They Held an Election and Almost Everybody Came!," *PS: Political Science and Politics* (1993): 695–700.
35. Stephen Knack, "Does 'Motor Voter' Work? Evidence from State-Level Data," *The Journal of Politics* 57 (August 1995): 796–811. Similar results can be found in S. Rhine "Registration Reform and Turnout Change in the American States," *American Politics Quarterly* 23 (1995): 409–426.
36. Stephen Knack, "Election-Day Registration: The Second Wave," *American Political Research* 29 (January 2001): 65–78.
37. For a thorough discussion of the development of racially discriminatory criminal disenfranchisement provisions, see John C. Rose, "Negro Suffrage: The Constitutional Point of View," *American Political Science Review* 1 (November 1906): 17–43.
38. 471 U.S. 222 (1985).
39. Quoted in Andrew L. Shapiro, "Challenging Criminal Disenfranchisement Under the Voting Rights Act: A New Strategy" *Yale Law Journal* 103 (November 1993): 548.
40. *Richardson v. Ramirez*, 418 U.S. 24 (1974).
41. The definition and distinction here is adapted from the classic work of Douglas Rae, *The Political Consequences of Electoral Laws* (New Haven: Yale University, 1967), 19.
42. For a concise guide to the New Zealand practice, see R. J. Johnston, "Seats, Votes, Redistricting, and the Allocation of Power in Electoral Systems," in Arend Lijphart and Bernard Grofman, eds., *Choosing an Electoral System: Issues and Alternatives* (New York: Praeger, 1984), 59–69.
43. For a full description of the process, see the web page for the Census, *http://www.census.gov/population/222/census/methodof.html*.
44. For a complete description of the various methods used, see David Butler and Bruce Cain, *Congressional Redistricting: Comparative and Theoretical Perspectives* (New York: MacMillan Publishing, 1992), 17–23.
45. Maurice Duverger, *Political Parties* (New York: John Wiley, 1963), 217.
46. The counterpart to "Duverger's law" is "Duverger's hypothesis," which states that proportional representation favors multipartyism.
47. For a discussion of formal models addressing "Duverger's law," see Kenneth Shepsle, *Models of Multiparty Electoral Competition* (New York: Harwood, 1991).
48. See especially Anthony Downs, *An Economic Theory of Democracy* (New York: Harper & Row, 1957).
49. Giovanni Sartori, "The Influence of Electoral Systems: Faulty Laws or Faulty Method?" in Bernard Grofman and Arend Lijphart, eds., *Electoral Laws and Their Political Consequences* (New York: Agathon Press, 1986), 43–68.

50.   Richard Niemi, Jeffrey S. Hill, and Bernard Grofman, "The Impact of Multimember Districts on Party Representation in U.S. State Legislatures," *Legislative Studies Quarterly* X (November 1985): 441–455.

51.   Ibid., 441.

52.   *Connor v. Johnson*, 402 U.S. 690 (1971).

53.   *White v. Regester*, 42 U.S. 755 (1973).

54.   Malcolm Jewell, "The Consequences of Single and Multi-member Districting," in Bernard Grofman, Arend Liphart, Robert Mckay, and Howard Scarrow, eds., *Representation and Redistricting* (Lexington, MA: Lexington Books, 1982), 129–135.

55.   Butler and Cain, *Congressional Redistricting*, 25.

56.   369 U.S. 186 (1962).

57.   377 U.S. 533 (1964).

58.   *Wesberry v. Sanders*, 376 U.S. 1 (1964).

59.   *Avery v. Midland County Texas*, 390 U.S. 474 (1968).

60.   The definition, one of many, comes from Bernard Grofman, "Criteria for Redistricting: A Social Science Perspective," *UCLA Law Review* 33 (1985): 100.

61.   One of the best articulations of this argument, especially for a lay audience, is Lani Guinier, *The Tyranny of the Majority* (New York: Free Press, 1994).

62.   Grofman, "Criteria for Redistricting," 92.

63.   See H. Peyton Young, "Measuring the Compactness of Legislative Districts," *Legislative Studies Quarterly* 13 (February 1998): 105–116. Young demonstrates among other things that a legislative district that is drawn to wind itself around like a coiled snake passes several tests of compactness, even though it is far from a natural shape for a legislative district.

64.   See Harry Basehart, "The Seats/Vote Relationship and the Identification of Partisan Gerrymandering in State Legislatures," *American Politics Quarterly* 15 (October 1987): 484–498; Gerald S. Gryski, Bruce Reed, and Euel Elliot, "The Seats-Vote Relationship in State Legislative Elections," *American Politics Quarterly* 18 (April 1990): 141–157; Edward R. Tufte, "The Relationship Between Seats and Votes in Two-Party Systems," *American Political Science Review* 67 (1973): 540–554; and Richard G. Niemi and Patrick Fett, "The Swing Ratio: An Explanation and an Assessment, *Legislative Studies Quarterly* XI (February 1986): 75–90.

65.   Richard K. Scher, Jon L. Mills, and John J. Hotaling, *Voting Rights and Democracy: The Law and Politics of Districting* (Chicago, Nelson-Hall, 1997), 127.

66.   Gary C. Jacobson, *The Electoral Origins of Divided Government: Competition in U.S. House Elections, 1946–1988* (Boulder, CO: Westview Press, 1990), 94.

67.   364 U.S. 339.

68.   See also *Bolden v. City of Mobile*, 446 U.S. 55 (1980).

69.   509 U.S. 630 (1993).

70.   *Shaw v. Hunt*, 116 S. Ct. 1894 (1996).

71.   See James Weinstein, "Organized Business and the City Commission and Manager Movements," *The Journal of Southern History* 28 (May 1962): 166–182; and Samuel P. Hays, "The Politics of Reform in Municipal Government in the Progressive Era," *Pacific Northwest Quarterly* 55 (October 1964): 160.

72.   For a complete discussion, see Everett Carl Ladd, *Negro Political Leadership in the South* (Ithaca, NY: Cornell University Press, 1966).

73.   Robert E. Lane, *Political Life: Why People Get Involved in Politics* (Glencoe, IL: The Free Press, 1959), 270.

74.   As examples, see Edward C. Banfield and James Q. Wilson, *City Politics* (Cambridge: Harvard University Press, 1964); Robert Dahl, *Who Governs* (New Haven:

Yale University Press, 1959); Gunnar Myrdal, *An American Dilemma* (New York: Harper, 1944); and James Q. Wilson, *Negro Politics* (Glencoe, IL: The Free Press, 1960).

75. *Kilgarlin v. Hill*, 386 U.S. 120 (1967).
76. Albert K. Karnig and Oliver Walter, "Election of Women to City Councils," *Social Science Quarterly* 56 (1976): 610.
77. Richard L. Engstrom and Michael D. McDonald, "At-Large vs. District Elections in the U.S.," in Bernard Grofman and Arend Lijphart, eds., *Electoral Laws and Their Political Consequences*, 224.
78. For a review of this newer research, see Charles S. Bullock, III, and Susan A. Mac-Manus, "Municipal Electoral Structure and the Election of Councilwomen," *Journal of Politics* 53 (February 1991): 75–89.
79. See Bullock and MacManus, "Municipal Electoral Structure." Also see Susan Welch and Albert K. Karnig, "Correlates of Female Office Holding in City Politics," *Journal of Politics* 41 (1979): 478–491. Welch and Karnig found a small but statistically significant relationship between election type and female representation. As they explain, however, election type explained less than 1 percent of the variance.
80. For an account of the legal standards, see *Thornburgh v. Gingles* 478 U.S. 30 (1986).

Chapter 2
The Nomination Process: Getting on the Ballot

In a conversation with one of his underlings, Boss Tweed, the dominant political figure in New York politics in the 1870s, emphatically pointed out the importance of the nomination process: "I don't care who does the electing, just so I do the nominating." Tweed knew, as contemporary office seekers know, that before you can run in a general election you have to get your name on the ballot. The laws and regulations that influence that process are often the key to eventually getting elected to public office. Every political party in the United States, including the Republicans and Democrats and the dozens of third or minor parties that fill the political landscape, go through the procedure of selecting candidates to run for office. Indeed, with over 500,000 elections held every four-year cycle in the United States, the campaign starting gate—the nomination process—is frequently a crowded and often complex course to navigate.

Our task in this chapter is to discuss the laws and regulations as they apply to the nomination process in national, state, and local elections in the United States. We are pursuing answers to two questions: how do laws effect which potential candidates get on the ballot, and do nomination laws and regulations have an impact on the campaign process? We argue that the laws, as they exist at the national, state, and local levels regarding the nomination process, are, indeed, significant and far-reaching and ultimately have an impact on the general election campaign process.

As we discuss the topic of nominations, it is important to keep one point in mind. The rules of the game controlling who gets nominated to run for elective office as a party or independent candidate are governed, for the most part, by state laws. Party rules, federal statutes, and court decisions play a more limited role in the process. And, as we shall see, the laws and regulations governing nominations in the United States often differ among the fifty states.

In the first part of this chapter we describe the historical development of the nomination process in the United States. We then examine nominations at the national level, briefly focusing on reforms in both the Democratic and Republican parties over the past three decades that have had such an important impact on the nomination process. We then turn to a discussion of primaries and caucuses at the national, state, and local levels as well the more limited use of state conventions. This section closes with a discussion of the impact of term-limits on ballot access.

Our discussion then turns to nomination rules and regulations as they apply to third party and independent candidacies and the subsequent difficulties facing these candidates in many states as they attempt to gain access to the ballot.

Finally, we summarize the impact of primaries and caucuses on the strategies of candidates in the pre-general election campaign environment and, indeed, the subsequent impact on the general election campaign strategy. We suggest answers to the question as to how the rules of the game affect and have an impact on getting on the ballot and campaigning in elections in the United States.

A Brief History of the Nomination Process: From the Founding to the 1970s

The history of the nomination process for public office in the United States spans 225 years of experiment and change. Americans have employed caucuses, conventions, and primaries at different times and under a variety of national, state, and local conditions since the framers met in Philadelphia in 1787 in an effort to amend the Articles of Confederation and ultimately to write a new constitution.

Interestingly, the major contemporary instrument of nominations and elections, the political party, was never even mentioned in the Constitution. The framers felt that political parties would be divisive in the political system. Yet the selection of candidates to run for political office necessitated a set of laws— or at the very least guidelines—by which factions, and later political parties, could run men, and eventually women, for public office. As you shall see, these laws and guidelines would evolve slowly over the next 225 years.

The Evolving Nomination System: Caucuses, Conventions, and Primaries

Initially, few formal rules governed the nomination process of the political system. At the national level, George Washington was selected unanimously as the first president by electors of the thirteen states (see Chapter 6 for a discussion of the electoral college). Few rules governed the selection of individuals seeking state or local office during the early years of the republic, although, as we discussed in Chapter 1, many states had citizenship, residency, and/or property ownership requirements. The earliest nomination practices centered on what is known as the **caucus**.

Caucuses   At the national, state, and local levels of government, informal groups of like-minded political leaders congregated at caucuses—meetings—and selected their choice of candidates without bothering with formal nominations. Indeed, up until the 1820s, the caucus was the instrument of choice for a candidate to gain access to office. At the state level of government, legislative caucuses were widely employed to select candidates for statewide and local offices.

At the national level, informal rules provided for the separate nomination and selection by legislative caucuses in Congress to select presidential and vice-presidential candidates from each of the factions or informal political parties. Because the parties did not initially slate a combined presidential and vice-presidential ticket, the selection of the president and vice-president was made from the top two candidates receiving the votes of the members of the electoral college regardless of the faction or party to which they belonged. Thus, in 1796, a not-so-insignificant imbroglio occurred when Federalist candidate John Adams was selected president and Democratic-Republican candidate Thomas Jefferson was selected vice-president.

By the time political parties began to take shape as formal political organizations in the 1830s, a new mechanism for the selection and nomination of candidates for political office, the **convention**, became popular.

Conventions   By the 1830s, we witnessed a shift, at the national scene, to the nominating convention as a means for selecting presidential and vice-presidential candidates. In 1831, a little-known minor party, the Anti-Masons, held a national convention in which delegates nominated the presidential and vice-presidential candidates selected from the various states. Shortly thereafter, national nominating conventions were held by the Whig party, the Democratic party, and the Republican party.

By mid-century (the 1840s), the convention system was gradually displacing the caucus system as a means of nominating state and local candidates for office. As James Davis would describe it, "[t] he . . . convention system was considered to reflect the 'popular will' because delegates to these conclaves had been chosen by the party membership at the precinct and county level. Throughout the nineteenth century, the nomination of all candidates for state and local office was strictly a party matter,"[1] one in which local conventions ruled the day.

The convention system remained the principal mode by which local, state, and national candidates were nominated for political office up until the beginning of the twentieth century. By the turn of the century, however, a new nominating instrument, the **primary**, began to take center stage.

Primaries   The Progressive movement, beginning around the turn of the twentieth century, kindled numerous election reforms, including the direct election of U.S. Senators and the women's vote. The era also heralded in the party primary system or direct election of party candidates.

The primary is an election in which registered voters in a party vote for and thus nominate the party's candidates for many state and local offices ranging from the city council to governor and senator. Primaries are also held every four years by the Democratic and Republican parties in many states to select delegates to the national presidential party conventions. The United States is the only nation on record employing the primary system for the selection of political party candidates. All other nations use a caucus or convention system.

Primaries are either "closed" or "open." In a closed primary, voters have to declare loyalty to the party holding the primary, generally by registering as a member of that party. In an open primary, any registered voter can participate in whichever primary he or she wishes to participate in, without declaring a party loyalty (we will shortly discuss several other variations of the primary).

Florida claimed the first use of primaries in 1901 in a statute that "gave state or local party officials the option to hold a primary election to choose any party nominee."[2] The primary was first widely employed in Wisconsin in 1903 when Robert M. LaFollette pioneered its use in selecting a party's candidates to run in the general elections and to select delegates to the national party conventions.

By the beginning of the twentieth century, many reformers and government officials feared that without a means of limiting access to the nomination ballot, we risked cumbersome long ballots with dozens if not hundreds of choices for each office. In order to control the escalating number of political parties and candidates seeking a spot on the ballot, at least two criteria often had to be met for a candidate to get on a primary ballot. Many states required a minimum number of petition signatures in order for a party or individual candidates to gain access to the ballot. And by the 1930s, in response to fears about socialism and communism, many states also required loyalty oaths by prospective candidates, outlawing any party or candidate calling for the overthrow of the government.

By the 1940s, most states provided for three means by which candidates could access the party primary ballot: the payment of a filing fee to the state, party, or both; the filing of a nomination petition with separate state laws determining the number of signatures necessary, often depending on the size of the electoral district; or a combination of both the filing fee and the nomination petition.[3]

By the 1950s, the primary nominating system had been adopted in a majority of the states, with Indiana the last state to adopt the system in 1976.[4] By the beginning of the twenty-first century, 80 percent of the states were using primaries as their vehicle for selecting delegates to the Republican and Democratic national conventions. Most states use the primary (sometimes in conjunction with or in lieu of a convention or caucus) as the means for nominating Democratic and Republican standard-bearers for their respective parties in local and state elections.

While state laws govern much of the activity surrounding the nomination process at all levels of government, political parties have, in recent history, attempted to reform the selection process. The most prominent reforms have affected the presidential nomination process.

The View from the Top: Reforms and the Presidential Nomination Process

Until the 1970s, nominations by the two major parties for president and vice-president were controlled, for the most part, by state party caucuses that selected delegates to the national conventions. Rules and regulations highly favored candidates supported by party leaders, providing relatively few independent-minded candidates the opportunity to get the Democratic or Republican nomination. In effect, what the collective state party leaders wanted, they got—the presidential nominee they felt had the best chance of winning the general election. By the late 1960s, tensions in the political system helped bring about a number of important reforms in the delegate selection process. The move for nomination reforms began in the Democratic party.

The Democratic Party: The McGovern-Fraser Reforms and Beyond

American politics is both a participant and observer sport and few Americans can resist the opportunity to tinker with the rules of the game that govern it. During the 1960s, that urge to tinker was kindled at the national level by a number of political and social conflicts including the civil rights movement, the war in Vietnam, and the women's movement.

The effects of these and other events resulted, in part, in a call for greater citizen participation in the political system and in efforts at reforming and democratizing the selection of the major party candidates for president of the United States. The old reliance on party leaders who dominated the selection of the party's presidential and vice-presidential candidates appeared to many Americans to be a throwback to the smoke-filled back rooms of the party organization machines.

After a tumultuous Democratic national convention in 1968, a convention racked by violence and the call by many for a more democratic process of selecting nominees to run for the office of the presidency, the Democratic party established a series of reform commissions. Beginning in 1969 with the McGovern-Fraser (1969–1970) and the O'Hara Commissions (1969–1972), on through the Mikulski (1972–1973), Winograd (1974–1978), Hunt (1980–1982), and Fairness Commissions (1985–1986), the Democratic party sought to use party rules as a means of regulating access to the presidential nomination ballot.

Cumulatively, the reforms brought about several important changes in the rules governing nominations for the Democratic candidates for the presidency and vice-presidency. The work of the combined commissions resulted in two major changes in the Democratic selection process. First, the number of primaries used in the selection of delegates to the Democratic national conventions was increased in an effort to open up participation to more women, young people, and minorities. Second, the commissions initiated a proportional representation rule that tied the number of delegates a candidate received in a primary to the proportion of the vote the candidate received in that primary.

Changes in the rules of the game brought about by the McGovern-Fraser Commission in 1970 (and modified in future commissions) did assure greater representation at the national conventions by rank-and-file delegates. But party leaders wanted also to guarantee that both party leaders and elected officials at the federal and state levels—the "professionals"—were also sufficiently represented at the national convention. The reforms of the Hunt Commission assured this outcome by establishing that a proportion of the delegates selected to go to the convention—known as "super delegates"—would come from the ranks of the party leaders and elected officials.

With the selection of delegates proportionally distributed to candidates based on the percentage of votes received by the candidate, James Davis argues "the shift in rules requiring delegates to run pledged to specific candidates transformed nominating campaigns into delegate-centered races rather than party-controlled nominations."[5] No longer did successful presidential party nominees have to rely on the various state party organizations and their leaders to get the nomination. Instead, the rules allowed for independence from the state party organizations and encouraged individual entrepreneurship by prospective candidates in seeking delegate support in each state.

At the national level, and just as importantly, at the state and local levels too, we saw a shift from **party-centered campaigns**—in which the political parties controlled the nomination process—to **candidate-centered campaigns**—in which individual candidates, relying on primaries, were able to get the party nomination without necessarily having the support of the party leaders.[6]

By the 1970s, individuals seeking the party's nomination could, with sufficient funding, bypass the party leaders, formerly the power brokers in the nomination process. They could directly appeal to primary voters in an effort to secure the largest proportion of the delegate pool possible. "The new presidential primaries, in effect, ended the smoke-filled room brokering process, whereby state party leaders used their controlled blocs of delegates to bargain with leaders from other states to decide on the most politically 'safe' candidate."[7] Successful party candidates did not have to be party insiders, thus encouraging a more competitive and open selection process.

This new and more open system incorporated by the Democratic party increased the number of challengers for the party's presidential nomination. Party outsiders, as was the case with Jimmy Carter in 1976, could get the Democratic nomination. The proportional distribution of delegates based on the percentage of votes that a candidate received in a specific primary also allowed long-shot candidates the opportunity to build incremental delegate support. They could use that support to negotiate the nomination or some other concession (for example, the shaping of the party platform) in a close-fought or deadlocked convention.

In effect, the rules governing the presidential nomination process significantly changed over time. Because party rules gave state party organizations less power over delegate selection, adequately funded candidates, who did not have the support of state party leaders, had a chance of getting the nomination by dint of hard work and the electioneering of prospective primary voters. Party leaders no longer selected a majority of the delegates attending the national conventions.

The changes in state laws and party rules created a more competitive arena for the Democratic nomination, a nomination process made more aggressive by changes in federal laws that provided for matching federal grants for qualified candidates during the primary season.[8]

In effect, the Democratic party reforms instigated in the 1960s and 1970s, the growth in the number of state-mandated primaries in the late 1960s, and new federal campaign finance laws written in the early 1970s, had a dramatic impact on the Democratic presidential nomination process. The changes kindled an increase in the number of challenges by candidates for the nomination who were not supported by the party leaders and who were not traditionally regarded as viable presidential candidates.

The new rules of the game, which had the impact of weakening the role of political parties in the nomination process, would, as we shall shortly see, trickle down the election ladder and weaken the role played by parties in the state and local nomination processes.

The Republican Party and the Limits of the Presidential Reform Process

Three Republican committees dealing with nomination reform evolved beginning in the 1960s: the Committee on Convention Reform (1966), the Delegates and Organizations Committee (1968–1971), and the Rule 29 Committee (1972).

Far less ambitious than the reforms instituted by the Democratic party, the Republican efforts provided for little meaningful change in the rules of candidate selection. As one observer of party reform concluded, "there is no constituency for reform within the Republican party."[9] While the "Rule 29 Committee" called for an "open door" policy encouraging greater participation by minorities, women, and young people, this was only a recommendation, one that was not binding on the state party organizations where the locus of power remained. For all intents and purposes, that same perspective permeates the Republican party today. For the Republican party, the party rules concerning the selection of delegates to the Republican national convention remain, for the most part, in the hands of the state party leaders.

However, as with the Democratic party nomination process, the Republican presidential nominating process was affected significantly by changes in state law regarding primaries and changes in federal law regulating campaign finance reform. With the broad-based adoption of the primary election system in a majority of states, more and more prospective Republican candidates sought delegate support from rank-and-file Republicans. This was the case in the 2000 Republican primaries, when no fewer than eleven candidates sought the presidential nomination. No longer did the Republican state party organizations have a lock on directing delegate support to a single candidate.

As in the case of the Democrats, the introduction of the state primary system—shifting the power of delegate selection from the state party organizations to the rank-and-file party voters—and the availability of federal financing for primary campaigns, changed the rules of the game. Republican candidates, including Senator John McCain in the 2000 Republican presidential primaries, who did not have the support of the state party bosses and who had more limited sources of campaign funding could now compete in the presidential nomination process.

While the national conventions remain important instruments for rallying the parties every four years, for the writing of a party platform, and for uniting delegates with diverse backgrounds around a single candidate, the role of the convention has been significantly reduced. Since the 1970s, the primary/caucus selection process of delegates predetermines, often months in advance of the convention, the successful nominees for both parties.

We now turn to a closer examination of primaries and caucuses—contemporary instruments for selecting national, state, and local party candidates—and the laws and regulations that control for and subsequently have an impact on the campaign process.

Primaries: Center Stage in the Nomination Process

While primaries date back to the early 1900s, it was not until the beginning of the 1970s that the primary system took center stage in the process of selecting party candidates to run in the general elections. Voters were increasingly demanding the opportunity to select their party's nominees for local, state, and national offices.

It is important to point out initially that primaries are state-centered elections. There are no national primaries. With the exception of the Federal Election Campaign Act, which places caps on how much money can be spent on presidential primaries if a candidate accepts federal matching grants (see Chapter 4 for details), and a scattering of Supreme Court cases dealing with the rights of voters to participate in primaries,[10] federal law has a limited bearing on regulating the primary process.

Articles I and II of the U.S. Constitution dealing with qualifications for serving in Congress and holding the office of the president have had a circuitous impact on the nomination process and access to the ballot. For a candidate to be eligible to hold the office of the president, he or she must be a natural-born citizen, thirty-five years or older, and a resident of the United States for at least fourteen years. Because the vice-president constitutionally succeeds the president in the case of the death, resignation, impeachment and conviction, or inability of the president to perform his or her duties, it is surmised that the vice-presidential candidate must also fulfill the same qualifications for holding office as the president.

Members of the House of Representatives, in order to qualify for office, must be at least twenty-five years of age, a citizen of the United States for at least seven years, and an inhabitant of the state in which he or she is elected. Members of the Senate must be at least thirty years old, nine years a citizen of the United States, and an inhabitant of the state in which they are chosen.

These constitutional prerequisites for holding federal office place citizenship and age restrictions on any individual who wishes to seek a party nomination for Congress or the presidency. State statutes, similarly, specify qualifications for holding statewide office. While varying from state to state, most state statutes include minimum age requirements for holding office, requisite state and/or U.S. citizenship, state residency requirements, and provisions specifying that a candidate be a qualified voter.

However, there is variation among the fifty states. For example, while a majority of states stipulate that a gubernatorial candidate must be at least thirty years of age in order to hold office, five states—California, Ohio, South Dakota, Washington, and Wisconsin—specify only a minimum age of eighteen. Indeed, in 2000, an eighteen year old was elected to Ohio's state House of Representatives. Eleven states have state citizenship requirements ranging from two to seven years (two states, Hawaii and Montana, simply require citizenship without stipulating years). A majority of the states specify in their statutes U.S. citizenship in order to qualify to hold the office of governor. Thirty-nine states have candidate residency requirements ranging from two to ten years while ten states stipulate that a candidate for governor must be a qualified voter. (See Table 2.1).

TABLE 2.1	State Laws Covering Qualifications for Running for Governor			
State	**Minimum Age**	**State Citizen (years)**	**U.S. Citizen (years)**	**State Resident (years)**
Alabama	30	7	10	7
Alaska	30	···	7	7
Arizona	25	5	10	···
Arkansas	30	···	*	7
California	18	···	5	5
Colorado	30	···	*	2
Connecticut	30	···	···	···
Delaware	30	···	12	6
Florida	30	···	···	7
Georgia	30	···	15	6
Hawaii	30	*	···	5
Idaho	30	···	*	2
Illinois	25	···	*	3
Indiana	30	···	5	5
Iowa	30	···	*	2
Kansas	···	···	···	···
Kentucky	30	6	*	6
Louisiana	25	5	5	···
Maine	30	···	15	5
Maryland	30	···	*	5
Massachusetts	···	···	···	7
Michigan	30	···	···	···
Minnesota	25	···	*	1
Mississippi	30	···	20	5
Missouri	30	···	15	10
Montana	25	*	*	2
Nebraska	30	5	5	5
Nevada	25	2	···	2
New Hampshire	30	···	···	7
New Jersey	30	···	20	7
New Mexico	30	···	*	5
New York	30	···	*	5
North Carolina	30	···	5	2
North Dakota	30	···	*	5
Ohio	18	···	*	*
Oklahoma	31	···	*	···
Oregon	30	···	*	3
Pennsylvania	30	···	*	7
Rhode Island	—	···	···	···
South Carolina	30	5	*	5
South Dakota	18	—	2	2
Tennessee	30	7	*	···
Texas	30	···	*	5
Utah	30	5	···	5
Vermont	···	···	···	4
Virginia	30	···	*	5
Washington	18	···	*	···
West Virginia	30	5	···	1
Wisconsin	18	···	*	···
Wyoming	30	···	*	5

SOURCE: The Council of State Governments, *The Book of the States*, 33 (2000–01): 17.

Key:
··· No formal provision.

*Formal provision; number of years not specified.

Local laws vary significantly regarding the general qualifications for candidates seeking offices ranging from county supervisors, assessors, and clerks to local city, town, and village councils and commissions. For the most part, state laws that provide local communities with home-rule power (the power to legislate and regulate in specified policy areas) give local communities considerable latitude in establishing requirements for running for local office as long as those statutes and regulations do not violate state and federal laws.

Clearly, the U.S. Constitution and the various state constitutions and statutes governing qualifications for holding office serve as an initial check or set of restrictions on who may or may not qualify for access to the nomination ballot. Once having met the qualifications to run for office, the rules of the game for access to a primary ballot lock in.

Primaries Rules in the Fifty States

As we have already noted, a **primary** is an election in which party members select candidates to run for office under the party banner.[11] No other form of access to the nomination ballot (and thus, ultimately, to the general election ballot) is used as widely in our nation as the primary.[12] In all of the fifty states, the rules of the game specify that major party candidates for most partisan and nonpartisan offices are required either to run in a primary election for federal, state, and local offices or the state's election codes specify some variation of the nomination process that can stipulate the primary as an option. Despite the patch work of state laws and regulations governing the nature and use of primaries, some generalizations are possible.[13]

Thirty-seven of the fifty states specify the primary as the sole means of nomination for all major political parties in statewide races.[14] The remaining thirteen states allow for exceptions to that practice. For example, in Alabama and Virginia, the state executive committee, an incumbent officeholder, or the governing body of any political party may choose, in lieu of a primary, to hold a state convention for the purpose of nominating candidates.[15] Connecticut, North Dakota, and Utah employ a state convention (meeting of locally designated party delegates) to select many statewide candidates, although stipulation is made in the election law for primaries if the candidates are challenged or if challengers petition to participate in a statewide primary.

At the local level, the nomination provisions in a majority of states include the use of primaries as the principal mechanism for the selection of major political party candidates to run in the general election. In most municipalities across the nation where parties contest local offices, local primaries are held on the same day as statewide primaries. Exceptions include Arizona, California, Illinois, Kansas, Louisiana, Massachusetts, Michigan, Mississippi, Montana, North Carolina, Tennessee, Virginia, and Wisconsin where local primary dates can vary from state primary dates.

Variations on the Primary System   In addition to the open and closed primaries discussed above, three other variations of the primary are found at the state and local levels.

As we noted earlier in this chapter, primaries are either "closed"—voters have to affirm loyalty to the party holding the primary in order to take part in it—or "open"—in which any registered voter can participate in one of the party primaries without registering or declaring support for that party. Thirty-seven states use a closed primary system; nine states use an open primary system. Three variations on the open and closed primary have been used in various states: nonpartisan, blanket, and run-off primaries.

The **nonpartisan primary** is most commonplace at the local level of government, although one state, Louisiana, uses a nonpartisan primary statewide.[16] In nonpartisan primaries, there is no party label on the ballot.

Members of the Progressive movement who were interested in reforming the political process introduced nonpartisan primaries around the turn of the twentieth century. Reformers felt that by excluding the party label from the primary (and general election) ballot, party machines would be destroyed—or at the very least, weakened—and issues and candidate qualifications would play a more prominent role in the campaign and election process.

In reality, many nonpartisan primaries involve candidates who are supported by local caucuses that often have strong partisan ties to the Republican or Democratic parties. The nonpartisan city council primaries in Chicago are an example of this phenomenon. Individuals seeking a seat on the Chicago city council (there are fifty seats representing the fifty wards of the city) run as nonpartisan candidates even though the media often reports the party identifications of the various candidates and the voters are more often than not aware of who is a Democrat and who is a Republican. This is true in many city, town, and village nonpartisan primaries and elections around the nation.

Until a U.S. Supreme Court ruling in 2000, a second variation on the primary was known as the **blanket primary**. In a blanket primary, a voter was permitted to vote in both the Republican and Democratic primaries although she could vote in only one party primary per office. If she voted in the Republican primary for president, she was not permitted to vote in the Democratic primary for president. However, on that same ballot, she could choose to vote in the Democratic primary for governor although the rules then foreclosed her right to vote in the Republican primary for governor.

The rules of the game for campaigns in states using blanket primaries complicated the lives of candidates who discovered that Republican voters could have a voice in selecting the Democratic nominee for a given office and Democratic voters could have a voice in selecting the Republican nominee for a given office. Both of the major parties disliked the rules that governed the blanket primary for they allowed for the crossover of voters from one party to the other, ostensibly in an attempt to vote for the weaker candidate of the opposition party. In 2000, the U.S. Supreme Court invalidated the blanket primary in a California case, calling it a "stark repudiation of freedom of political association that stripped political parties of the ability to control their own nominating process and define their identity."[17]

The Supreme Court ruling may also invalidate the blanket primary used in two other states, Washington and Alaska, although these states have already indicated a willingness to investigate other variations of the blanket primary (see the case of Louisiana below) as an alternative nomination process.

The third variation on the primary is the **run-off** primary. In eleven states—Alabama, Arkansas, Florida, Georgia, Louisiana, Mississippi, North

Carolina, Oklahoma, South Carolina, South Dakota, and Texas—if no candidate receives a majority of a party's primary vote, the two leading vote-getters compete with each other in a run-off primary. Historically, the run-off primary was most popular in the South where the Democratic party dominated politics until the 1980s and where the outcome of the Democratic primary for most federal, state, and local offices often determined who would win the general election. In recent years, as a result of a strong, two-party competitive system for many offices in the South, the importance of the Democratic primary in determining the outcome of the general election has declined significantly. No longer is victory in a Democratic primary in many southern states an assurance that an individual will win the general election. In fact, across the nation there are no states that can be classified as one-party states.

A variation on the blanket and run-off primary exists in Louisiana. Under the Louisiana primary system, candidates for all parties at the state and local level compete on one nonpartisan ballot and the candidate receiving a majority of the vote is declared the winner. If no candidate receives a majority of the vote, the two highest vote-getters compete in a nonpartisan, run-off election to determine who will serve in office.

The advent of the primary system in its various manifestations at the state and local levels of government has clearly had an impact on the campaign and election process. Chief among those impacts is that the primary provides candidates who lack party organization support the opportunity to challenge the party organization's favored candidate (assuming one exists).

With the arrival of the primary system the number of candidates seeking party nominations has increased under two conditions: when no incumbent is running in the primary (called an open-seat primary), and in one-party dominant elections in which the primary is very competitive for the majority party. The primary has also promoted a significant increase in the number of candidates in presidential primaries. But the rules of the game provide other conditions that have to be understood and fulfilled by the prospective candidate for a party's nomination if he or she expects to be able to compete in the primary nomination process.

State Primaries and Access to the Ballot

Access to the primary ballot in the United States transpires through the nomination of individuals as major party candidates, third-party candidates, or as independent candidates. In most cases the rules governing that access are established by state statute, with political parties playing a limited role or no role at all in the nomination process.

That the states would play a significant role in establishing the rules governing ballot access was inevitable once states got into the business of printing election ballots. Before the advent of the Australian or secret ballot in the United States in 1888, the printing of local, state, and national ballots was left in the hands of the political parties who generally printed ballots with only the names of their candidates listed. An individual who wished to split his vote between candidates of both major parties (or a third-party or independent candidate) had to write in the name of that candidate. By the beginning of the twentieth century all states took on the responsibility of printing their election ballots. With this new role the states acquired significant control over the rules that governed access by prospective candidates to a party primary ballot. As one observer pointed out, "States have been generally endowed with the authority to regulate primary elections 'because of the substantial role primary elections have in the overall electoral system.'"[18]

This is not to suggest that political parties do not have an impact on influencing candidate access to the primary ballot. While it is true that "[m]any state party officials are forbidden from taking sides in the [primary] process by either party rules or state law,"[19] seven states provide for a compulsory preprimary endorsement of candidates for statewide office by means of a state convention. State conventions generally favor the candidate of the party leaders, whose choice is often placed first on the primary ballot. Preprimary endorsements also generate fewer primary challenges against incumbents. The power of these endorsements, almost always supporting incumbents, often discourages challengers from entering the primary election.

In addition to states that have statutes requiring preprimary endorsements by party organizations, several state party organizations engage in extralegal endorsements at state conventions or through the preprimary practice of party slate making. However, while these practices provide the parties with influence over the selection of the party candidates in a few states, in most states, statutes provide the state with the dominant role in the nomination process.

Filing Fees and Petitions   The two most widely adopted state requirements for determining the placement of a candidate's name on a primary ballot are the payment of a filing fee and the presentation of a properly completed petition with a requisite number of signatures on it.

The filing fee is regarded as a controversial and restrictive system for accessing the ballot by the courts, specifically when it is the sole means by which an individual can gain access to a primary ballot. It is argued that some prospective candidates simply cannot afford to pay a fee. Nevertheless, a majority of states require a filing fee or monetary deposit in order to gain access to the ballot. Fewer than 25 percent of the states, however, require minor parties and independents to pay a filing fee.

The filing fee is justified on the grounds that it discourages frivolous candidates from seeking the nomination. The fee also defrays some of the costs to the state associated with administering a primary. Fees vary from state to state and from office to office. For example, in Texas, filing fees are $2,500 to run for the U.S. House of Representatives, $3,000 for any statewide office, $1,000 to run for the state senate, and $600 to run for the state house. Florida assesses a double fee for candidates seeking federal and statewide offices: a state filing fee of 3 percent of the annual salary for the office and a party assessment fee of 2 percent of the annual salary.

In a case brought before the U.S. Supreme Court in 1974, the Court ruled a filing fee unconstitutional unless an alternative means of access to the ballot was provided.[20] The Court argued that the sole use of filing fees was an unfair and restrictive provision of the state law, limiting access to the primary ballot.

While states can choose to legislate filing fees, alternative provisions for getting on the ballot must be offered to individuals who cannot or choose not to pay the fee.

The most acceptable alternative to the filing fee that has been condoned by the courts is the use of petitions. Prospective candidates must accumulate a requisite number of signatures in order to win a place on the primary ballot. The number of signatures required varies from state to state, municipality to municipality, and from office to office. For example, in Illinois, in 2000, 25,000 signatures were required to get on the presidential ballot in that state.

Other constraints employed by states to control for access to the ballot include early filing deadlines and the imposition of geographically based distribution requirements regarding the collection of petition signatures. An early deadline can impose burdens on a prospective candidate ranging from the inability to organize a petition drive in a timely fashion to the inability to recruitment campaign workers and to raise campaign funds in a timely fashion.

Geographically based distribution requirements on the collection of petition signatures may also burden a candidate who has limited funds and volunteers and subsequently less access to different regions of a voting district or state. For example, in a statewide race, geographically based distribution requirements may include the collecting of a specified number of petition signatures from every county in the state. Thus, a prospective candidate may have problems soliciting the necessary number and distribution of signatures to get on the primary ballot.

Cross-filing   Finally, the ability for candidates to cross-file and run in the primary of more than one party can have an impact on the success of a candidate in the general election.

Three states—Connecticut, New York, and Vermont—permit a candidate for state or local office to seek concurrently the nomination of more than one party.[21] For example, state laws in New York permit a candidate to run as both a major party and minor party candidate (if the minor party uses a convention system for selecting its candidates). Thus, a Democrat capturing her party's nomination in a state or local primary and who also wins the nomination, for example, of the Liberal party, can be assured her name will appear on both the Democratic and Liberal party ballots. This is true of a successful primary candidate in the Republican party who can often count, at the state and local level, on the nomination of the Conservative party to supplement his general election vote totals. Elections in New York State have been influenced by a candidate's success—or failure—in receiving the endorsement of both a major and minor party and the subsequent votes the candidate receives from the third party's supporters.[22]

Establishing the ground rules for a candidate to gain access to the ballot is not a simple issue easily resolved by the states or the courts. Most observers would agree that open access to the ballot would lead to long ballots that inevitably would overwhelm the voter. In turn, a too-restrictive system is likely to lock out individuals who, by some measure, deserve legitimate access to the ballot. New York State law regarding primary access covers over 350 pages of complicated text.[23]

Whatever the regulations are in a state regarding access to the primary system, it is clear that ballot access rules have an impact on the strategies and tactics employed by a candidate in the electoral process. We now turn to the caucus system of nomination.

The Caucus: A Limited Role in State Politics

The caucus, the gathering of like-minded political leaders to caucus—meet—and nominate a candidate to run for office, was the most commonly used nominating system after the founding of the nation. Today, state law determines whether a primary or caucus system is used in the nomination of party candidates. As already indicated, most states use the primary system in selecting Democratic and Republic candidates for statewide offices. One exception is Kansas, which provides that any party that receives less than 5 percent but more than 1 percent of the vote cast for statewide offices in the general election must nominate candidates by either caucus or convention.[24] In effect, the caucus plays a very limited role in the modern two-party nomination process.

A number of states provide in either their statutes or state constitutions that local communities may avoid the cost of using primaries by using local caucuses in the selection of partisan and nonpartisan candidates. This often makes sense given the high cost of primaries and low voter turnout in many communities.

At the national level, only about a quarter of the states use the caucus system to select delegates to the Republican and Democratic national conventions, including Virginia and Maine.[25] Officially known as a caucus-convention system, the selection process begins with precinct caucuses and ends with a statewide convention. Iowa, the first state to use the caucus every four years to select Democratic and Republican convention delegates, kicks off the candidate selection process in February of presidential election years. Initially, caucuses are held in over 2,100 Iowa precincts where delegates are selected to attend county caucuses in March. Caucus-conventions are held in each of the 99 counties in March to select delegates who will go on to congressional district conventions in May when delegates are chosen to attend the national party conventions. National convention-bound delegates meet at a state convention in June to select at-large delegates to the national conventions.

The significant attention that the Iowa caucus receives every four years has done little to popularize caucuses in other states. The caucus remains a state or local option for states and local communities and, as we shall shortly see, is mostly used by third parties.

The Convention: Outdated but Surviving

While most states require the use of primaries for all state nominations, sixteen states either permit or mandate the use of statewide conventions. In almost all cases, the use of a party convention provides for greater control by the political parties over the nomination process. Party leaders generally have greater influence over convention delegates then they do over primary voters.

Variations on the rules governing the convention provide for some diversity among the states. For example, in Alabama and Virginia, the state executive committee or other governing body of the political parties may choose to hold a state convention in lieu of a primary. In Colorado, a preprimary convention may be held by a party for the designation of candidates for statewide office. Candidates receiving 30 percent or more of the vote are certified as the candidate for the office they seek. In Connecticut major parties hold conventions for the purpose of endorsing candidates. If anyone receiving at least 15 percent of the delegate vote wishes to challenge the winner of the convention, a primary election is held to determine the party's nominee in the general election.

Similar procedures (with variations on the delegate votes necessary for a nomination and the means of challenging the convention results) exist in New York, North Dakota, and Utah. Michigan uses primaries for some statewide offices, including the gubernatorial, congressional, state legislative, and the circuit and appellate court races, while employing a state convention for the selection of the party candidates who want to run for lieutenant governor, secretary of state, and attorney general.

Iowa offers an interesting innovation on the convention/primary process. If no party candidate receives at least 35 percent of the Democratic or Republican primary vote for statewide office, that party calls a state convention where the nomination and selection is made.

The most visible use of the convention system is not at the state or local level but at the national level where every four years the Republican and Democratic parties hold their national conventions to nominate their presidential and vice-presidential candidates formally. In recent years, party rules have diminished the role the conventions play in the selection of the party nominee. Today, with approximately 80 percent of the delegates to the conventions elected in primaries, it is often no surprise by convention time whom the nominee will be. Party rules do give party conventions the responsibility for writing national platforms that often serve as an excellent blueprint forecasting the policies a successful candidate will work for once elected to the presidency.

In states that provide for the convention system as an alternative to a primary, incumbents are often favored. Alternatively, a small but active group of delegates at a state convention can dominate a deliberation process in support of a specific candidate. Thus, campaign strategy is affected to some degree by the work of the convention and the rules that govern it.

Term Limitations and the Nomination Process

A recent change in some states' electoral laws have had a significant impact on the nomination process: legislation implementing term limitations at the state and local levels of government. A growing number of states and local municipalities have legislated term limits—a restriction on the number of terms an individual can serve—for statewide offices, state legislative offices, and a variety of local offices, including terms for mayor and city council. While the consequences of term limitations have an important impact on many aspects of the representative and policy-making processes, its impact on the nomination process is far from subtle.

The implementation of term limits has resulted in a rise in the turnover of candidates seeking their party nomination for statewide and local offices. Statutes preventing incumbents from running for reelection because they have been "termed-out," have resulted in a growing number of "open-seated" races for the party nomination in which none of the candidates are an incumbent. Because incumbents generally have a significant advantage in being renominated in a primary, caucus, or convention, the increase in the number of open seats has attracted many candidates who might otherwise not seek public office. One clear incentive for seeking the nomination for a political office occurs when you will *not* be challenging an incumbent whose advantages often include high visibility, name recognition, and a record of service to her or his constituents.

The impact of term limits on the nomination process is made clearer by an examination of recent legislative races in Michigan, one of eighteen states that provide for term limitations for their state senate and house. In 1998, 67 of the 110 members of the state house were termed-out of office, unable to run for reelection.[26] As a result, 494 individuals filed to run in the primaries for the Michigan House, the highest number in over thirty-five years.[27]

In general, most states that have adopted term limits restrict the maximum length of time an individual can hold office in the state house or senate to between eight and twelve years. In addition to term limitations in the state legislatures, thirty-eight states have legislated gubernatorial term limits. (See Table 2.2).

Local term limits date back in some states to the 1850s. Eight of the ten largest cities in the United States have municipal term limits, including New York City, Los Angeles, Houston, Dallas, San Francisco, New Orleans, Cincinnati, Phoenix, Philadelphia, San Antonio, Denver, and Kansas City. Nearly 3,000 cities have placed limits on the service terms of mayors and members of their city councils. "Although term limits remain infrequently used at the local level, they have received much more widespread attention in the past five years and their use at the local level has certainly increased."[28]

Recently, state legislators in Oregon, Missouri, and several other states as well as city councils in a number of municipalities including New York City, considered legislation that would relax or even rescind time limits that have been imposed on legislator and council terms. The impetus behind these moves includes the concern that any valued members of these legislative bodies are being termed-out at a time when their knowledge, expertise, and experience are needed.

At the national level, U.S. House and Senate offices are not subject to term limitations.[29] However, with the ratification of the Twenty-Second Amendment to the Constitution in 1951, individuals serving in the office of the president are limited to two terms of office. The impact on the nomination process at the presidential level has been significant. Political parties can expect an open-seat election at least every eight years. The only incumbent to serve more than two terms was Franklin D. Roosevelt and no incumbent president since Dwight Eisenhower has had the option of running for more than two terms.

Because prospective presidential candidates must be ready to seek the open seat at least every eight years, the nomination process is more open to challenges under term limitations than before the Twenty-Second Amendment.

TABLE 2.2   Term Limits in the States

State	State Gubernatorial Term Limits	State Legislative Term Limits*
Alabama	2 consecutive terms allowed; terms last 4 years.	None
Alaska	2 consecutive terms allowed; terms last 4 years.	None
Arizona	2 consecutive terms allowed; terms last 4 years.	House: 4 terms (8 years); Senate: 4 terms (8 years)
Arkansas	2 consecutive terms allowed; terms last 4 years.	House: 3 terms (6 years); Senate: 2 terms (8 years)
California	2 consecutive terms allowed; terms last 4 years.	Assembly: 3 terms (6 years); Senate: 2 terms (8 years).
Colorado	2 consecutive terms allowed; terms last 4 years.	House: 4 terms (8 years); Senate: 2 terms (8 years)
Connecticut	None	None
Delaware	2 consecutive terms allowed; terms last 4 years.	None
Florida	Governor limited to 8 consecutive years in office.	House: 4 terms (8 years); Senate: 2 terms (8 years)
Georgia	2 consecutive terms allowed; terms last 4 years.	None
Hawaii	2 consecutive terms allowed; terms last 4 years.	None
Idaho	Governor limited to 2 consecutive 4-year terms, then eligible to serve again after a 4-year respite.	House: 4 terms (8 years); Senate: 4 terms (8 years)
Illinois	None	None
Indiana	Governor limited to 2 consecutive 4-year terms, then eligible to serve again after a 4-year respite.	None
Iowa	None	None
Kansas	2 consecutive terms allowed; terms last 4 years.	None
Kentucky	2 consecutive terms allowed; terms last 4 years.	None
Louisiana	2 consecutive terms allowed; terms last 4 years.	House: 3 terms (12 years); Senate: 3 terms (12 years)
Maine	2 consecutive terms allowed; terms last 4 years.	House: 4 terms (8 years); Senate: 4 terms (8 years)
Maryland	2 consecutive terms allowed; terms last 4 years.	None
Massachusetts	None	None
Michigan	2 consecutive terms allowed; terms last 4 years.	House: 3 terms (6 years); Senate: 2 terms (8 years)
Minnesota	None	None
Mississippi	2 consecutive terms allowed; terms last 4 years.	None
Missouri	2 consecutive terms allowed; terms last 4 years.	House: 4 terms (8 years); Senate: 2 terms (8 years)

SOURCE: U.S. Term Limits web site, *www.termlimits.org,* February 27, 2001.

*The following states' legislative term limits are consecutive: Arizona, Florida, Louisiana, Maine, Ohio, South Dakota, and Utah.

TABLE 2.2 Continued

State	State Gubernatorial Term Limits	State Legislative Term Limits*
Montana	Governor limited to 8 years in a 16-year period.	House: 4 terms (8 years); Senate: 2 terms (8 years)
Nebraska	2 consecutive terms allowed; terms last 4 years.	None
Nevada	2 consecutive terms allowed; terms last 4 years.	Assembly: 6 terms (12 years); Senate: 3 terms (12 years)
New Hampshire	None	None
New Jersey	2 consecutive terms allowed; terms last 4 years.	None
New Mexico	2 consecutive terms allowed; terms last 4 years.	None
New York	None	None
North Carolina	Governor limited to 2 consecutive 4-year terms, then eligible to run after a 4-year respite.	None
North Dakota	None	None
Ohio	Governor limited to 2 consecutive 4-year terms, then eligible to run after a 4-year respite.	House: 4 terms (8 years); Senate: 2 terms (8 years)
Oklahoma	2 consecutive terms allowed; terms last 4 years.	12-year combined total for both houses.
Oregon	Governor limited to only 8 years.	House: 3 terms (6 years); Senate: 2 terms (8 years)
Pennsylvania	2 consecutive terms allowed; terms last 4 years.	None
Rhode Island	2 consecutive terms allowed; terms last 4 years.	None
South Carolina	2 consecutive terms allowed; terms last 4 years.	None
South Dakota	2 consecutive terms allowed; terms last 4 years.	House: 4 terms (8 years); Senate: 2 terms (8 years)
Tennessee	2 consecutive terms allowed; terms last 4 years.	None
Texas	None	None
Utah	If governor serves 12 consecutive years he/she cannot seek re-election.	House: 6 terms (12 years); Senate: 3 terms (12 years)
Vermont	None	None
Virginia	Governor cannot serve 2 consecutive terms, but can seek re-election after a 4-year respite.	None
Washington	None	None
West Virginia	2 consecutive terms allowed; terms last 4 years.	None
Wisconsin	None	None
Wyoming	Governor limited to 2 terms in a 16-year period.	House: 6 terms (12 years); Senate: 3 terms (12 years)

The following states' legislative terms limits are lifetime: Arkansas, California, Michigan, Missouri, Nevada, Oklahoma, and Oregon.

The following states' legislative term limits are a time-out four years or longer: Colorado, Idaho, Montana, and Wyoming.

The Rules of the Game as They Apply to Third-Party and Independent Candidates

In our earlier discussion in this chapter, we reported that states are often faced with a dilemma regarding access to the ballot by third parties and independent candidates. Many observers agree that open access to the ballot might lead to very long and cumbersome lists of candidates and inevitable confusion for voters. In turn, a too-restrictive system could lock out individuals who, by some measure, may deserve legitimate access to the ballot.

Most states have chosen to legislate very restrictive laws regarding ballot access for third parties and independent candidates. The motivation for this certainly involves concerns over unwieldy and long ballots. But restrictive laws have also been prompted by the desire of both the Republican and Democratic parties and their elected officials to protect the traditional two-party system and to minimize the possibility of access to the election process by third parties. Whatever the justifications, minor parties and independent candidates often have a difficult time getting on a federal, state, or local ballot, although the courts have intervened in recent years to open up the process.

While we have had over 900 third parties in our 225-year history, third-party and independent candidates have been relatively unsuccessful, since the 1950s, in getting elected to public office. In recent years a number of third-party and independent presidential candidates—George Wallace (1968), John Anderson (1980), H. Ross Perot (1992 and 1996), Pat Buchanan (2000), and Ralph Nader (2000)—have attracted considerable media attention during their campaigns. In 1992, Ross Perot amassed a respectable 19 percent of the popular vote. However, only the Republican party, a minor party that would evolve into a major party with the presidential election of Abraham Lincoln in 1860, successfully captured the office of the president. Only one member of Congress has been elected as a third-party candidate since 1952—James Buckley, a New York Conservative Party candidate elected to the Senate in 1971—and only one independent candidate—Bernard Sanders from Vermont—has been elected to the House of Representatives since the 1950s.[30]

At the state and local levels, third-party and independent candidates have also lacked any broad-based electoral success. As one student of political parties has observed, "minor-party candidates . . . have fared poorly in state legislative contests . . . and local enclaves of significant minor party strength have been reduced to a small, albeit colorful, handful."[31]

Nevertheless, every election year, thousands of independents and dozens of minor political parties seek access to state and local ballots via primaries, caucuses, and conventions, or the petition process. Under some circumstances they have been successful. In 1998, Reform Party candidate Jesse Ventura, a former professional wrestler, was elected governor of Minnesota, one of only a handful of third-party or independent candidates who have successfully won statewide office in recent years.

While in most states major parties are authorized to use primaries, paid for by the state, to select their nominees for national, state, and local offices, most state laws specify that minor parties that already qualify to be on the general election ballot must select their nominees through a caucus, a convention, or by petition.

By their very definition, independent candidates are either unaffiliated with a political party or belong to a political organization that is not recognized by the state as a political party. Thus, independents generally do not take part in the nomination process but rather gain access to the ballot through the payment of a filing fee, a nomination petition, or both. Nominating petitions, like primaries and conventions, are intended to establish a minimal level of popular support for the candidate, deterring frivolous candidates.

In many states how a new political party qualifies for getting on the ballot is often problematic for that party.[32] States often require that new political parties demonstrate minimum voter support in one of a number of ways: (1) by filing a petition for party recognition signed by the requisite number of registered voters; (2) by attaining a minimum level of registered voters who claim party membership or affiliation; (3) by conducting a nominating convention with a minimum number of supporters in attendance; (4) by meeting certain organizational requirements (such as having local caucuses or committees); or (5) by meeting some combination of these methods.[33]

The U.S. Supreme Court has, in recent years, lowered the barriers placed by many state laws on third-party and independent candidate access to the ballot. In a seminal ballot access case in 1968,[34] the Court ruled that Ohio's access rules for minor parties in presidential elections were unconstitutional, restricting the right of voters to advance certain political beliefs by placing too great a burden on the party through an excessive and discriminatory petition system. In 1979, the Supreme Court admonished the states for limiting access to minor parties. The Court found that:

> The States' interest in screening out frivolous candidates must be considered in light of the significant role that third parties have played in the political development of the nation. Abolitionists, Progressives, and Populists have undeniably had influence, if not always electoral success. As the records of the parties demonstrate, an election campaign is a means of disseminating ideas as well as attaining political office . . .[35]

Nevertheless, state laws and regulations often constitute a difficult obstacle course for third parties and independent candidates seeking to gain access to the election ballot. Early filing deadlines and the number of signatures necessary to be placed on the ballot can constitute an obstacle, as well as a financial burden, for third-party and independent candidates. Ralph Nader, the Green Party presidential candidate in 2000, found this to be the case. After a day of collecting signatures to get his name and party on the presidential ballot in Wyoming, a group of Nader volunteers carelessly left a clipboard filled with petition signatures in a local restaurant. The clipboard was never recovered. Nader was soon informed by electoral officials that his petition to get on the statewide ballot had fallen short of the required signatures—as it turned out, just about one clipboard's worth of signatures. Nader would eventually run as a write-in candidate in the state.

In a recent election held in Texas, minor parties and independent candidates for state office had to file notice of their candidacy ten months in advance of the November general election, a decision, for some candidates, that was difficult to make so early in the election year. New political parties needed more than 40,000 signatures in order to get placed on the general election ballot, while independent candidates had to procure the signatures and registration numbers of over 60,000 voters who had not participated in another party primary. The process of collecting signatures is not easy and serious minor parties and candidates often need to hire political bounty hunters—paid collectors—to get the requisite valid signatures at up to $2.25 per signature.[36]

The Trail from the Nomination to the General Election Campaign: Some Implications and Conclusions

Our review of the ballot access process suggests that statutes and constitutional provisions that regulate ballot access in the United States have an important impact on the nomination process and the decisions, strategies, and tactics of election campaigns.

As the rules of the game have evolved, one of the most important forces has been the emerging role of state and local primaries and their subsequent impact on the role of political parties in the nomination process at the national, state, and local levels of government.[37] While it is accurate to state that many primaries go uncontested or weakly contested throughout the United States, many candidates, under the right conditions, can and do successfully challenge for the major party nominations through primary elections at all levels of government, a development much less likely to occur under the old party-centered system.[38] Because of changes in the rules of the game, political parties, for so many years the gatekeepers to the nomination process, no longer dominate the recruitment and selection process.

This is not to suggest that political parties do not play a role in the nomination system. As we have already indicated, some states have statutes allowing political parties to endorse primary candidates, providing the party with an important tool in influencing the nomination process. Jewell and Olson have outlined the significant influence of party endorsements in states including Connecticut, Delaware, Colorado, North Dakota, Rhode Island, Utah, Illinois, New Mexico, Wisconsin, and New York.[39] (Party endorsements are most effective when parties also provide their candidates with money, volunteers, and organizational support.)[40] In addition, many primaries go uncontested, allowing the parties the opportunity to have more influence over the selection process.

But as Maisel has pointed out, "in the majority of states, party organization plays no preprimary role at all."[41] The primary, according to Keefe, increases party campaign costs, reduces the party's capacity to reward its members by guaranteeing a nomination, isolates the party from primary candidates who establish their own power bases or who are antagonistic to the party, and increases the possibility of intraparty competition, conflict, and dissent causing deep wounds that may be slow to heal.[42] The primary also increases the likelihood of selecting a party candidate who is poorly qualified or who may take issue positions that are repugnant to the party leaders and supporters. Clearly, the laws and regulations relating to primaries have altered the campaign and election landscape.

The influence of primaries and the rules that govern them as they apply to ballot access extends to other domains in the nomination process. As we have pointed out, the use of petitions and filing fees to qualify for primary races can place significant burdens and restrictions not only on individuals seeking major party nominations but on third-party and independent candidacies, too. And open primaries provide the opportunity for voters to cross over from one party to the other, thus potentially weakening the selection of the party's nominee by allowing nonparty members, who lack a commitment to the party, a voice in deciding whom its candidates will be.

Certainly, the "front-loading" of presidential primaries—the bunching of as many as two-thirds of election year state primaries early in the primary season— makes it difficult for relatively unknown or long-shot candidates to gather the momentum necessary to win the nomination. This was the case in the presidential primaries in the year 2000, when over two-thirds of the states held their primaries by the end of March.

Recently, the National Association of Secretaries of State approved a proposal that would establish by the year 2004 four regional presidential primaries in the East, West, Midwest, and the South. The regional primaries would be staggered, taking place in March, April, May, and June. The regions would rotate the month in which their states would participate in the primary in succeeding presidential election years. States would not be required to hold their contest on the same day of the month, and New Hampshire and Iowa would be permitted to maintain their leadership position in the presidential selection process. Whether or not a regional primary plan evolves appears to be highly questionable. Any plan—including that of the National Association of Secretaries of State—will have to be approved in each of the fifty states.

The very timing of presidential primaries by state law can have a significant effect on the outcome of the nomination process, generally favoring the early and very visible frontrunners.[43] The state laws that determine when a presidential primary will take place also delineate when primaries will be held for most statewide and many local offices. Thus, early presidential primary dates also generally favor state and local frontrunners and incumbents seeking every office from governor to the village, town, or city council.

Other statutory, constitutional, and institutional influences discussed in this chapter that have had an impact on the rules of the game governing the nomination process include the use of caucuses and conventions, the courts, term limitations, cross-filing, and statutory and constitutional qualifications for holding office. To what end do these rules have an impact on the soon to follow general elections? The trail leading from the nomination to the general election for any office closely links the nomination processes to the general election.

The most obvious link is that the nomination process establishes who the contending personalities will be in the general election and thus directly influences both the temperament of the general election campaign and issue priorities. It is not inconsequential, then, that factors that dictate the ease or difficulty of access to the primary ballot eventually have a very important impact in the United States on general elections and their outcome.

Office qualifications will determine eligibility to serve in office and thus will dictate initial requirements for gaining access to the general election ballot. Term limits dictate whether an incumbent will run in a primary, thus potentially influencing the direction that a general election will take. The ability to cross-file on more than one party ticket can dictate the breath of support a candidate in the general election may receive as a consequence of being listed on multiple ballots. The ease with which a third-party candidate or independent can get access to the ballot may affect the issues of the general election campaign and the contentiousness of the contest. A divisive primary, caucus, or convention may hurt a candidate in the general election.[44] Front-end loading of primaries, caucuses, and conventions can give significant advantage to the early frontrunners and favorites, forecasting many months in advance who the successful candidate will be in the general election. Money spent in getting the nomination may, particularly in local and state elections, reduce the financial resources available to a candidate for the general election campaign ahead.

All of these factors suggest that the statutes governing the nomination process—at the local, state, and national levels—have a significant influence on the selection of party and independent candidates. They also reinforce the strong link between the ballot access process and the general election.

We turn next, in Chapter 3, to a discussion on campaign financing.

Endnotes

1. James W. Davis, *U.S. Presidential Primaries and the Caucus-Convention System: A Sourcebook* (Westport, CT: Greenwood Press, 1997), 11.
2. Ibid., 13.
3. Edward D. Feigenbaum and James A. Palmer, *Ballot Access 1: Issues and Options* (Washington, DC: National Clearing House on Election Administration, Federal Election Commission, 1988), 17.
4. John F. Bibby, *Politics, Parties, and Elections in America*, 3rd ed., (Chicago: Nelson-Hall Publishers, 1996), 132.
5. Davis, *U.S. Presidential Primaries*, 28.
6. John F. Bibby, *Politics, Parties, and Elections in America*, 3rd ed. (Chicago: Nelson-Hall Publishers, 1996), 131-132; John Frendreis and Alan R. Gitelson, "Local Parties in the 1990s: Spokes in a Candidate-Centered Wheel," in John C. Green and Daniel M. Shea, eds., *The State of the Parties: The Changing Role of Contemporary American Parties*, 3rd ed. (Lanham, Maryland: Rowman & Littlefield Publishers, 1999), 135-153.
7. Davis, *U.S. Presidential Primaries*, 28.
8. While we will discuss the rules of the game regarding campaign financing and spending in more detail in Chapters 3 and 4, it is important to note that with the passage in 1971 of the Federal Election Campaign Act and subsequent amendments, along with the passage of the Revenue Act of 1971, candidates meeting minimal qualifications (see Table 3.2) could receive federal matching grants from the federal government to pay for their presidential primary campaigns.
9. William J. Crotty, *Party Reform* (New York: Longman, 1983), 227.
10. See, for example, *California Democratic Party v. Jones* (S.C. 99-401) for the most recent court case affecting the primary system. See also *United States v. Classic* (313 U.S. 299), *Smith v. Allwright* (321 U.S. 649), and *Terry v. Adams* (345 U.S. 461).
11. Alan R. Gitelson, Robert L. Dudley, and Melvin J. Dubnick, American *Government*, 6th ed. (Boston: Houghton Mifflin Company, 2001), 181. Note differences between open and closed primaries.
12. It is noteworthy to point out that no other nations employ the primary as a means of selecting party candidates to run for political office.
13. Feigenbaum and Palmer, *Ballot Access1*, 29.

14. *Book of the States*, 2000-01 edition, Volume 33 (Lexington, Kentucky: The Council of State Governments, 2000), 164–165.

15. *Book of the States*, 5.3, 164–165.

16. Nebraska has nonpartisan state legislative primaries.

17. Quoted by Linda Greenhouse, "Court Rejects One-Ballot Primary as Limit on Party's Right to Shape Its Identity," *The New York Times* (June 27, 2000): A19.

18. Feigenbaum and Palmer, Ballot Access 1, 15.

19. L. Sandy Maisel, Cary T. Gibson, and Elizabeth J. Ivry, "The Continuing Importance of the Rules of the Game: Subpresidential Nominations in 1994 and 1996," in L. Sandy Maisel, ed., *The Parties Respond: Changes in American Parties and Campaigns*, 3rd ed. (Boulder, CO: Westview Press, 1999), 148–149.

20. *Lubin v. Panish*, 415 U.S. 709 (1974).

21. Bibby, *Politics, Parties, and Elections*, 137–38.

22. Ibid., 138.

23. Paul Allen Beck, *Party Politics in America*, 8th ed. (New York: Longman, 1997), 204.

24. *Book of the States*, 164–165, Table 5.3.

25. Davis, *U.S. Presidential Primaries*, 47.

26. National Conference of State Legislators.

27. "Term Limits Kick in for Politicians," Associated Press Release, August 8, 1998.

28. Tari Renner and Victor S. DeSantis, "Municipal Form of Government: Issues and Trends," in *The Municipal Year Book 1998* (Washington, DC: International City/County Management Association, 1998), 38. See also Danielle Fagre, *Microcosm of the Movement: Local Term Limits in the United States*, Study for the U.S. Term Limits Foundation, 1995.

29. In 1995, the U.S. Supreme Court ruled unconstitutional the laws of twenty-three states that established congressional term limits (*U.S. Term Limits v. Thornton*, 1995).

30. Beck, Party *Politics in America*, 51–53. On May 24, 2001, U.S. Senator James M. Jeffords of Vermont declared he was no longer a member of the Republican party, subsequently confirming that he regarded himself as an independent. The decision by Jeffords, who has one of the most liberal voting records in the Senate among Republicans, came after a series of policy disputes with the White House and the Senate Republican leadership. For purposes of committee assignments, Jeffords declared that he would align himself with the Democratic party. If he chooses to run for reelection to the Senate at the end of his present term in 2006, he will run as an independent from the state of Vermont.

31. Beck, *Party Politics in America*, 52.

32. Feigenbaum and Palmer, *Ballott Access1*, 53.

33. Ibid., 54.

34. *Williams v. Rhodes*, 393 U.S. 23 (1968).

35. Feigenbaum and Palmer, *Ballot Access 1*, 14.

36. R.G. Ratcliffe, "New Parties Face Daunting Task to Get on Ballot," The Houston Chronicle (May 6, 1996): section a, 21.

37. Bibby, *Politics, Parties, and Elections in America*, 131–137.

38. Bibby, *Politics, Parties, and Elections*, 144. Limited interparty competition and no incumbent.

39. Malcolm E. Jewell and David M. Olson, *American State Political Parties and Elections* (Homewood, IL: Dosey Press, 1978), 94–104.

40.   William J. Keefe, *Parties, Politics, and Public Policy in America*, 8th ed. (Washington, DC: CQ Press, 1998), 88.
41.   Maisel, *The Parties Respond*, 165.
42.   Keefe, *Parties, Politics, and Public Policy in America*, 88.
43.   David Dodenhoff and Kenneth Goldstein, "Resources, Races, and Rules: Nominations in the 1990s," in L. Sandy Maisel, ed., *The Parties Respond: Changes in American Parties and Campaigns,* 3rd ed. (Boulder, CO: Westview Press, 1999), 200.
44.   Keefe, *Parties, Politics, and Public Policy in America,* 121.

Chapter 3
The Money Constituency

M ention the words "campaign financing" in almost any forum and you are likely to generate an abundance of commentary, mostly negative, on the role money plays in the American campaign process. This should not come as any surprise to us. For the 2000 elections, all presidential and congressional candidates, in addition to the political parties, political action committees, interest groups, labor unions, and corporations spent over $3 billion. This sum represented more than a 50 percent increase over spending in the presidential/congressional races in 1996.

Much of the debate and controversy over campaign financing in the United States centers on the laws, regulations, and rules that govern the process at the national, state, and local levels of government. In this chapter we will focus on the rules covering the campaign contribution process at the federal, state, and local levels of government. Chapter 4 will include, among other topics, the rules and laws governing the disclosure and expenditure of money in campaigns.

We begin this chapter with a discussion of the role of campaign financing at the federal level, starting with a review of the history of campaign financing and reform prior to 1971. We then examine the reforms and regulations established by the Federal Election Campaign Act of 1971 and its amendments in 1974 and 1979 which have such a significant impact on individual, corporate, union, and political action committee funding of congressional and presidential campaigns.

Our analysis continues with a discussion of campaign funding laws and reforms at the state and local levels, once again focusing on the theme of the chapter, campaign contributions. Finally, we summarize and review the impact of recent changes in the laws and regulations governing campaign financing in federal, state, and local election campaigns.

Campaign Contributions at the Federal Level

It is appropriate, for at least two reasons, to begin our discussion of the laws and regulations governing campaign contributions by focusing initially on the federal level. First, recent state and local reforms regarding the campaign financing process have their roots in changes and reforms at the national level. Much of the activity in recent years regarding campaign finance reform at the state and local level has come as a consequence of or a reaction to efforts at reform of federal campaign finance laws. Second, a good deal of attention, by the media, the public, and candidates, regarding campaign finance laws and reform has centered on federal elections, specifically presidential and congressional campaigns. The 2000 presidential primary campaign was made conspicuous by the very strong interest that Republican presidential hopeful Senator John McCain and Democratic presidential aspirant Bill Bradley placed on federal campaign finance reform. Certainly the public is more aware of campaign finance reform at the federal level than it is of reform in state and local government.

We turn first to a brief history of laws governing campaign financing, a chronicle that then leads us to a discussion of the contemporary rules and regulations that govern campaign contributions in federal elections.

A Brief History

Anthony Corrado, a student of campaign finance reform, reminds us that concerns over the issue of campaign financing and its potential and real impact on the election process started long before Watergate, a major scandal during the Nixon presidency that involved, among other things, the revelation of widespread violations in the soliciting of political campaign contributions. While the Watergate era during the early 1970s was marked by increased apprehension over the impact of money on the outcome of the election process, concerns regarding the role of money in campaigns goes back as far as colonial times. George Washington was accused in 1757 of campaign-spending irregularities in seeking a seat in the Virginia House of Burgesses.[1] Washington was said to have purchased enough wine, beer, rum, and hard cider to provide each of the 391 voters in his district with one and a half quarts of the alcohol. One hundred years later, Abraham Lincoln spent over $100,000—regarded as an enormous sum of money in 1860—on his successful bid for the presidency. It was not, however, until the turn of the century and the Progressive movement of the 1890s and 1910s that we saw our first significant attempts at campaign finance reform.[2]

By the 1890s, millions of dollars were being solicited and contributed to the presidential elections, with many political reformers fearful that money was buying influence in the halls of both the White House and Congress. In an effort to respond to the calls for reform, the Tillman Act was passed in 1907 forbidding corporations and national banks from making any contributions to presidential and congressional campaigns. This prohibition continues today although, as we shall see shortly, the evolving role of "soft money" in federal elections—money that does not fall under federal regulation—has weakened considerably the impact of the Tillman Act on campaign finance regulation and the prohibition placed on corporations from donating money to federal election campaigns.

In 1910, the Federal Corrupt Practices Act, also known as the Publicity Act of 1910, was enacted by Congress requiring the reporting of all campaign receipts and expenditures of national party committees and party committees operating in two or more states. The impact of this bill on campaign finance reform was minimal. It involved only a single postelection report with no disclosures made during the campaign itself. An amendment to the act in 1911 sought to strengthen the law by first providing for preelection reports on receipts and expenditures in Senate and House campaigns, and second, by establishing spending limits in both Senate and House races. The latter provision was struck down as unconstitutional by a Supreme Court ruling in 1921.[3]

It was not until the notorious Teapot Dome scandal in 1924 involving President Warren Harding's Secretary of the Interior, accused of taking bribes to lease government property to oil companies, that federal campaign regulations were further revised. The result was the Federal Corrupt Practices Act of 1925. The act reasserted and tightened earlier laws dealing with disclosure of contributions and expenditures in federal elections and revised spending limitations in the Senate and the House of Representatives.[4]

The Federal Corrupt Practices Act was ineffective for it did not provide for the efficacious enforcement of its provisions, most of which were ignored or easily avoided. No individual was ever prosecuted for violating any parts of the Corrupt Practices Act, and only two individuals were excluded from office for violating the act's provisions—in both cases in the election immediately following the enactment of the law in 1925.

It was not until 1939 and the enactment of the Hatch Act, also known as the Clean Politics Act, that campaign reform showed its head again at the federal level. The Hatch Act, supplementing the provisions of the earlier Pendleton Civil Service Act of 1883, forbid federal employees from participating in federal elections and also prohibited the soliciting of campaign contributions from federal employees.

While amendments in 1940 to the Hatch Act sought to reform further the federal campaign process by imposing limits on individual campaign contributions to candidates for federal office and political parties, for all practical purposes the limits were, as with past acts, unenforceable. By establishing multiple campaign committees, candidates and parties could legally solicit contributions of up to $5,000 from individuals to each of the established committees. Candidates could create dozens—even hundreds—of campaign committees to circumvent the law.

A more significant, although limited, reform occurred in 1943 with the passage of the Smith-Connally Act, which prohibited labor unions from contributing union funds to federal campaigns. This act, which expired shortly after the end of World War II, was reenacted as part of the Taft-Hartley Act of 1947. It served to put the labor unions on the same footing as corporations which were prohibited from donating corporate funds to federal election campaigns by the Tillman Act of 1907.

Although a number of commissions would seek to establish campaign reform during the 1950s and 1960s, including one commission formed by President Kennedy, which unsuccessfully called for matching funding of presidential races, little legislation of any consequence was enacted during the first two decades of the post–World War II era. In 1966, Congress enacted the Long Act, a bill designed to diminish the influence of wealthy contributors to presidential

TABLE 3.1	Campaign Reform Acts: 1907 to 1947	

Year	Act	General Purpose
1907	Tillman Act	Forbids corporations and national banks from making contributions to presidential and congressional elections.
1910	Federal Corruption Act (Publicity Act of 1910)	Requires the reporting of all campaign receipts and expenditures of national party committees and party committees operating in two or more states.
1925	The Federal Corruption Practices Act of 1925	Tightened up earlier laws dealing with disclosure of contributions and expenditures in federal elections.
1939	Hatch Act (Clean Politics Act)	Forbids federal employees from participating in federal elections. The Act also prohibits the soliciting of campaign contributions from federal employees.
1943	Smith-Connally Act	Prohibited, during World War II, labor unions from contributing union funds to federal campaigns.
1947	Taft-Hartley Act	Replaced the Smith-Connally Act after World War II, placing labor unions on the same footing as corporations under the Tillman Act of 1907, which prohibited corporate funds from being donated to federal election campaigns.

races. The bill called for the public funding of political parties who would pay for presidential races. Ensuing acts of Congress one year later permanently postponed its enforcement.

In effect, with the exceptions of the Tillman Act, the Hatch Act, and the Taft-Hartley Act, none of the campaign finance reforms and regulations enacted during the first 175 years of our nation's history had any practical or long-term impact on the federal campaign finance process. The nation would have to wait until 1971 before a serious effort was made regarding genuine attempts to reform the campaign finance process (see Table 3.1).

The Federal Election Campaign Act

The first modern effort to enact effective legislation dealing with the reform of federal campaign financing occurred in 1971 with the passage of the Federal Election Campaign Act (FECA). The impetus for reform built during the 1960s. A major catalyst was the negative publicity generated by the significant amounts of money that were spent on the 1968 presidential campaign.

The passage of legislation—more effective than the previous ineffectual attempts at campaign finance reform—was no small task. The legislation's authors soon discovered that opponents of campaign finance reform forcefully, and often effectively, argued against any restrictions on campaign contributions. They argued that there was a fine constitutional line between placing limits on campaign contributions in federal elections and suppressing the right of individuals to speak out in politics by donating money to political campaigns. Placing limitations on the right of an individual to support her or his favorite candidates with a campaign contribution potentially threatened the First Amendment right of free speech. As one contemporary antireform lawyer leading the fight to foil any new campaign finance laws has argued, any efforts at legislating limits on campaign financing and spending, which is an expression of freedom of speech, "is off-limits to regulation, cannot be regulated."[5]

In 1976, the Supreme Court clarified the relationship between the First Amendment and limitations on campaign contributions in their ruling in *Buckley v. Valeo*.[6] The Court argued that while campaign expenditure limits in federal elections created serious and constricting restrictions relative to the free speech issue, Congress could legislate broad limitations on contributions to federal elections. The decision specified, however, that those restrictions could not be so inhibiting as to limit severely a campaign's financial resources or significantly block the support that an individual wished to give to a candidate. In effect, Congress was given pivotal power by the Supreme Court to establish campaign contribution limits in federal elections.[7]

Federal laws governing campaign contribution limitations cover a number of funding sources including individuals, political action committees (PACs), multicandidate committees, and political parties.

Individual Contributions   Individual contributions to federal election campaigns are limited to no more than $1,000 per candidate per election. Technically, an "election" includes general, primary, and run-off contests as well as special elections that may take place outside normal election periods. (For example, in the case of the death or resignation of a member of Congress, a special election may be held to fill the unexpired term of office.) Thus, an individual can contribute up to $1,000 to each of these elections.

This provision of the law was clearly aimed at limiting the campaign contributions of individual "fat cats," who were often perceived as buying influence in the policy-making process. The FECA also limits the total contributions an individual can make to one or more of the national party committees in a calendar year to no more than $20,000.[8] Individuals are further limited to no more than a $5,000 contribution to any other distinct political committee including PACs. An individual can make a maximum total contribution to all federal campaigns, party organizations, and political committees of no more than $25,000 in a calendar year.

As Trevor Potter points out, there are exclusions in the statute including donations of personal time, home hospitality (up to $1,000 per candidate per election), and personal travel (up to $1,000 per candidate per election and up to $2,000 per year for party committees).[9] Candidates in congressional elections are also permitted to loan as much of their own money to their campaign as they want. As we shall see shortly, the capability of making what are known as "soft money" contributions to nonfederal committees, parties, and accounts provides individuals with the ability to skirt the rules of the game as they apply to individual contribution levels in federal campaigns.

PAC Contributions   The rules governing federal campaign contributions also have an impact on other institutions central to the campaign finance process. Corporations, trade associations, and unions, which are prevented by law from raising money or making contributions to federal campaigns, can organize and pay administrative costs for PACs, which do have the power to raise and contribute money to federal campaigns.

A PAC may contribute up to a maximum of $5,000 to a congressional campaign with no limit on the total aggregate contributions they can make. A PAC may be unaffiliated—that is, have no ties to any corporation, trade association, or union—but still represent an ideological position or a candidate or officeholder (the latter are often referred to as leadership PACs). PACs may also make contributions of up to $20,000 per year to political party organizations.

Multicandidate Committees   A second type of campaign committee is the multicandidate committee, defined by the FECA as any organization with fifty-one or more individuals making contributions to at least five congressional candidates (some PACs are classified as multicandidate committees). Multicandidate committees may contribute no more than $5,000 to any individual candidate or candidate committee in a given election, no more than $15,000 to a national party committee, and no more than $5,000 to any other political committee in a calendar year.

Party Committees   Finally, national and congressional party campaign committees (the Republican National Committee, the National Republican Senatorial Committee, the National Republican Congressional Committee, the Democratic National Committee, the Democratic Senatorial Campaign Committee, and the Democratic Congressional Campaign Committee) have the same contribution limits placed on them as multicandidate committees with the following exceptions:

- Party committees can shift unlimited amounts of money to other party committees including state party committees.
- The two national party committees and the two U.S. Senate campaign committees may contribute up to $17,500 to individual Senate candidates per election; the national party committees and the two U.S. House campaign committees may contribute up to $5,000 to a House candidate's campaign per election.
- State political parties may contribute unlimited amounts of money to certain party-building activities that may have an impact on federal elections—for example, voter registration drives and get-out-the-vote drives.
- Party organizations (as well as PACs) may "bundle" individual contributions to candidates. With bundling, the party urges individual contributors to send them checks made out to a candidate. That check, along with others made out to the candidate's campaign, will be bundled together as part of a large contribution and will be delivered to the candidate by the party. In effect, federal law regards the contributions as being made by individuals but the party gets credit for having organized the donations and for delivering the collective amount (often totaling in the tens or hundreds of thousands of dollars) to the candidate's campaign. (This tactic is not limited to political parties. Emily's List, an interest group that supports many women's issues, pioneered the use of bundling, often relying on public figures like singer Barbra Streisand to solicit contributions to their cause.)

Under federal law, parties appear to have a distinct advantage over other groups and individuals because they have a higher ceiling on contribution levels. As a consequence, parties are an attractive conduit for contributions to

> **TABLE 3.2** Provisions of the Federal Election Campaign Act of 1971 and as Amended Affecting Campaign in Federal Elections

- Established a bipartisan, six-member Federal Election Commission to administer and enforce all federal regulations dealing with contributions and expenditures as they apply to congressional and presidential campaign funding.

- Established maximum individual, political action committee (PAC), and multicandidate committee contribution limitations for primary, runoff, and general elections:

  Individuals: $1,000 for individuals per candidate per election,* $5,000 per year to any PAC, and $20,000 per year to a national party committee. Total contributions by an individual in any calendar year cannot exceed $25,000.
  PACs: may contribute up to $5,000 per candidate per election with no cap on total contributions a PAC can make in a year.
  *Multicandidate Committees:*** may contribute up to $5,000 per candidate or candidate committee per election, a maximum of $15,000 to a national committee of a political party, and up to $5,000 to a PAC or any other political committee in a calendar year.

- National Party and Congressional Campaign Committees: may contribute up to $5,000 to each House of Representatives candidate. The national party committee and the senatorial campaign committee for each party may contribute up to $17,500 to each of their Senate candidates in any election cycle.

- Corporations, unions, banks, government contractors, and foreign nationals and corporations are barred from making contributions to federal elections.

- Contributions are illegal if the money is provided by one individual but made in the name of another individual.

- Contributions in cash may not exceed $100.

SOURCE: William J. Keefe, *Parties, Politics, and Public Policy in America*, 8th ed. (Washington, DC: CQ Press, 1998), 155.

*Primary, runoff, and general elections, in addition to special federal elections called because of the death or resignation of a congressional candidate, are regarded as separate elections.

**A multicandidate committee is defined as any committee with fifty or more contributors making contributions to five or more candidates for federal office.

candidates and independent efforts made in support of candidates. Paul Allen Beck points out that "the parties have been able to circumvent the $5,000 limit on their contributions to candidates by providing valuable services, acting as conduits for individual contributions to candidates (so-called bundling), channeling soft money to the state parties, [we will discuss soft money shortly] making coordinated expenditures for the party ticket as a whole, and investing in long-term state and local party building."[10]

The Federal Election Campaign Act and subsequent amendments constitute a menagerie of rules and regulations governing federal campaign contributions (see Table 3.2). These statutes include the prohibition of certain groups—national banks, corporations, and labor unions—from directly contributing to federal campaigns. In addition to these organizations, direct and indirect contributions from foreign nationals are prohibited in any federal, state, and local election.[11] Federal contractors and nonprofit organizations are also banned from making contributions to federal candidates and party committees.

Public Funding in Presidential Elections

The Federal Election Campaign Act and the Revenue Act of 1971 provide for the public funding of presidential campaigns. Congressional campaigns are not publicly funded.

Major party candidates for the presidency can elect to receive matching federal grants for presidential primary races if they qualify and agree to certain limitations, including caps on contributions and spending limitations during the primaries. In effect, presidential campaigns are partially publicly funded. To participate in the matching fund program candidates must raise $100,000 by collecting a minimum of $5,000 in 20 different states. In an effort to lessen the role of large donors the law allows only the first $250 of any contribution to be counted toward determining eligibility. Furthermore, to receive the matching funds, the candidate must agree to abide by overall spending limits and spending limits for each state. The overall spending limit is defined as $10 million (in 1974 dollars) plus an adjustment for inflation. In 2000, that amounted to a spending ceiling of $40.53 million for the primaries. Spending ceilings in each state are set at $200,000 (again 1974 dollars) plus the cost-of-living adjustment or $0.16 times the voting-age population of the state, whichever is greater. (See Chapter 4 for further discussion of spending limits when a candidate accepts federal funding in presidential primaries.) With the exception that individual contributions are still restricted to no more than $1,000, presidential candidates who choose not to accept public funding are not bound by the limitations specified in the law. Thus, candidates rejecting federal matching grants in primaries are not restricted in how much of their own money they can spend, can spend unlimited amounts of money in the primaries, and are not constrained in any way by individual state caps on spending. In effect, there are two different sets of rules that a candidate can operate under in presidential primaries.

In 2000, only two candidates for the Republican nomination, George W. Bush and Steve Forbes, chose not to accept federal-matching funding. Bush relied on individual and PAC contributions totaling approximately $100 million to fund his campaign, thereby avoiding the spending limits in state primaries. Forbes, a multimillionaire who inherited a family fortune, also chose to fund his own primary campaign without federal funding in order to avoid restrictions on spending limits.

Major party candidates also can qualify for full funding for the general election race ($67.56 million in 2000) if they agree not to accept any private contributions for the campaign (or to spend money in excess of the federal funding). Candidates can refuse to accept public funding, thus removing any restrictions on the total contributions they can solicit, although no major party candidate has chosen this option. Both Republican George W. Bush and Democrat Al Gore chose to take advantage of public funding during the 2000 general election campaign.

Minor party and independent candidates may qualify for lesser sums provided that their candidate received at least 5 percent of the vote in the previous presidential election. This was the case in the 2000 presidential campaign for the Reform party, which qualified for $12.6 million in federal campaign funding because its 1996 presidential candidate, Ross Perot, received 8 percent of the vote. New parties and independent candidates can retroactively qualify and apply for partial federal funding after a presidential race if they receive at least

5 percent of the vote in the election. Since no third-party candidate in the 2000 presidential elections received at least 5 percent of the vote, no third party qualifies at this time for public funding for the 2004 presidential elections.

The Revenue Act of 1971 provides for the federal funding of presidential primaries and the general election. Every individual and couple filing a federal tax form has the option of voluntarily requesting that $3 of the tax that they are paying be placed in a segregated fund known as the Presidential Election Campaign Fund. That money is applied to the payment of matching grants in the presidential primaries as well as full funding in the presidential general election. While a majority of the public supports some form of public funding of presidential elections, the public has never been enthusiastic about designating part of their tax return to the Presidential Election Campaign Fund. In 1976 when the act first became effective, 27.5 percent of the tax-paying public indicated a willingness to contribute to the fund. By 1997, that public support had dropped to only 12.2 percent.[12]

While significant pressures still exist for major party candidates to raise money in the primary stage of a presidential race, both matching federal grants in the primaries and full federal funding in the general election have, in effect, changed the rules of the game. Certainly, some of the pressures associated with seeking contributions in presidential contests have been reduced. We'll have more to say about this in the chapter's concluding section on campaign finance reform.

Soft Money: The Big Loophole

Soft money contributions provide the national political parties with a significant loophole by which federal campaign contribution laws can be eluded. By definition, soft money contributions, a term coined by political writer Elizabeth Drew,[13] are financial donations to the national Republican and Democratic political parties that are passed through to state parties.[14] The federal government does not regulate these monies, although contributions of $250 or more must be reported to the Federal Election Commission (FEC) and, according to federal law, soft money funds may not be raised for or spent directly on federal elections. Nevertheless, soft money contributions have a significant impact on federal elections.

As we noted earlier, corporations, unions, PACs, and individuals are limited by federal law as to the amount of money they can legally contribute to political parties for presidential and congressional campaigns (see Table 3.2). A contribution or expenditure that is defined and limited under federal law is designated as "hard money." However, under the FECA and its amendments as well as Supreme Court rulings, national parties are empowered to raise unlimited and unregulated soft money contributions from PACs, corporations, unions, and individuals and to filter those contributions to the state party organizations for purposes of party-building activities including get-out-the-vote and voter registration drives.

In 1976, the Supreme Court ruled that the national parties were permitted to raise unlimited funds—soft money—for the use of state parties to finance generic campaign advocacy or issue advertisements. The Court stated that those ad campaigns could not be coordinated with a candidate's campaign and that words including "elect," "vote for," or "vote against" could not be used in the advertisements targeted in support of or opposed to a specific candidate.[15] The advertisements could be directed toward the general support of a party or candidate's issue positions.

In addition, soft monies were also permitted by federal law to be filtered by the national parties to the states for nonfederal campaigns, including races for the governorship, state contests, and races for the state legislator and local campaigns. Support of these campaigns is often of great interest to the national parties for two reasons. First, in addition to supporting the party's candidates in important statewide races and state legislative races, they provide further advertising and promotion both directly and indirectly for the party's congressional and presidential candidates.

Second, the outcome of state legislative elections that follow the national census every ten years can have a significant impact on the makeup of the House of Representatives. After the census is taken, shifts in population around the nation will affect the distribution of the 435 seats in the House of Representatives. Any loss or gain of House seats for a state after the census will generally necessitate a redrawing of congressional district lines in the state. Members of the state legislature and the governor have primary responsibility for the redrawing of district lines, a process that can favor one party or the other depending on who is doing the drawing. Thus the national parties have a vested interested in this process. The 2000 census, for example, resulted in Arizona and Texas gaining two seats in the House of Representatives, while California, Colorado, Florida, Georgia, Montana, and Nevada all gained one seat. In turn, New York and Pennsylvania were targeted to lose two seats, while Connecticut, Illinois, Mississippi, Ohio, Oklahoma, and Wisconsin all lost one seat.

One important rational for soft money contributions is that it is justified on the grounds that it helps strengthen political parties at the state and local levels through party-building activities and through issue advocacy supported by the party's candidates. In addition, soft money contributions assist in promoting voter registration and get-out-the-vote efforts, an important objective of any representative democracy.

Critics of soft money argue that it is "sewer money" which, in effect, circumvents reform efforts at limiting the role of "fat cat" contributors including individuals, PACs, corporations, and unions seeking special influence in the policy-making process. Soft money, critics argue, can buy the influence of elected officials as effectively as direct hard money contributions to candidates.

Critics also argue that soft money contributions often provide very strong, if indirect, support for specific congressional or presidential candidates.[16] Voter registration drives and get-out-the-vote efforts are often targeted for populations most likely to support a party's candidates at all levels of government. Even generic issue advocacy campaigns benefit congressional and presidential candidates when they emphasize policy positions supported by the party's candidates or are critical of policy positions supported by the opposition candidates.

As we shall see in the concluding section of this chapter, there are clear justifications both for and against the raising of soft money for federal campaigns. Whatever the case may be, it is obvious that soft money has a significant impact on federal campaigns. In 2000 alone, total soft money contributions to the Republican and Democratic parties were estimated to exceed $500 million, a significant increase over the 1996 elections. Between 1991 and 1999, the

American Federation of State, County, and Municipal Employees union made soft money contributions of over $3.6 million to the Democratic party. The Philip Morris Company soft money contributions to the Republican party during that same period totaled over $6.2 million.[17] Contributions by many individuals, corporations, and unions exceeded $100,000.[18]

According to Anthony Corrado:

> This nonfederal money quickly became known as "soft money," because it was not subject to the "hard" limits of federal law. National committees could solicit unlimited amounts from donors throughout the country, and then use the money to . . . redistribute these funds to those states where they were considered most necessary. As long as the contributions were legal under state law [*and did not violate federal restrictions on campaign fundraising for federal elections*], the gifts were permissible. So a national party fundraiser could solicit $1 million from a donor and use the monies for a variety of purposes. . . . In essence, the new rules gave party organizations a green light to engage in unrestricted fund-raising.[19]

The impact of soft money contributions is not a neutral influence on the campaign process. First, the Republican party has historically been more successful than the Democratic party in raising soft money although the Democratic party has done well in recent years. Second, soft money provides the national parties with the opportunity to free up hard money funds—otherwise spent on party building activities, overhead costs, voter registration drives, and get-out-the-vote efforts—for direct campaign spending under the FECA regulations.

We will return to the effects of federal reform on presidential and congressional campaign contribution limits in the final section of this chapter. We now turn to a discussion of the laws and regulations regarding campaign contributions as they apply to state and local elections.

Campaign Contributions at the State Level

While most public attention regarding campaign funding reform has focused on federal elections, the fifty states have been active in recent years, to varying degrees, regarding the regulation of state and local campaign finance reform.[20] The picture of reform at the state and local level, however, has been erratic. We turn first to the states in our continuing analysis of the rules of the game governing campaign financing.

The Fifty States

As was true in our discussion on ballot access and the laws governing the nomination process in Chapter 2, the preponderance of election laws dealing with campaign financing and contributions in the United States fall under the jurisdiction of the individual fifty states. Not surprisingly, any examination of campaign reform and regulation regarding contributions to state and local political campaigns involves a closer examination of those regulations, regulations that vary considerably across the nation. We turn initially to a brief review of the history of laws governing state campaign financing, a chronicle that then leads us to a discussion of the contemporary rules that govern campaign contributions in state elections.

A Brief History: The States

Campaign financing at the state level has been an issue of concern for much of our nation's history. Early records indicate, for example, that in 1828 a candidate for the governor of Kentucky solicited contributions in amounts ranging from $5,000 to $10,000, sums that were regarded as considerable during the early days of our nation.[21]

The earliest recorded efforts at reforming the campaign process at the state level took place around the turn of the twentieth century in response to the growth of political party machines at both the state and local levels of government.[22] Some of those efforts were radical if short-lived. For example, Oregon and several other states passed legislation that paid for the distribution of candidates' campaign statements and the printing of brief candidate statements on the voting ballots.[23] Several states, including New York (1890), Massachusetts (1892), and California (1893), required disclosure statements listing campaign receipts and expenditures. Others legislated regulations dealing with the size of campaign contributions and the prohibition of donations to campaigns from corporations and other businesses.

There is little if any evidence that efforts at campaign finance reform effectively dealt with campaign contribution abuses or that those laws were even enforced. Two states, California and Colorado, serve as important case studies in early state reform.

In 1893, the California legislature passed a comprehensive law governing state campaign funding reforms. The statute, The Purity of Elections Act, established limits on campaign expenditures, prohibited independent campaign spending, forbade the shifting of campaign funds from one candidate to another, and established strict disclosure rules which, if violated, would require that the elected official be removed from office. However, as a consequence of several rulings by the California Supreme Court, the legislation was effectively eviscerated and the act was finally repealed by the state legislature in 1907.

Colorado was no more successful in its early efforts at campaign finance reform. In 1909, the state legislature passed the first statute in the nation providing for the public financing of state elections. State political parties were given public funds for campaign financing based on the party's vote in the previous gubernatorial election. Parties were restricted from accepting any additional funding from other sources and candidates were only permitted to use party funds or personal funds in their campaign as long as total expenditures did not exceed a spending limit of 40 percent of the salary of the office the candidate was seeking. As in the case of California's reform efforts, the legislation never took effect. The Colorado Supreme Court declared the statute unconstitutional in 1910, thus ending the earliest effort at establishing public funding of political campaigns in the United States.

Campaign Finance in the States

In the aftermath of the revelation of widespread violations in the soliciting of political campaign contributions during the 1972 presidential race and the Watergate scandal in 1973, many states pushed for campaign finance reform within their own state boundaries. In some states, loopholes or slow implementation have eroded some of those reforms. In other states, we have seen innovative attempts at reforming the campaign finance process.

One must be careful in characterizing all state statutes dealing with campaign finance as reform efforts. The seriousness with which state legislators have taken campaign finance reform has been irregular over the past thirty years with some states providing for significantly stricter provisions than others.

The variations among the states regarding legislation governing contributions by organizations and individuals are significant. In Florida, corporations, labor unions, PACs, and individuals are permitted to contribute a maximum of $500 to any candidate seeking state office. In New York, corporations are limited to no more than $5,000 per candidate in a calendar year, while individual contributions are governed by a formula that takes into account the vote the party received in a specific election district, averaging an estimated $5,600 in a state assembly campaign.[24] Other states, including Alaska, Arizona, Colorado, Connecticut, New Hampshire, North Carolina, North Dakota, Pennsylvania, and Rhode Island have banned any direct campaign contributions by labor unions or corporations, while states including Idaho, Illinois, Missouri, New Mexico, Utah, and Virginia have no restrictions on contributions to state office campaigns from corporations and unions.[25]

Laws governing individual contributions to campaigns in the various states vary as widely as corporate and labor union regulations vary. Alabama, Indiana, Iowa, Mississippi, New Mexico, North Dakota, Pennsylvania, Utah, and Virginia place virtually no limitations on contributions to state-office campaigns by individuals, candidates, or their family members.[26] Illinois provides for unlimited contributions with the exception of generally banning donations to judicial candidates.

The fifty states also vary in their regulations regarding political party contributions to statewide and legislative candidates. Seventeen states place virtually no restrictions on party contributions; the remaining states place limitations ranging from $1,000 per slate per election in Kentucky to $50,000 for statewide offices in South Carolina.[27] In some states, political parties are not permitted to make any contributions to judicial candidates. In addition to regulating who can make campaign contributions, a majority of states have laws that restrict when contributions can be made to a candidate. Those states prohibit contributions to state legislative and statewide office holders while the state legislature is in session or during the period thirty days before or after the legislature has met.[28]

As has been the case at the federal level, the issue of freedom of speech and the right to contribute money to campaigns has raised its head in recent years in state races. While many states have placed contribution limits on corporations, unions, PACs, and individuals (see Table 3.3), a number of state and federal court decisions have found some state restrictions unconstitutional and in violation of the First Amendment right of freedom of speech. Cases in Missouri and Oregon have involved the overruling of contribution limits that were regarded as too restrictive and thus unjustified.

Public Funding in State Campaigns

As in the case of presidential elections, the question of public funding of statewide and legislative races has undergone a renewed interest by some legislators and reformers in recent years. Twenty-four states provide for some variation in public funding of statewide and legislative offices. Twelve states including Alabama, Arizona, California, Idaho, and Virginia provide for the

TABLE 3.3   State Campaign Finance Laws:* Limitations on Contributions in Eight Selected States

State	Corporation	Labor Union	Individual
Alabama	Limited to $500 to any candidate, political committee, or political party per election.	Unlimited	Unlimited
California	Limits of $1,000 per candidate per special election or special runoff election only. Certain jurisdictions have local limits on contributions to candidates.	Limits of $5,000 for a broad-based political committee; and $2,500 for a political committee per candidate per special election or special runoff election only. Certain jurisdictions have local limits on contributions to candidates.	Limit of $1,000 per person per special election or special runoff election. Certain jurisdictions have local limits on contributions to candidates.
Colorado	Prohibited	Prohibited	Unlimited
Florida	Limited to $500 per candidate per election.	Limited to $500 per candidate per election.	Limited to $500 per candidate per election. Unemancipated children under 18 limited to $100 per candidate per election. Some restrictions on judges and judicial personnel.
Illinois	Unlimited	Unlimited	Unlimited but generally prohibited for judicial candidates and judicial employees.
Oregon	Unlimited	Unlimited	Unlimited
Pennsylvania	Prohibited	Prohibited	Unlimited
Texas	Unlimited to political parties, except during 60 days before election, and to political committees to support or oppose a measure.	Unlimited to political parties except during 60 days before election and to support or oppose a measure.	Unlimited

SOURCE: *The Book of the States, vol. 33,* 2000–01 edition. (Lexington, KY: The Council of State Governments, 2000), Tables 5.10 and 5.11. Data on all other states not covered in this table can be found in this publication.

*Data collected as of December 31, 1999.

distribution of public funds to political parties designated by taxpayers who agree to a surcharge—a charge above and beyond the taxpayer's normal tax responsibility—or a tax check-off system—a charge in which the taxpayer approves the allocation of a small sum of her or his taxes to pay for the public financing of campaigns.[29]

Other states provide for direct public funding out of the state budget for gubernatorial candidates (Florida, Maryland, Massachusetts, Michigan, Minnesota, New Jersey, Vermont, and Wisconsin) and other statewide offices (Minnesota, Wisconsin). Four states—Maine, Minnesota, North Carolina, and Rhode Island—provide public money to both political parties and candidates. Minnesota, Nebraska, and Wisconsin are the only three states that provide for direct comprehensive funding of state legislative races.

Public monies for the support of state campaigns are disbursed as either an outright grant or a matching grant. With few exceptions, states that directly fund campaigns—bypassing the political parties—use a matching grant system similar to that used at the federal level in presidential primaries. For every dollar raised by a candidate that is a qualified contribution, she or he receives a one-to-one or two-to-one matching grant from the state (with a specified cap in total matching funds). In Maryland, qualified candidates for the governor's race receive a flat grant for the general election.

Whether the public funding of state campaigns will become more widespread is speculative at best (see Table 3.4). Maine's public financing program, which is a voluntary system providing public funding if a state legislative candidate accepts spending limitations, has met with mixed acceptance and endorsement by candidates.

Soft Money at the State Level

As in the case of federal campaign financing, few issues raise as many red flags and generate more heated discussion at the state level than the use of soft money to circumvent campaign finance laws. While a majority of states provide for some level of campaign finance regulation, most also allow for the establishment of soft money accounts. These accounts, according to Michael Malbin and Thomas Gais, "are not used to contribute directly to candidates . . ." and thus are exempt from state regulation.[30] As in the case of the state of Washington, other states often permit soft money accounts. State, county, and often legislative party committees are allowed to:

> set up separate, segregated accounts for specified activities: organizational overhead, voter registration, absentee ballot information, and get-out-the-vote campaigns. All of these activities must be conducted "without promotion of or advertising of political candidates."[31]

This stipulation in the law in the state of Washington applies even to indirect references to candidates.

In effect, the raising of soft money in many states is critical to statewide and legislative campaigns. Soft money directed at voter registration drives or get-out-the-vote campaigns frees up "hard money"—money that is legally collected for a campaign—for other uses including direct campaign support. Many states allow for the use of soft money in "issue campaigns" in which indirect support of candidates is often implied in campaign advertisements.

In states that have strict regulations regarding campaign contributions to state races it is clear that soft money accounts are proliferating as a means of bypassing state laws that place limits on corporate, union, PAC, and individual contribution levels. In states like Virginia and Illinois that allow for unlimited contributions from corporations, unions, PACs, and individuals, soft

TABLE **3.4**	Public Financing of Some or All State Elections*	
State	**Provisions for Public Financing**	**No Provisions for Public Financing**
Alabama	X	
Alaska		X
Arizona	X	
Arkansas		X
California	X	
Colorado		X
Connecticut		X
Delaware		X
Florida	X	
Georgia		X
Hawaii		X
Idaho	X	
Illinois		X
Indiana	X	
Iowa	X	
Kansas		X
Kentucky	X	
Louisiana		X
Maine	X	
Maryland	X	
Massachusetts	X	
Michigan	X	
Minnesota	X	
Mississippi		X
Missouri		X

SOURCE: *The Book of the States, vol. 33*, 2000–01 edition. (Lexington, KY: The Council of State Governments, 2000), Table 5.13. For states providing for public funding of state elections, specific provisions can be found in the above publication, Table 5.13.

*Data collected as of December 31, 1999.

money accounts are of little significance or importance in filling campaign coffers.

Campaign Contributions at the Local Level

Few studies have systematically collected data and analyzed campaign finance reform legislation and initiatives at the local level of government in the United States. There are, however, some generalizations that can be made regarding local campaign finance law.

According to Craig Holman, co-executive director of the Center for Governmental Studies, a local community's ability to legislate campaign finance reform "depends on whether a state constitution permits some degree of local action

TABLE **3.4** Continued		
State	**Provisions for Public Financing**	**No Provisions for Public Financing**
Montana		X
Nebraska	X	
Nevada		X
New Hampshire		X
New Jersey	X	
New Mexico	X	
New York	X	
North Carolina	X	
North Dakota		x
Ohio	X	
Oklahoma		X
Oregon		X
Pennsylvania		X
Rhode Island	X	
South Carolina		X
South Dakota		X
Tennessee		X
Texas		X
Utah	X	
Vermont	X	
Virginia	X	
Washington		X
West Virginia		X
Wisconsin	X	
Wyoming		X

and how the courts in that state define what constitutes a 'local action' versus a 'state interest.'"[32] Holman goes on to explain that

> [i]n California, for example, both the state constitution and the statutory Political Reform Act permit some degree of local autonomy, which has been upheld by the courts. Local jurisdictions that desire to codify their own rules of conduct organize their jurisdiction as a charter county or charter city (as opposed to a general law county or general law city).[33]

As a charter city, a municipality in California can modify the state's campaign laws—enhancing or strengthening the law or imposing new requirements—as long as those modifications do not violate state or federal mandates.[34] In effect, local communities in California and across the nation have limited autonomy regarding the enactment of campaign finance laws. Even so, a number of cities have adopted local campaign laws including partial public financing schemes in Austin, New York City, Los Angeles, Long Beach, Tucson, Sacramento County (California), and King County (Washington).[35]

Twenty-seven states have state laws regulating local campaign financing. In 1974, the California state legislature passed the Political Reform Act that gives local communities the power to legislate campaign finance reform as long as those laws apply only to local candidates and committees within the local jurisdiction. Since that legislation, a number of charter communities have initiated their own disclosure laws, contribution and spending limits, and financing laws for local campaigns (e.g., Los Angeles and Long Beach).

In 1996 in California, Proposition 208 established state and local spending limits with the option for local communities to enact stricter contribution and spending limits for local candidates "by a vote of the governing board, or weaken the state contribution and spending limits on local candidates by a popular vote."[36] However, in 1998, the federal court found many of the provisions of Proposition 208 unconstitutional, thus rendering most efforts at implementing the proposition useless. Nevertheless, home rule provisions in the state have provided almost fifty cities and towns with the legal tools necessary to enact some measures of campaign finance reform.

In 1996, Michigan enacted legislation governing both state and local campaign financing. The law, as it applied to local communities, established contribution limits based on a local electoral district's population. Counties supervise the campaign finance laws for Michigan cities, towns, and the counties.

Initiatives on campaign finance reform have also taken place at the local level. Prominent among those municipalities is New York City. In 1988, New York City enacted the Campaign Finance Program. The act established a voluntary plan in which local candidates who accepted limits on the amount of money they raised and spent on their campaign were eligible to receive public matching funds for contributions made by New York City residents.[37] For example, a candidate for the mayor's office has to agree to accept no more than $4,500 from any individual (combined contribution for the primary and the general election). A city council member can accept no more than $2,500 in contributions from an individual.[38]

The rewards for participating in this voluntary program are significant. Public funding by the city, intended to increase the value of small contributions by New York City residents, is very generous. The program "matches each dollar a New York City resident gives up to $250 ($125 in a special election) with four dollars in public funds up to $1,000 ($500 in a special election)."[39] Contributions from outside the city cannot be matched with public funds. Under the law, program participants are not permitted to accept contributions from corporations. Any political committee wishing to donate money to a New York City campaign must first register with the Campaign Finance Board.

In recent years, most candidates for the New York City Council and essentially all candidates for citywide offices have participated in the campaign finance reform program. If a citywide candidate chooses not to participate in the program, she or he must still abide by a state law that establishes a contribution limit of $45,000 per donor.[40]

In addition to New York City, at least seventy-seven other cities and towns in twelve states and Washington, DC, as of 2000, have enacted local campaign finance reforms, some dating back to the late 1960s.[41] The reforms range from the enforcement of local contribution limits and time limits on fundraising to the public financing of elections.

How quickly and to what degree local communities will continue to enact campaign reform legislation is still unclear. While campaign finance reform has been implemented in communities ranging in size from New York City with a population of over 7 million people to Alta, Utah, with a population of 397 citizens, the intense and often conflicting politics of campaign finance regulations still appear to impede widespread use of reforms at the local level.

Campaign Financing: Some Conclusions

In our introduction to this chapter, we suggested that few issues in American politics provoke more discussion and controversy than the financing of election campaigns. Americans are suspicious of a political campaign system in which millions of dollars must often be raised to compete effectively in a congressional or gubernatorial race. At the local level, many races ranging from mayor and county supervisor to the state legislature are becoming more expensive undertakings.

The consequences of reform action and regulation have been mixed in terms of their impact on the campaign finance process. What conclusions can we draw when scrutinizing the state of campaign financing in the United States?

We initially argue that the laws and regulations that govern federal, state, and local campaign financing are often complex and frequently abused. Early reforms and laws at the federal and state level were, more often than not, ineffective if not unenforceable. Not until the early 1970s did we see a concerted effort at all levels of government to reform the process by which candidates, party organizations, PACS, corporations, and unions could participate in the raising and collection of campaign contributions. The central goal has been to reduce the influence of individual "fat cats" in the election process and to place limitations on corporate, union, and political organization activity. How have the rules of the game regarding campaign finance reform fared at the federal, state, and local levels?

Federal Level

While the Federal Election Campaign Act has checked some campaign finance abuses, the impact of unlimited soft money contributions has effectively circumvented federal statutes that sought to curb the influence of large individual, corporate, and union donations to both congressional and presidential races.

Part of the problem may be that hard money caps on individual, PAC, and party contributions to congressional and presidential candidates have not been adjusted since the inauguration of the limits by the FECA in the early 1970s. Thus, soft money has flowed indirectly into campaign coffers while hard money contributions have remained fixed. Maximum individual contributions ($1,000) and PAC contributions ($5,000) to federal campaigns have remained unchanged over the past thirty years with no indexing taking inflation into account. In effect, since the early 1970s, hard money has lost approximately two-thirds of its value in 2001 dollars. At the same time, the cost of presidential and congressional elections has increased many fold between 1971 and 2001, often, it has been argued, providing candidates with no other alternative than to indirectly fund their campaigns with soft money contributions.

Clearly, the availability of unregulated soft money in federal campaigns provides the single greatest impediment to the effective regulation of campaign financing. Soft money can be collected in unlimited amounts for party building, independent campaign efforts, and issue campaigns, all benefiting candidates while not violating federal law. But there are at least three other rules of the game that effectively influence the raising of funds for federal elections.

The first rule allows unlimited contributions by a congressional candidate to her or his own campaign. Not surprisingly, wealthy candidates have been known to provide significant financial support to their campaigns by means of personal fortunes. In 1994, Republican Michael Huffington spent $27.9 million of his own money in his effort to win a senate seat in California—an election that he lost. In 2000, Jon Corzine, seeking the Democratic nomination for the U.S. Senate seat in New Jersey, spent over $60 million, mostly his own money, on a successful campaign. Candidates with enough personal resources need not be concerned by rules and regulations that restrict contributions from individuals and other groups. It is relevant to point out also that wealthy and successful candidates like Jon Corzine are often highly valued by the political parties. This is true for two reasons. First, wealthy candidates can and often do fund most of their own campaign. The parties need not exert effort or time on their part to help raise campaign funds for the candidate and can direct party resources to other, more needy candidates. Second, a party candidate that counts on his own personal wealth to fund his campaign will often indirectly benefit other candidates from his party lower down on the ticket. Such was the case with Jon Corzine's campaign when it was found that his ability to spend large sums of money on his campaign helped also to draw attention to other Democratic candidates on the ticket who benefited by the media attention. Not surprisingly, the Democratic Senatorial Campaign Committee was overjoyed with the Corzine candidacy.

The second rule of the game that has influenced federal election campaign financing has been the public funding of presidential campaigns. The law provides that candidates seeking the presidential nomination of the Republican or Democratic party are eligible for matching grants if they qualify for the funds and if they adhere to requirements regarding disclosure laws and spending limitations.

But public funding is not a neutral concept. As political scientist Paul Allen Beck reminds us, "[b]y providing a sizable financial 'grubstake' to the major-party candidates at the beginning of their campaigns and effectively denying it to others until after the election, they have increased the competitive disadvantage of third-party and independent candidates."[42] Minor parties receive only a small portion of the maximum grant received by major-party candidates and only after the election.

Finally, in federal elections political parties appear to have a distinct advantage over other groups and individuals because they have a higher ceiling on contribution levels. As a consequence, parties are an attractive conduit for contributions to candidates and independent efforts made in support of candidates. For many individuals who see political parties as an important mediating force in campaign contribution reform, this advantage is both welcome and desirable. For opponents of political parties, the advantage that parties have in raising campaign contributions is seen as a defeat for campaign finance reform.

Any conjecture regarding further reform at the federal level is at best speculative. At least two considerations stand in the way of further reform in campaign contribution rules.[43]

First, court cases, including *Buckley v. Valeo* and *Colorado Republican Campaign Committee v. Federal Election Commission*, have directly and indirectly supported the right of individuals, corporations, PACs, and other groups to make soft money contributions to federal election campaigns. As long as the rules of the game allow soft money contribution loopholes to exist, it is unlikely that any efforts at reform in the realm of campaign financing will be meaningful. For change to occur, the U.S. Supreme Court will have to reverse its past position on soft money, further limiting its use or declaring it unconstitutional. That does not seem to likely in the near future. It is also unlikely, at least in the near future, that an amendment to the Constitution will be enacted that would ban soft money in federal elections. It appears that support does not exist at this point in time to amend the Constitution.

Second, Congress could pass legislation acceptable to the federal courts that would place limitations on federal campaign financing. As recent congressional debate has made clear, the issue of campaign reform and specifically the placing of limits on campaign contributions are highly partisan and ideological. Perhaps one-party control of both the office of the presidency and the two houses of Congress may generate campaign finance reform in Congress. The results of the 2000 elections did not bring about effective one-party control of either house with the Senate initially split 50–50 and the Republicans, controlling the House of Representatives by a razor-thin margin. In May 2001, Senator James Jeffords left the Republican party and declared himself an independent. This left the Democrats with a 50–49 majority and a razor-thin control of the Senate. But even in a Congress controlled by a single party, it is, at best, speculative as to how soon changes in the rules of the game will come about. Many incumbents, both Republican and Democratic, are wary of any significant modifications in the campaign contribution laws that got them elected and are likely to be very hesitant regarding the enactment of any statutes that hinder the traditional advantage that incumbents have in raising campaign funds. In short, the rules of the game tend to favor incumbents. As painful as the process may be for them— in a Senate campaign that will cost $4 million, a candidate has to raise approximately $15,000 per week over six years—incumbents are hesitant to tinker with the rules of the game regarding federal campaign funding.

There is reason to speculate on change, however, as we move into the twenty-first century. The burden of campaign fundraising is getting increasingly prohibitive—even for financially well-endowed candidates. It is not unusual for a competitive candidate in a large state to spend over $20 million on the race. In the New York Senate race in 2000 between Democrat Hillary Rodham Clinton and Republican Rick Lazio, the two candidates collectively raised over $60 million. Even the cost of running for a House seat can be astronomical. In 2000, in one California congressional race (the 27th congressional district), the two candidates collectively had to raise over $10 million.

The unremitting task of raising campaign funds coupled with public pressure to legislate new reforms has, in recent years, instigated a more realistic move toward reform legislation in Congress. Senators John McCain (R-Arizona) and Russ Feingold (D-Wisconsin) have led the way toward reform, introducing in recent congresses a bill that would ban soft money and bundling in federal elections as well as establish closer oversight of independent expenditures in campaigns. They also called for an increase in the maximum allowable contribution to candidates. On April 3, 2001, the Senate passed the McCain–Feingold bill providing for the most wide-ranging overhaul of federal campaign finance law since the 1971 Federal Election Campaign Act.

If Senate approval of the McCain–Feingold bill is a good sign for proponents of campaign finance reform at the federal level, there are reasons to believe that the process may be stalled in the House where there was, during spring 2001, growing resistance to the McCain–Feingold legislation. The fate of campaign finance reform will rest on the ability of proponents in the House to rally support around a complex issue. Even if a campaign finance reform bill is passed by both houses of Congress and signed into law by the president, there is little doubt that opponents will challenge the statute as unconstitutional. More than likely, the Supreme Court will have the final word on the legislation.

State Level

If our national representatives are cautious about fiddling with the rules of the game as they apply to campaign contributions, state officials are equally hesitant. As one scholar put it, most states have been less than willing to display "consistency and vigor" in enforcing those campaign laws that are on the books.[44] More often than not, state agencies, given the responsibility of monitoring contributions to state campaigns, are either underfunded, understaffed, or both.

Many states provide for limited regulation of campaign financing, while other states, including Colorado, Illinois, Missouri, and Utah, provide for virtually no regulation. A major initiative that a number of states have taken, providing public funding for statewide and legislative races, has met with limited success. One recent study found that "[t]ypically, public financing programs break down at the very first step, by failing to provide enough money so that there will be sufficient incentive for candidates to participate."[45] The authors of that study also found declining participation in state income-tax check-off and add-on programs that traditionally support the public funding programs—a trend that is evident at the federal level, too.

It is important to note that some states have been active in legislating campaign finance regulations. The data does reflect an activity level over the past twenty-five years unprecedented for any other time period in our history. But even when the rules of the game encourage campaign finance reform, reality sets in and more often than not provides us with a complex and disappointing picture of the effectiveness of many programs. As one student of state politics suggests, "It is hard to escape the feeling that much of the campaign reform effort has been a waste of time."[46]

Through the use of bundling of campaign contributions and soft money donations, individuals, PACs, corporations, and unions often circumvent state campaign contribution limits and restrictions, thus skirting the intent, if not the let-
ter, of laws governing campaign financing. Funds are also funneled through
legislative leadership committees and state party organizations with little ability
to pinpoint accurately where the contributions originated.[47]

There are some signs, however, that a number of states are ready to enact
laws that will deal with the complex issues surrounding campaign finance
reform. Some of those reforms include voluntary contribution limits by candidates, limits on when contributions can be made (often restricting or prohibiting contributions when the state legislatures are in session or thirty days before
and/or after a session), restrictions or prohibitions on corporate, PAC, and
union contributions, and the providing of more information on the occupations,
employers, and economic interests of contributors.[48]

While skepticism may be in order regarding the effectiveness of state laws
governing campaign finance regulations, there is still some reason to believe
that even incremental changes in the laws and regulations will have some
impact on the rules of the game.

Local Level

As we've already discovered, state law dictates the extent to which local communities can establish campaign finance laws independent of state regulations. When state law does give local communities the power to enact campaign finance laws, those laws cannot conflict with existing state and federal
regulations.

In thirteen states and the District of Columbia, the law provides some latitude
for municipalities and counties in instituting contribution limits. In five states,
local communities have provisions for public campaign financing programs.
However, most states do not provide for laws allowing local communities to
enact campaign finance reform.

The laws and regulations as they apply to campaign finance reform have not,
however, been entirely stagnant. In Fort Collins, Colorado, contribution limits
have been set at $50 for any candidate running for local office. In Tucsan, Ari-
zona, Long Beach, California, Los Angeles, and New York City, public financing
models have been adopted. Westminster, Colorado, and the cities of Chula
Vista, Santa Ana, Modesto, and Costa Mesa, California, all have conflict of interest laws requiring that city council members abstain from debating and voting
on issues that affect contributors who have reached a specific threshold in contributions to their campaigns. Little Rock, Arkansas, and thirteen other cities
have established restrictions on when campaign contributions can be made to
local candidates. Alta, Utah, Austin, Texas, Concord and Indi, California, Aspen
and Crested Butte, Colorado, and Richmond, Washington, have all established
ordinances that publicize contribution and spending patterns of local candidates. All of these efforts are aimed at reforming the campaign finance process
in local communities.[49]

As we noted earlier in this chapter, how quickly and to what extent local
communities will enact their own campaign reform legislation is still unclear.
While changes in the law are being implemented in a number of states, the

politics of campaign finance reform still appear to impede widespread use of reforms at the local level. This has been true in recent years at all levels of government.

A recent newspaper editorial commented that campaign finance reform is always a work in progress.[50] This is equally true for any analysis of campaign finance disclosure and expenditure rules. In Chapter 4 we turn to this subject and other rules of the game that govern the campaign process.

Endnotes

1. *Dollar Politics* (Washington, DC: Congressional Quarterly, 1982).
2. For one of the most comprehensive reviews of campaign finance law and reform at the federal level, see Anthony Corrado, Thomas E. Mann, Daniel R. Ortiz, Trevor Potter, and Frank J. Sorauf, eds., *Campaign Finance Reform: A Sourcebook* (Washington, DC: Brookings Institution Press, 1997).
3. *Newberry v. United States,* 256 U.S. 232.
4. For an exhaustive review of the Federal Corrupt Practices Act of 1925 as well as other laws regarding campaign finance reform in the United States prior to 1971, when the present Federal Election campaign Act was enacted, see Corrado, et al., *Campaign Finance Reform,* ch. 2.
5. Eliza Newlin Carney, *National Journal* (February 17, 2001): 472, quoting election lawyer James Bopp.
6. *Buckley v. Valeo,* 424 U.S. 1 (1976).
7. For a detailed review of federal campaign law, see Trevor Potter, "The Current State of Campaign Finance Law," in Corrado, et al., *Campaign Finance Reform,* ch. 1.
8. In addition to the Republican National Committee and the Democratic National Committee, both major parties have Senate and House campaign committees that contribute to their respective house campaigns.
9. Potter, "The Current State of Campaign Finance Law," 6.
10. Paul Allen Beck, *Party Politics in America*, 8th ed. (Washington, DC: Congressional Quarterly Press, 1997), 296.
11. 2 U.S.C. 441e.
12. Internal Revenue Service, "Taxpayer Usage Guide," 1997.
13. *Politics and Money* (New York: Macmillan, 1983), ch. 15.
14. The term "soft money" also encompasses money spent on "issue advertising," campaign and party administrative costs, generic party building, and generic advertising by a political party. See Michael J. Malbin and Thomas L. Gais, *The Day After Reform* (Albany, NY: The Rockefeller Institute Press, 1998), 12. See also David B. Magleby, ed., *Outside Money: Soft Money and Issue Advocacy in the 1998 Congressional Elections* (Lanham, MD: Rowman & Littlefield Publishers, 1998).
15. *Colorado Republican Federal Campaign Committee v. FEC,* 165 S. Ct. 2309 (1996).
16. See John Bibby, *Politics, Parties, and Elections in America*, 3rd ed. (Chicago: Nelson-Hall Publishers, 1996), 214–215.
17. *Washington Post,* (January 6, 2000): A11.
18. Corrado, *Campaign Finance Reform,* 167.
19. Ibid., 172–173. Words in italics are ours.

20. For one of the most comprehensive and recent studies of campaign financing at the state level, see Malbin and Gais, *The Day After Reform*.

21. Quoted from George Thayer, *Who Shakes the Money Tree? American Campaign Practices from 1789 to the Present* (New York: Simon and Schuster, 1974) in *A Brief History of Money in Politics: How Americans Have Financed Elections in the Past* (Report of the Center for Responsive Politics, 1998), 1.

22. Much of the material discussed in this brief overview of the history of state campaign finance laws and initiatives comes from the Center for Responsive Politics, *A Brief History of Money in Politics*, 1998 Website.

23. Ruth Jones, "The Historical Context of Campaign Finance Regulations" (unpublished manuscript), August 6, 1994.

24. See Ann O'M. Bowman and Richard C. Kearney, *State and Local Government* (Boston: Houghton Mifflin, 1999), 134; and Malbin and Gais, *The Day After Reform*, 17.

25. Edward D. Feigenbaum and James A. Palmer, *Campaign Finance Law 2000* (Washington, DC: Federal Election Commission, 2000), Table 2-A.

26. *Book of the States*, vol. 33 (Lexington, KY: The Council on State Governments, 2000), 186–195.

27. Sigenbaum and Palmer, *Campaign Finance Law 2000*, Table 2-B.

28. Ibid., Table 2A.

29. Ibid., Table Chart 4.

30. Malbin and Gais, *The Day After Reform*, 120.

31. Ibid., 120.

32. E-mail communication with Craig Holman, Executive Director of the Center for Governmental Studies, Los Angeles, January 14, 1999.

33. Ibid

34. Ibid.

35. "State Issue Brief: Campaign Finance Reform," Common Cause, January 1994, reported in a Committee for Responsive Politics report, "A Brief History of Money in Politics, The States: Laboratories of Reform" (1995).

36. Holman e-mail communication. According to Holman, "Proposition 208 has since been temporarily suspended by a federal district court, leaving no limits on money at the state level but all local limitations continue to remain in full effect."

37. New York City campaign races covered by the program included the following offices: mayor, public advocate, comptroller, borough president, and the city council.

38. "The Board and Its Mandates," New York City Campaign Board, 1999.

39. Ibid., 10. According to the New York City Campaign Finance Board, the total amount of public funding that a candidate can receive is capped at 55 percent of the spending limit. For the general elections in 2001, the spending limit for mayoral candidates accepting public funding is $5,231,000.

40. Clifford J. Levy, "New York Council Approves Stiffer Campaign Fund Rules," *The New York Times* (August 28, 1998): A1 and B2.

41. The National Civic League has taken the lead in cataloging a list of local communities throughout the United States that have undertaken campaign finance reform. The report, written by Ric Bainter and Paul Lhevine, provides important information and tables on this subject. See *Local Campaign Finance Reform: Case Studies, Innovations and Model Legislation*, 1st ed., A Report by the National Civic League, 1998.

42. Beck, *Party Politics in America*, 295.
43. This final section draws on Beck, *Party Politics in America*, 297-298.
44. Robert J. Huckshorn, "Who Gave It? The Enforcement of Campaign Finance Laws in the States," *Journal of Politics* 47 (August 1985): 773.
45. Malbin and Gais, *The Day After*, 164.
46. Rob Gurwitt, "The Mirage of Campaign Reform" *Governing* (August 1992): 50.
47. David M. Hedge, *Governance and the Changing American States* (Boulder CO: Westview Press, 1998), 67.
48. Ibid., 68.
49. See *Local Campaign Finance Reform*, chs. 1-5.
50. Editorial, "Time to Make a Good Law Better," *New York Times* (March 2, 1998): A 26.

Chapter 4
Campaigning to Election Day

At their best, political campaigns inform and engage citizens. Ideally, they also stimulate the deliberative process and link citizens and leaders in ways that bolster public perceptions of political legitimacy. But of course, in the final analysis, political campaigns are about winning votes. Political campaigns use information to persuade voters. The point of political campaigns is to identify likely supporters, attract new supporters, and energize these two groups to turn out at the polls on election day.

Fashioning campaigns is a demanding process. Although the goal is simple, the best way to reach it is seldom clear. As one veteran campaigner told a researcher, "I don't know very much about elections. I've been in a lot of them."[1] Much of what goes on in a campaign is justified on the grounds that it's always been done that way. Alternatively, when a candidate wins after trying something new, the tactic is widely adopted by others in subsequent elections. Lacking certainty as to what works, candidates are always in search of the strategy or tactic that will make the difference and assure their victory.

Despite this endemic uncertainty, all campaigns operate within a series of givens which shape the strategic options available to the candidate. Among these givens is the office sought and the size and geographic distribution of the constituency. Another of these givens is the campaigner's status as an incumbent or challenger. The resources available to and the strategies adopted by incumbents and challengers are of necessity very different. Contestants for open seats employ yet another set of tactics. Also important in planning a campaign is the partisan balance among the candidate's constituency. Although partisan attachments may not be as decisive in determining electoral outcomes as was once the case, the majority of voters still identify with one party. Obviously, candidates of the majority party are not guaranteed election, but partisan strength in the constituency affects campaign strategy. Minority party candidates face additional restraints not felt by the majority party office seeker.

In addition to these contextual factors, campaigns also take place against the backdrop of national, state, and local laws and regulations. It is true that there is very little regulation of the content of American political campaigns. Still the strategies and tactics available to campaign organizers are affected by the laws and regulations promulgated by governments. In both direct and indirect ways, campaigns are shaped by governmental policies. Campaign strategies must take into account the election year calendar. What other offices are in play during the election year does much to shape campaigns, for instance. Similarly, campaigns often must be conducted under a maze of campaign expenditure limitations. Finally, the various rules and regulations governing the press shape the way candidates use the media.

Electoral Calendars

Consider, for example, the seemingly trivial issue of the election calendars. When are the elections held? All elections for national office are held on the first Tuesday after the first Monday in November in even numbered years. (For an explanation of why this day was chosen, see Chapter 5.) But this is not necessarily true for state and local elections. Fives states—Kentucky, Louisiana, Mississippi, New Jersey, and Virginia—elect their governors and most statewide offices in the odd numbered years. Louisiana, Mississippi, New Jersey, and Virginia, but not Kentucky, also hold state legislative elections in the odd numbered years. Furthermore, thirty-six states hold their gubernatorial elections during what are called the off-years—the even numbered years when there is no presidential election. At the local level there is even greater variability, as elections may be held not only in odd numbered years, but during months other than November.

From a campaigner's perspective these calendar issues have weighty consequences, because other races on the ballot have an impact on the campaign. Contested elections at the top of the ticket may, for instance, increase voter participation across the board. The immense voter and media attention given to presidential elections assures that these elections are "high stimulus" contests affecting all other races on the ballot.[2] Presidential campaigns also soak up massive resources making them unavailable to other campaigns. Not surprisingly, turnout for congressional elections is, on average, some 15 percentage points higher in presidential election years than in off-years. Turnout in gubernatorial elections is also higher when they are held in conjunction with U.S. Senate elections.[3] But the increased turnout also introduces national issues and political trends into state and local elections. In order to insulate gubernatorial elections from national trends and issues, seventeen states between 1952 and 1988 moved their elections to the off-years. Probably not coincidentally, during this period the number of contested gubernatorial elections increased, especially in the South. Separated from high stimulus national elections, minority party gubernatorial contestants were encouraged to seek the office, without fear of being overwhelmed by coattails.[4] Similarly, local elections may be affected by particularly competitive gubernatorial elections. Local elections are often insulated from state tides by scheduling them in odd years or in months other than

November. But again this insulation from larger political trends comes at the cost of turnout. High stimulus presidential elections, especially when they are close, mobilizes voters across the board. Removing the high stimulus contests reduces voter involvement.

This staggering array of elections, especially when combined with the growth of primaries, may constitute one explanation of the declining voter turnout in American elections. According to Richard Boyd, the concurrent election of governors and presidents increases the attractiveness of elections for voters and therefore increases turnout by about 6 percentage points; separating the two then necessarily depresses turnout. Additionally, the more frequently elections are scheduled, the less likely it is that individuals will vote in any of them. It may be, Boyd suggests, that frequent elections, especially when they are part of a year-long sequence of nomination and general election, simply "satiate people's interest in politics." As he argues:

> ... precisely because electoral participation is for many a matter of civic obligation, frequent elections may lead to the *satisfaction of the norm* and a less compelling call from the conscience to vote in the next election. Considering the large number of elections for federal, state, and local governments in the United States, it is not surprising that when civic norms collide with personal obligations or convenience even a conscientious voter may think, "I have done my duty; I can skip this time."[5]

Interestingly, some scholars have suggested that the frequency of elections may at least partially explain the low voter turnout in Switzerland. Swiss voters, like their American counterparts, are noted among democracies for their low participation rate at the polls and their high frequency of elections.

Electoral calendars are only one example of laws and regulations affecting political campaigns, however. More direct influences can be seen in the various regulations of campaign spending. It is not simply the case that raising campaign funds is the only regulated activity, so too is reporting and spending those funds. Similarly, relations between campaign organizations and the mass media are conducted in the shadow of a variety of laws and regulations at all levels of government.

Reporting and Spending the Money

As we noted in Chapter 3, Americans have always been suspicious of money in elections. Efforts to reform campaigns and lessen the role of money are not recent in origin. Although efforts to minimize the role of big donors by restricting contributions has received considerable attention, regulatory efforts have also attempted to bring accountability to the process through reporting requirements. Less successful have been the repeated efforts to legislate expenditure ceilings.

Reporting Requirements

One of the earliest campaign reform efforts undertaken at the national level was the Corrupt Practices Act of 1910—also known as the Publicity Act of 1910.[6] Under this act, all party committees operating in two or more states were required to report all expenditures made in connection with campaigns for the

U.S. House of Representatives. Bold on its face, the Corrupt Practices Act was at best a tepid effort to reform campaign finance. Because the act applied only to committees operating in two or more states, it only affected the national party committees and the congressional campaign committees. Not even the candidates themselves were covered by the act. Moreover, the limited reporting that was required occurred after the election. There was no preelection reporting requirement. Dissatisfaction with the 1910 act led, in 1911, to amendments that strengthened the reporting requirements. Under the amendments, both House and Senate campaigns were required to report receipts as well as expenditures. Furthermore, campaign committees were compelled to file reports both before and after elections, including primary elections.[7]

In the wake of the infamous Teapot Dome scandal, Congress revisited the issue of campaign finance regulation with the Federal Corrupt Practices Act of 1925. On paper the 1925 act greatly strengthened the existing reporting requirements. Pivotal to the 1925 act was the requirement that all multistate political committees file quarterly reports that documented every contribution in excess of $100. The reporting requirements were ineffective, however. The problem was that the act made no provisions for disseminating the reports, nor did it state who had access to the reports. Once filed, the reports were kept a couple of years and then destroyed. More telling, the law made no provisions for punishment of those who failed to comply.

These weak reporting requirements were more effectively addressed in the Federal Election Campaign Act (FECA) of 1971. Through this act, Congress set strict disclosure requirements on federal candidates and political committees. Reporting of campaign contributions and expenditures were extended to primaries and other aspects of the nomination process previously not covered. Ironically, the 1971 act provided an excellent documentation of the campaign finance practices of the 1972 election—one of the nation's more scandal-plagued elections. Indeed, the scandals that attended the 1972 election led to several reform amendments to the Federal Election Campaign Act. Most significantly for the disclosure requirements, the 1974 amendments made the newly created Federal Election Commission (FEC) responsible for gathering and reporting campaign disclosure statements. For the first time, an agency was clearly responsible for disseminating this information. Finally, the disclosure requirements were modified in 1976 when Congress exempted from filing reports any candidate who raised or spent less than $5,000. Similarly, candidates were freed of the need to report contributions or expenditures under $200. Of course, these reporting requirements apply only to the so-called "hard money"; "soft money" used for nonfederal activity is not subject to federal disclosure laws, although it may be reportable under state laws.

Given the long struggle to require disclosure in federal elections, it is somewhat surprising that all fifty states and the District of Columbia have some sort of campaign finance reporting procedure. As would be expected, these laws and their enforcement vary considerably. Nebraska, for instance, requires all candidate committees, political party committees, independent committees, and ballot question committees to file disclosure statements, but only if they receive or spend more than $2,000 in a calendar year. Pennsylvania, on the other hand, requires any candidate or political committee receiving or spending more than $250 to file disclosure statements. What needs to be reported also varies across the states. Twenty-one states require candidates and political committees to itemize all contributions of more than $100. Colorado, Michigan, and Wisconsin demand substantially more itemization—all contributions in excess of $20 must be listed separately. In New Jersey only contributions surpassing $300 need to be itemized in the reports. Interestingly, only three states use the federal standard of $200. Paralleling the contribution standards are the requirements for itemizing expenditures. Generally the minimum expenditure that needs to be separately reported is the same as the contribution trigger. But again there are significant differences. Many states require the itemization of all or almost all expenditures. Iowa illustrates the requirement, requiring the itemization of all campaign expenditures larger than $5.

State disclosure laws are sometimes applicable only to statewide offices, but many states also regulate some or all local races. Ohio law, for example, applies to all candidate campaign committees, political action committees (PACs), legislative campaign funds, and political parties, but it excludes campaign committees for candidates for municipal office paying less than $5,000 a year. Also excluded are candidates for local school boards and township trustees certifying that their aggregate contributions will not exceed $2,000. Where state law does not extend to local elections, communities often have the option of imposing their own disclosure requirements.

Does all this disclosure have an effect? Anecdotal evidence often conjures up the image of potential donors scared off by the possible public exposure, but given the amounts of money that continue to pour into campaigns this does not seem to be a serious problem. On the theory that political activities should occur in the light of day, disclosure laws comprise a valuable source of information. As a result of the FECA, federal campaign practices are clearly more documented than in the past, although the rising dependence on soft money threatens the validity of the reports. In the final analysis, however, the disclosure laws are only useful if the data are quickly and easily available. At the federal level, the Federal Election Commission makes campaign reports available for public inspection within 48 hours of receipt. Distribution of these reports could become more effective if the electronic filing system that the commission has initiated becomes mandatory. Nevertheless, enforcement of the law is greatly hampered by a lack of congressional support. Congress has never provided sufficient funding for the commission's operation. Structurally, the FEC is hampered by the fact that its chair can serve for only a single year, depriving the commission of consistent leadership. Moreover, under law violators have little to fear from the commission. Investigations are long and complex, often including several procedural hurdles that severely burden the FEC's small investigative staff. Not surprisingly, these investigations can take months and even years to complete. When improper filings are determined the civil fines levied against violators may not exceed $5,000 or the amount contested, whichever is greater. (If the commission concludes that criminal prosecution is warranted, its only recourse is to refer the matter to the Department of Justice.) In 1979 Congress further weakened the commission's ability to deter illegal operations when it prohibited random audits of congressional campaigns.[8]

At the state level, regulatory efforts are generally considerably weaker. Most states have weak enforcement procedures and little by way of effective disclosure. Only a few states make the data readily available, even fewer if the standard is readily available in a timely fashion. Indeed fewer than half the states make any provision for the publishing and dissemination of the data.

Controlling the Spending

More controversial than reporting requirements have been the multiple efforts by Congress and various state legislatures to control the spending in political campaigns. Congress first legislated spending limits in the 1911 amendments to the Corrupt Practices Act of 1910. As amended, the law attempted to regulate both primary and general election campaigns by limiting total expenditures for House candidates to $5,000 and capping Senate campaigns at $10,000 or, if it was less, the amount set by state law. This striking attempt to constrain election spending soon ran afoul of the U.S. Supreme Court, however. According to a bare majority of the Court, in *Newberry v. United States* (1921), congressional authority over elections did not extend to the nomination process. The badly divided Court opined that when the Constitution referred to elections it meant the "final choice of an officer by duly qualified electors," and that primaries were "in no real sense part of the manner of holding the election."[9]

Congress returned to the issue of expenditures in the Federal Corrupt Practices Act of 1925. This time Congress made no attempt to regulate primaries, but it did set spending limits on House and Senate general election bids. House candidates could not spend more than $5,000 and Senate campaigns were limited to $25,000, unless state law set a lower limit. Because there were no meaningful enforcement provisions to the act, the spending ceilings were generally ignored. Nevertheless, Congress made no attempt to correct the deficiencies in the expenditure limits for almost five decades.

Not until the early 1970s did Congress become sufficiently motivated by the rapidly escalating costs of political campaigns to make yet another attempt at regulating expenditures. Central to the Federal Election Act of 1971 was a series of targeted spending limits applied to all federal campaigns. Rather than cap total spending, the act limited the amount that federal candidates could spend on media in each election—primary, run-off, and general elections. Specifically the act constrained spending on media to $50,000 or $0.10 times the voting age population of the office's constituency, whichever was greater. Additionally, the act prohibited candidates from spending more than 60 percent of their media money on radio and television advertising. It is possible that these restrictions did dampen media spending, but in the 1972 election, the only election to fall under these provisions, total spending by the candidates increased dramatically. President Richard M. Nixon spent twice as much in 1972 as he had in 1968. Similarly, the Democratic candidate, George McGovern, spent four times as much as the 1968 standard bearer, Hubert H. Humphrey. Given the act's failure to curb the growth of election related expenses, the 1974 amendments to the Federal Election Act replaced the media limits with ceilings on all spending and combined with the Revenue Act created a tax check-off scheme for public funding of presidential elections.

Statutory limits on campaign spending had a short life, however. In the Supreme Court's 1976 *Buckley v. Valeo* decision, the spending limits for House and Senate races, as well as the constraints placed on independent expenditures, were ruled unconstitutional. According to the Court the spending of money in a political campaign is an exercise of the First Amendment right to freedom of speech. Limitations on campaign spending constitute, the Court concluded, unacceptable restrictions on First Amendment freedoms. Whatever the wisdom of the Court's decision, the effect was to declare large parts of the act unconstitutional, forcing Congress to rewrite the law before it went into effect. Less noticed, but no less important, the *Buckley* decision struck down several state laws limiting spending in state elections. Because campaign spending is, the Court argued, protected by the First Amendment, neither the national government nor state governments may curb its exercise. Only the expenditure limits attached to the public funding of presidential elections won the Court's approval; because participation in the program is voluntary, the Court found no First Amendment violation. (Table 4.1 summarizes the provisions.)

TABLE 4.1   Important Provisions Limiting Campaign Spending in Federal Elections

- Presidential candidates who accept public financing may spend no more than $10 million plus a cost of living adjustment in the prenomination stage of the campaign. (In 2000, the candidates were entitled to $40.53 million.)

- Presidential candidates who accept public financing in the prenomination stage must stay within specified expenditure limits set for each state.

- Presidential candidates who accept public financing may not spend more than $20 million plus a cost-of-living adjustment in the general election. (In 2000, candidates were entitled to $67.56 million.)

- Presidential and vice-presidential candidates who accept public financing may spend no more than $50,000 of personal funds in their campaign.

- Each party may spend up to two cents per person of the voting-age population on behalf of its presidential candidate. (In 2000 this figure was $13,680,292.)

- The national party committees as well as their congressional and senatorial campaign committees may spend on behalf of their House and Senate candidates. Each committee may spend up to $10,000 plus a cost-of-living adjustment for each House member in states with more than one Representative. If the state has only a single Representative, the limit is the same as that set for the state's Senators. For the Senate, the committees may spend $20,000 plus a cost-of-living adjustment or two cents per person of the voting-age population in the state, whichever is greater.

- There are no limits on how much House and Senate candidates may spend.

- Senate and House candidates may spend an unlimited amount of their own money.

- There are no limits on how much an individual or group may spend on behalf of a presidential or congressional candidate so long as the expenditures are independent—not coordinated with or controlled by the candidate.

- Political parties may make unlimited expenditures on behalf of presidential and congressional candidates, so long as they are independent expenditures.

SOURCE: William J. Keefe, *Parties, Politics, and Public Policy in America* (Washington, DC: Congressional Quarterly Press, 1998), pp. 155–156.

To receive the matching funds, the candidate must agree to abide by overall spending limits and in the prenomination stage to spending limits for each state. The overall spending limit is defined as $10 million (in 1974 dollars) plus an adjustment for inflation. In 2000, that amounted to a spending ceiling of $40.53 million for the primaries. Spending ceilings in each state are set at $200,000 (again 1974 dollars) plus the cost-of-living adjustment or $0.16 times the voting age population of the state, whichever is greater.

Candidates who opt for the matching funds have to calculate the spending limitations into their campaign strategy. Most troublesome to the campaigns are the individual state limits, particularly as they are applied to the early contests (see Table 4.2). Given the need to do well in the early stages of the nomination process, candidates have traditionally spent disproportionately in Iowa and New Hampshire. To get around the state spending limitations, "campaign workers commute to Iowa and New Hampshire from neighboring states, eating, sleeping, and renting cars from outside these states whenever possible so that the expenditures will not be applied to the Iowa and New Hampshire totals."[10] In the New Hampshire primary, most of the cost of television advertisements run out of Boston stations and can therefore be assigned to the Massachusetts account instead of New Hampshire.

TABLE 4.2 State-by-State Expenditure Limits for the 2000 Presidential Candidates in the Prenomination Stage

State	Expenditure Limit	State	Expenditure Limit
Alabama	$1,785,746	Montana	$675,600
Alaska	$675,000	Nebraska	$675,600
Arizona	$1,861,413	Nevada	$712,353
Arkansas	$1,022,048	New Hampshire	$675,600
California	$13,091,507	New Jersey	$3,318,547
Colorado	$1,616,576	New Mexico	$675,600
Connecticut	$1,326,338	New York	$7,434,843
Delaware	$675,600	North Carolina	$3,086,141
District of Columbia	$675,600	North Dakota	$675,600
Florida	$6,237,680	Ohio	$4,547,058
Georgia	$3,097,491	Oklahoma	$1,338,228
Hawaii	$675,600	Oregon	$1,345,255
Idaho	$675,600	Pennsylvania	$4,940,528
Illinois	$4,835,675	Rhode Island	$675,600
Indiana	$2,385,679	South Carolina	$1,583,606
Iowa	$1,162,032	South Dakota	$675,600
Kansas	$1,056,638	Tennessee	$2,239,209
Kentucky	$1,618,738	Texas	$7,742,376
Louisiana	$1,719,807	Utah	$768,563
Maine	$675,600	Vermont	$675,600
Maryland	$2,087,334	Virginia	$2,814,820
Massachusetts	$2,544,039	Washington	$2,307,850
Michigan	$3,947,125	West Virginia	$758,293
Minnesota	$1,089,842	Wisconsin	$2,108,953
Mississippi	$1,089,608	Wyoming	$675,600
Missouri	$2,199,213		
Total	$40,536,000		

The overall spending limits have generally been less of a problem for candidates. Because the eventual nominees have tended to emerge early in the process, facing little more than token opposition in the latter stages, the overall spending limit seldom presents a problem for the organizations. In 1996, however, Robert Dole exhausted the allowable expenditures at the nomination stage and had to rely on soft money expenditures until the general election campaign began.

Nominees of the two major parties are automatically eligible to receive a public grant to cover campaign expenses. The $20 million grant provided for in the original act is adjusted for inflation each presidential election year. In 2000, the grant amounted to $6.56 million per candidate. Campaign organizations opting to receive the grant must agree to spend no more than the grant received and they must refrain from accepting private contributions. They must also agree to subject themselves to frequent auditing by the FEC.

Of course, candidates are not required to accept public funds at either stage of the election. Candidates who choose not to participate in the public funding program may spend as much as they wish. George W. Bush, for example, shunned federal funding in his 2000 nomination campaign; instead he raised and spent close to $100 million. Those who, like Bush, refuse public funds can still solicit private contributions, but donors are subject to the law's contribution and reporting provisions.

In addition to these direct disbursements, presidential nominees as well as House and Senate candidates may benefit from national party expenditures known as "coordinated expenditures." Parties may, in coordination with the candidates, spend money on their behalf, but only in the general election. Because these monies are spent in coordination with the candidate and the party they share control over their use. This is over and beyond the contributions that the parties may make to the candidates, and from the parties' perspective, coordinated expenditures are preferable because they allow the parties to influence campaign tactics. Coordinated expenditures generally take the form of services paid for by the party, services such as polls, advertisements, issue position research, fundraising activities, and direct mailings. Like candidate spending there are limits on coordinated expenditures. Under the 1974 act the national parties were allowed to spend a maximum of $10,000 for each House candidate, unless the seat was the state's only one, then the maximum was set at $20,000. In Senate elections the act permitted national parties to expend as much as $20,000 or two cents times the state's voting age population, whichever was greater. The presidential limits were set at two cents times the nation's voting age population. All of these were indexed for inflation. These limits do not apply to soft money expenditures or party and interest group activities known as "issue advocacy spending."

Issue advocacy spending includes all party and interest group advertisements urging support for the party and candidate issue positions that are not coordinated with the candidate and do not specifically entreat voting for or against a particular candidate. According to the Supreme Court's 1996 decision in *Colorado Republican Federal Campaign Committee v. FEC*, issue advocacy ads are legal so long as no candidate is targeted through the use of words such as "elect," "vote for," or "vote against."[11] Initially parties and interest groups were cautious in the use of the issue advocacy status, but by 2000 the floodgates had opened. Issue advocacy has become a major tool to circumvent campaign contribution and expenditure limits. In the 2000 race for California's 27th congressional district twenty-nine goups not affliliated with the political parties spent between $2.1 and 2.3 million to influence some 600,000 California voters.[12] This is undoubtably only the beginning of issue advocacy spending, because interest groups in particular can use it to avoid the campaign finance laws and still help candidates that they support.

State parties are also allowed to make coordinated expenditures to House and Senate candidates. State party organizations seldom have the resources to take full advantage of the opportunity, however. If they lack the resources they may enter into what are called "agency agreements" with a national party commit-tee. Under "agency agreements" a national party committee agrees to act as the agent for the state party, thereby transferring the state party's spending quota to the national committee. This allows the national party committee to increase its coordinated expenditures.[13] If the state party has the money, but places a high-er priority on statewide elections, the national parties may induce the state orga-nization to engage in a "money swap." In this case, the national party offers to make contributions to state candidates equal to or greater than the amounts they would like the state party to spend on House or Senate elections in exchange for the state's quota. This gives the national party additional money to fund House and Senate elections and may pad the state party coffers.

Unregulated are those expenditures by individuals and PACs known as "inde-pendent expenditures." Individuals and PACs may spend unlimited amounts urg-ing voters to vote for or against a candidate so long as they do not coordinate these efforts with the candidate or the candidate's organization. The only restriction is that the spending must be disclosed to the Federal Election Commission. Similarly, the expenditure of soft money is not limited by federal regulations because it is not covered by the Federal Election Act as amended in 1974. Even national party orga-nizations may make soft money expenditures. The national party organizations may use soft money to defray a portion of their administrative costs and a share of the costs of voter registration and get-out-the-vote drives even when these are designed to benefit national candidates. National parties may transfer their soft money to state organizations that actually conduct voter drives or they may use soft money as part of a "money swap." The main benefit for the national parties is that soft money expenditures preserve their hard money resources.

Some states have also attempted to limit campaign spending, but they have been hampered by the Supreme Court's decision in *Buckley v. Valeo* Six states responded to the Court's decision by instituting voluntary spending caps. (See Table 4.3 which lists the states and provide summaries of their programs.) In Colorado voters approved, in 1996, a ballot initiative that creates a system of vol-untary expenditure limits. Gubernatorial candidates who agree to abide by the system are limited to expenditures not exceeding $2 million, while candidates for lieutenant governor may not spend more than $100,000. Candidates for other statewide offices may, if they agree to participate, spend no more than $400,000, while state senators' and representatives' expenses are capped at $75,000 and $50,000, respectively. Because the program is voluntary, no candi-date is required to comply with these limits, but state law offers positive induce-ments for participation. Candidates who agree to the limits are allowed to adver-tise that fact in their political messages. Those who do not agree to the limits must indicate their noncompliance in all of their political advertisements. More-over, the general election ballot clearly identifies those who have and have not accepted the voluntary limits. Several other states have sought to control cam-paign spending by instituting some form of public financing scheme containing

TABLE 4.3	Campaign Expenditures Limits for State Offices

State	Provision
Colorado	Voluntary campaign spending limits. • $2 million for governor • $400,000 for secretary of state, treasurer, and attorney general • $100,000 for lt. governor • $75,000 for state senate • $50,000 for state house of representatives
Florida	Publicly financed candidates and those agreeing to voluntary limits. • $5 million for governor and lt. governor • $2 million for cabinet
Hawaii	Voluntary election year limits. • governor—$2.50 × qualified voters • lt. governor—$1.40 × qualified voters • state representatives and senators—$1.40 × qualified voters • mayor—$2.00 × qualified voters • others—$.20 × qualified voters
Kentucky	Candidates accepting public financing limited to • $1.8 million in primary • $300,000 in a primary runoff • $1.8 million in general election
Michigan	Gubernatorial candidates who accept public funds limited to $2 million per election.
Minnesota	Candidates accepting public subsidies are limited in election years to (adjusted each election year, figures shown are 1994). • $1,926,127 governor/lt. governor • $321,023 attorney general • $160,514 other statewide offices • $43,150 state senate • $24,083 state representative • Nonelection year limits are 20% of election year limits
New Hampshire	Candidates may agree to limit campaign expenditures made by candidate, political party, and immediate family on candidate's behalf in primary or general election in accordance with maximum expenditure schedule.
New Jersey	Spending limits for gubernatorial candidates (adjusted for each election year, shown are 1997 dollars.) • $3.1 million in primary • $6.9 million in general election • candidate receiving public funding is limited to $25,000 in primary and $25,000 in general election from candidate's personal funds
North Carolina	Candidates for state office in general election who receive public matching funds are subject to expenditure limits defined for each election year.
Oregon	Candidate for statewide or state legislative office may agree to limit expenditures to the statutory limit in primary or general election by filing a declaration of limitation on expenditures, but are not bound by the declaration if an opposing candidate has not filed the declaration or has filed the declaration but has exceeded the applicable limit.
Rhode Island	Limited only for those who accept public funding.
Texas	Voluntary limits on aggregate expenditures for judicial offices only.
Wisconsin	State office candidates who receive election campaign fund grant may not expend more for a campaign than amount specified in the authorized disbursement schedule unless opponents not accepting grant do not agree to comply with the limit voluntarily.

spending limits. Kentucky's public financing program caps the spending of participating gubernatorial candidates at $1.8 million in the primary and another $1.8 million in the general election contest.

These voluntary public funding programs at the state level are permissibly applied to state candidates, but they may not be extended to U.S. Representatives or Senators. Thus a Minnesota scheme that would have limited the spending of U.S. House and Senate candidates if they accepted state funding was set aside by the Federal Election Commission. Minnesota was, the commission reasoned, preempted from regulating federal officials by federal statute.[14] Likewise, a New Hampshire law that sought to restrict party spending on behalf of federal candidates was superceded, the commission ruled, by federal law allowing such activities.[15]

After all this reform effort the only certainty is that campaign spending continues to increase. With each election cycle the total costs grow and anecdotal evidence also turns up new spending records. What then has been the impact of the reforms? That, of course, is difficult to answer because it is unclear what campaigns would look like without the current regulations. Reformers continue to protest the Supreme Court's language equating spending with speech, but there has been no successful challenge to the doctrine. Unless the Court overturns or significantly modifies the *Buckley* decision it is unlikely that effective spending limits will be possible. In the wake of *Buckley* those wanting spending caps on elections are left with few options. One option would be a constitutional amendment overturning the decision. Such amendments are regularly put forth in Congress, but the difficulty of securing the sufficient number of states for ratification makes this is an unlikely option. Public funding is, of course, another option, but it has never gained significant political support. Indeed, in the immediate post–*Buckley* era there was a flurry of public financing schemes adopted by state and local governments, but interest in such schemes seems to have subsided. Incumbents are reluctant to change a system that they have learned to work and reformers are often suspicious that public funding and the spending ceilings that come with it may protect incumbents. Because a lesser-known challenger needs to spend a great deal of money just to be recognized, some observers worry that limiting spending will simply advantage incumbents. It is not even clear that the public funding of presidential elections will continue to be viable. When candidates can, as George W. Bush did in 2000, raise millions (in his case $100 million) in a few short months, the temptation to forgo public financing and the limits that come with it will be great.

The campaign finance laws have had another impact, however. At the very least they have been a contributing factor to the increasing nationalization of political campaigns. The complex rules have encouraged the participation of national forces in formerly local elections and created a demand for professionals with expertise in the campaign finance rules. Soft money, money swaps, and coordinated expenditures under agency agreements have provided new sources of money making and have contributed to the escalation of spending in races around the country. As Salmore and Salmore pointed out in the mid-1980s, "Candidates who in the past had run modestly financed campaigns, depending upon party workers and local party financial support, found themselves seeking funds from individuals nationwide who shared their positions and from the national party apparatus (until recently a shell) rather than from the enfeebled state and local organizations."[16] Additionally, the evolving role of interest groups in issue advocacy means more nationalization of the issues, as these groups use their money to promote their national agenda.

Campaigns and the Media

For an increasing number of election contests, campaigning is a media affair. Unable to reach the voters directly, candidates use the press to communicate with voters. Of course this is a risky undertaking given that campaign organizations do not control the media. (Gone are the days when the political parties owned major newspapers.) Reliance on the press makes the development of a media strategy central to campaign planning. Candidates may and do use the media in two different ways: "free press" (news coverage) and paid advertising.

The mix of tactics employed by a campaign will depend on many factors. Obviously the more interested the media are in the race, the more coverage it will be afforded. In such cases, free press takes on great importance. A candidate attuned to the needs of the press may leverage that into favorable coverage. Indeed a well-run campaign will try to spoonfeed the press, controlling reporters' agenda in an effort to control the content of the news. Keeping the reporters happy and informed becomes a high priority in the campaign. Staffers will routinely supply reporters with daily schedules, advance copies of speeches, and access to telephones all in an effort to facilitate coverage.[17] On the other hand, if the press has no interest in the campaign there will be little free press. Of course, candidates have some ability to influence the amount of press interest, but this is often quite limited. A congressional candidate running from a district carved from an urban area may find that the press has little interest in an election that does not cover the entire metropolitan market. Under these circumstances even the most skillful candidate may find adequate free press a dream. Lacking free press candidates must shift the emphasis to paid advertisements. Of course, this is an expensive strategy not available to low-funded candidates, but in well-funded races that attract little press attention this is likely to be the only strategy available.[18]

Strategic considerations for dealing with the press are then largely products of the interaction between media imperatives and constituency considerations. Nevertheless, public policies and regulations form a background for these strategic considerations. This is true in the general sense that the structure and operations of the media have been shaped by countless government policies. As Timothy Cook reminds us, " . . . it is clear that, at any stage in American history, the production of news was centrally aided and abetted by political and governmental policies and practices. Whether explicitly or implicitly, what government decided and what it did toward the news media helped to impel the media to take the shape they ultimately have today."[19] But government policies regarding the media also shape campaigns in several specific ways.

Regulating Broadcasting

Illustrative of governmental policies impacting media campaigns are the regulations that have been attached to securing and maintaining a broadcast license. Because demand for the airwaves is high and the availability of frequencies for transmission limited, the Communications Act of 1934 created the Federal Communications Commission (FCC) and empowered it to issue licenses to operate. Licensees were to be granted use of the airwaves so long as they acted in the "public interest, convenience, and necessity."[20] The act itself never defined the public interest. As a result the phrase has provided what Newton Minow, a former FCC commissioner, called, "the battleground for broadcasting's regulatory debate."[21] Over the years, rulings of the FCC, congressional legislation, and court decisions have defined, at least broadly, the meaning of the public interest, convenience, and necessity. Until the 1980s, for example, licensees were required to provide minimum levels of public service programming or risk losing their license. (Although the denial of a license renewal for any reason has been a rarity.) In 1981, the FCC, as part of the Reagan administration's commitment to deregulation, abolished the public service requirement for radio stations. Public service requirements for television were dropped in 1984.

In addition to the public service requirement, the FCC also sought to encourage open discussion of political issues. To this end, in 1949 the FCC issued the so-called "fairness doctrine." Accordingly, radio and television broadcasters were required to provide reasonable amounts of airtime to controversial issues of public importance and a reasonable opportunity for the expression of contrasting viewpoints on the issues. Eventually the FCC extended the fairness doctrine to cover not just issues, but people. Thus if a broadcast attacked an individual, the fairness doctrine required the station that aired the attack to notify the person who was attacked and provide that person with an opportunity to reply. So if a station editorialized against a candidate, that candidate needed to be notified and given a reasonable chance to respond. The fairness doctrine, like the public service requirement, was rescinded by the FCC in 1987. Noting that the electronic media were, in most parts of the country, more competitive than newspapers, supporters of deregulation argued that competition among broadcast outlets would provide for the open and vigorous debate desired by the fairness doctrine. The doctrine was, according to a majority of the commissioners, unnecessary.

By rescinding the fairness doctrine the FCC left only one major regulation affecting political campaigns on the books. Under Section 315 of the Communications Act broadcasters must, if they open their airways to one candidate, provide the same opportunity to other qualified candidates. To be legally qualified to take advantage of the rule a candidate must have announced for the office and have met all legal requirements for candidacy. This so-called "equal time" rule means that if a broadcaster makes free time available to one candidate it must make equivalent free time available to all other qualified candidates.[22] Similarly, if the station sells time to one candidate, it must allow all other candidates to buy time. Broadcasters do not have to give free time to all candidates, if one buys the time. They simply must make the same options available to all qualified candidates.

News Coverage, Debates, and Other Exceptions to the Equal Time Rule

There are exceptions to the equal time rule, however. Equal time need not be provided in response to regularly scheduled newscasts, documentaries, or news coverage of live events. It is this last category, news coverage of live events, which allows for the broadcast of candidate debates. Such debates do not invoke the equal time rule if they are sponsored by organizations other than the broadcasters (e.g., League of Women Voters) and are covered live and in their entirety. Where previously presidential debates were organized on an ad hoc basis by organizations like the League of Women Voters, they are now sponsored by contributors, including major corporations, to the congressionally created Commission on Presidential Debates (CPD).

A nonprofit entity, the CPD was created in 1987 to provide an umbrella agency for sponsoring presidential debates. The CPD solicits and accepts contributions from corporate and private individuals to sponsor presidential and vice-presidential debates and to undertake educational and research efforts related to the debates. Chaired by Frank J. Fahrenkopf, Jr., former chair of the Republican party, and Paul G. Kirk, Jr., former chair of the Democrat party, the commission is, by law, bipartisan—made up of five Democrats and five Republicans. Most importantly, as the organizer of the debates, the CPD decides who is eligible to participate. Under the law creating the CPD, corporations may make contributions for staging the debates so long as the participants are determined by "pre-established objective criteria." Moreover, the law makes it clear that nomination by a major party may not be the sole criterion.

Thus in 1996 it was the CPD, not the networks, that decided that neither Ross Perot nor Natural Law Party candidate John Hagelin were entitled to participate in the debates. When months after his exclusion, the Federal Election Commission finally ruled on Perot's appeal of the CPD decision, the decision was left standing. The Federal Election Commission, in 1998, accepted the CPD's judgment that Perot was not a viable candidate—even though he had qualified for the ballot in all fifty states and had received federal campaign funds. Similarly, Ralph Nader and the Green Party were excluded from the 2000 debates, because, in the judgment of the commissioners, he was not a viable candidate.

Ironically, about the same time that the Federal Election Commission was deciding the legality of Perot's exclusion, the U.S. Supreme Court was granting wide discretion in this matter to public broadcasters. While broadcasters can cover a live political debate sponsored by someone else, the fact is that below the vice-presidential level there have been few eager sponsors. An important source of debate sponsorship for these less visible campaigns has, for some years now, been public broadcasting stations, over two-thirds of which are owned by states. In these instances the public station sponsors and covers the debates. Reasoning that if the state-owned stations were required to include every candidate the stations would probably cancel the events, the Court in 1992 ruled that public broadcasting stations need not include in their debates all candidates for a given office. The Court did not even require that the public broadcasters develop pre-established objective criteria as is required of the CPD. It seems likely then that minor or third parties in these less visible elections will find it even more difficult to receive media attention.

Regulating Print Media

Print media are subject to far less regulation than broadcasters. Nothing highlights the differential treatment of the broadcast media and the print media better than the application of the fairness doctrine before its demise. Newspapers and magazines have never been subjected to the fairness doctrine, because they enjoy First Amendment protections from governmental regulation. To illustrate the difference one need only look to a pair of Supreme Court cases decided just five years apart. In the first, Timothy Cook, a liberal political commentator, was the subject of a critical radio commentary by the Reverend Billy James Hargis. Cook requested free airtime from Red Lion Broadcasting, the owner of the station that had aired the original commentary. Red Lion refused Cook's request and he then filed a complaint with the FCC. The FCC ruled in Cook's favor and suspended the station's license for failure to comply with the fairness doctrine. After years of legal wrangling the issue reached the Supreme Court where the FCC's actions were upheld. "It is," the majority said, "the right of the viewers and listeners, not the right of broadcasters, which is paramount."[23]

Five years later the Court had before it a very similar case, but this one involved a newspaper. Mr. Pat Tornillo, a candidate for the Florida House of Representatives, was the target of a *Miami Herald* editorial questioning his fitness for office and criticizing his leadership of the teachers' union. Florida had, at the time, a "right to reply" statute that required newspapers attacking candidates for public office to make available equal space to rebut the criticism. Mr. Tornillo requested the opportunity to respond, but the *Herald* refused to print his reply. In upholding the *Herald's* right to refuse publication of the rebuttal Chief Justice Burger argued that:

> A newspaper is more than a passive receptacle or conduit for news, comment, and advertising. The choice of material to go into a newspaper, and the decisions made as to limitations on the size of the paper, and content, and treatment of public issues and public officials—whether fair or unfair—constitutes the exercise of editorial judgment. It has yet to be demonstrated how governmental regulation of this crucial process can be exercised consistent with First Amendment guarantees of a free press as they have evolved to this time.[24]

Not only is the printed press free of the equal time rule, it is also unfettered by anything like the fairness doctrine. Newspapers and magazines are more fully protected by the First Amendment. This lack of regulation of the printed press probably has little effect on national and statewide campaigns of high visibility,[25] but at the local level the freedom of the print media is likely to have significant effect. Candidates for local offices often depend heavily on local newspaper endorsements. The backing by the local newspaper can make or break many candidates.[26] Unable to command much attention without the local newspapers, candidates for local offices spend a great deal of their campaign efforts courting newspaper editors.

Paid Advertising

Paid political advertising is a lightly regulated activity, still it is governed. The content of political advertising is freer of regulation than commercial advertisements. Managers of the media routinely refuse to run or edit advertisements that they feel are in bad taste or offensive to their audience. When it comes to candidate advertising, however, this option is not available. It is here that the differences between normal commercial speech and political speech become apparent. Take the case of indecent speech. In 1978 the Supreme Court ruled in the case of *Federal Communications Commission v. Pacifica Radio* that the FCC had the power to restrict the use of indecent language over the airwaves. At issue was the broadcasting of a George Carlin album entitled simply and descriptively, "Filthy Words." Two years later, Barry Commoner, a 1980 presidential candidate, was allowed to use in a radio commercial one of the prohibited words in Carlin's monologue.[27] Again the point is that the content of candidate advertising remains uncensored.

This is not to say that there are no regulations affecting candidate advertising. The Federal Election Campaign Act of 1971, for instance, created the "lowest unit rate" rule for political candidates. What this means is that starting sixty days before an election (forty-five days for primaries) broadcasters must charge candidates the lowest rate charged to any other customer.[28] (This rule does not apply to political parties or PACs.) Unfortunately in tight elections the rule seems to do little to keep costs down. The problem is that there is a finite amount of airtime. As the campaigns heat up and the demand for time increases, even the lowest unit rate climbs. Illustrative of this are the changes in the lowest unit rates of one Philadelphia television station. In September of 2000, a thirty-second spot ad on the station cost $1,250 . By November first of that year the station charged $1,650 for the same thirty-second ad.[29] As the election drew nearer, and time became more scarce, the station, responding to market forces, raised the lowest unit rate.

Moreover, candidates are not always in a position to accept the lowest rate. Commercial time is generally sold as preemptible and nonpreemptible time (also known as fixed-rate). While preemptible time is the cheapest (the lowest unit rate), it contains no guarantee as to when the advertisement will be aired. Preemptible time, as the name implies, means that the ad may be preempted if another buyer offers to pay the higher rate for that time slot. Because political advertisements are perishable commodities—airing a political commercial after the election is an obvious waste of money—candidates are often forced to opt for the more expensive nonpreemptible times.[30]

National campaigns awash in money may not be severely harmed by the rising advertising rates, but the same cannot be said for state and local candidates. Because in a presidential election year presidential candidates, national parties, and PACs are all vying for the same limited time, the costs can easily escalate beyond the reach of candidates for state and local races. Indeed, preliminary analysis of the 2000 election suggests that electronic media costs have escalated at an extraordinary rate. Some estimates put the electronic media costs for the 2000 election at just under $1 billion. With the increasing use of issue advocacy advertising by interest groups all paying for nonpreemptible time, these costs will only grow and candidates will find it increasingly difficult to make their voices heard even in the paid media environment.

Low-Cost Advertising

Some states have also attempted to regulate nonbroadcast political advertising by prohibiting anonymously published campaign literature. The state of Ohio, in an effort to prevent fraudulent and libelous statements in the midst of campaigns, required distributors of the materials to identify themselves on the literature. Such regulations, the Supreme Court concluded, violate the First Amendment without serving any sufficient state interest.[31] By this decision the

Supreme Court legitimated a series of Federal Election Commission rulings that had limited state power in this area. Going back to the late 1970s, the FEC had ruled that states could not require campaign ads to include: (1) the candidate's party affiliation;[32] (2) the names of campaign officers responsible for the ads;[33] (3) specific wording in campaign logos;[34] or (4) anti- littering warnings.[35] On the other hand, several states prohibit the distribution in nonpartisan elections of any campaign materials containing political party endorsements. The California Constitution forbids political parties and their central committees from endorsing, supporting, or opposing candidates in nonpartisan elections for city, county, and judicial offices. Furthermore, the City of San Francisco deletes from the personal statements contained in the pamphlets of political candidates any reference to party endorsements. Although challenged as a violation of the First Amendment, the Supreme Court let the San Francisco practice stand.[36]

At the local level the regulatory activities of campaign advertising tend to focus on the display of signs, posters, and billboards. Although these advertising techniques may not be central to a national campaign or even a statewide race, in local politics these are likely to be major techniques for publicizing candidates. Local officials concerned about preserving the aesthetic beauty of their communities often seek to limit or even ban the display of signs, billboards, and placards. Although the courts have often spoken on this issue they have, as one commentator noted, left "a collection of mixed and ambiguous signals."[37] Ordinances that seek to control the display of signs on private residential property are apparently the least defensible. Courts have consistently struck down ordinances prohibiting all political signs within town limits, because they regulated private residential property,[38] and efforts to restrict the number of signs residents may display.[39] But the courts have been more willing to tolerate restrictions on the display of signs on public property. In 1984 the Supreme Court granted local governments broad leeway in regulating political signs when it ruled that cities may prohibit the posting of signs on utility poles. Although a common practice with a long history, Justice Stevens argued that the fact that the poles can be used for that purpose does not mean that the use is required. Indeed, Justice Stevens seemed to suggest that a government's right to regulate its property is virtually the same as that of a private property owner.[40] If this is so, ordinances that ban political advertising on all public property would appear constitutional. Lacking clear precedents, municipal governments currently practice a wide array of limitations, including size, shape, and duration requirements that may or may not be constitutional. This form of political advertising which serves as the backbone of thousands of low-budget local election campaigns is, in many jurisdictions, highly regulated and even prohibited.

Libel

Given the rise of negative campaigning in American politics, the applicability to political campaigns of libel laws takes on some importance. Can candidates sue their opponents and the news media if they feel that they have been defamed? The short answer is yes, they can and do file suit. But the fuller story is that winning a libel suit is difficult and time consuming. Under the Supreme Court's ruling in *New York Times v. Sullivan* (1964)[41] public figures—those who willing put themselves before the public—must demonstrate that not only were the statements false, but that they were made with "actual malice." With regard to political candidates (and all public figures) "actual malice" means that the defamatory statement must be proven to have been made " . . . with knowledge that it was false or with reckless disregard of whether it was false or not." Needless to say, this is a very high burden of proof which makes recovering unlikely.

Illustrative of the kind of cases raising the issue of libel during a campaign is the 1991 mayoral run-off election in Houston. Late in a very tight campaign a local broadcaster reported that one of the candidates, Sylvester Turner, had participated in defrauding an insurance company. In the six days between the report and the election, Mr. Turner's poll numbers dropped and he lost the election by 8 percentage points. Following the election Mr. Turner sued the station and its reporter for libel. At the trial it was discovered that the story was given to the reporter by a private investigator working for the opposing campaign. The jury, concluding that the accusations were false and made with actual malice, awarded Mr. Turner $5.5 million. On appeal, the decision was overturned because the appellate court was unconvinced that the statements were made with "actual malice."[42] More importantly, although candidates in Mr. Turner's position may, on occasion, secure compensation from a suit, that will not overturn the election.

Truth in Political Advertising

Given the limited utility of libel laws for political candidates who feel that they have been wronged by an opponent's advertising, it may be that other solutions are needed. Indeed, several media outlets have created "ad watches" whereby reporters evaluate the truthfulness of candidate advertising. These have been generally instructive, but of limited utility. Given the volume of political advertising, the media cannot evaluate even a substantial portion of the ads. They simply cannot give the ads the space or airtime needed to cover the extensive advertising adequately.

Another solution sometimes offered is to treat political advertising like commercial promotions. When it comes to the promotion of commercial products the Federal Trade Commission has the authority to prescribe penalties for false advertising claims. Perhaps the FEC could be empowered to police political advertising. Tempting though it may be, using the FEC in this role is unlikely to meet with much success. Because the truth or falsity of a political ad is likely to be much more difficult to assess than the truthfulness of a commercial product's claim, any policing of political ads will necessitate a great deal of subjectivity. Given the bipartisan nature of the FEC, it is unlikely that it could resolve partisan disputes over the truthfulness of ads, and it is doubtful that such decisions could be made while the campaign was in progress. Thus the commission, even if could come to agreement, would be unlikely to do so until long after the campaign.

Getting Out the Vote

As the campaign comes to a close candidates and parties will increase their efforts to get out the vote. In many elections an important part of this effort is the staffing of phone banks to remind likely supporters of the need to vote. The night before the election and election day these phone banks go to work on lists of voters. Just how effective these efforts are remain speculative, but in the uncertainty of a political campaign the efforts cannot be ignored.

In addition to phone banks, candidates and parties recruit workers to pass out literature and sample ballots at the polling places. This activity is carefully regulated by the states. Every state has laws regulating electioneering at the polls, but of course these regulations differ. North Dakota and Vermont prohibit electioneering within the building where the voting takes place. Most states, however, limit these activities by specifying the distance that campaign workers must keep from the polling place. These distances range from 10 feet in New Hampshire to 600 feet in Kentucky.

States also differ on provisions for compensating campaign workers engaged in these get-out-the-vote activities. Although it is illegal in most states, some states allow the candidates and parties to provide what is called "walking around money." This money, generally cash payments on the morning of the election, is given to campaign workers distributing literature or canvassing door-to-door on election day. The money may, for example, be used to compensate campaign workers for their expenses encountered in driving voters to the polls. Thought by many to be a means of promoting vote-buying, the practice remains an important part of elections in some states. Moreover, the Federal Election Commission has ruled that federal laws placing limits on campaign expenditures do not preempt state laws on this subject.

Conclusions

American political campaigns are conducted against the backdrop of state, local, and national policies and regulations that shape the strategies and tactics available to candidates. These regulations also impact voter response to campaigns. Even a seemingly trivial question like the timing of elections may have consequences for campaign organizers and voters. The altering of election calendars to minimize the importance of high visibility races affects not only the way candidates run their campaigns, but also how voters respond to the campaigns. Staggered election calendars are, for example, thought to be an explanation for declining voter turnout.

Candidates must also conduct their campaigns within the context of various disclosure and campaign spending regulations promulgated by the national governments and the states. Candidates for national offices are now responsible for reporting their receipts and expenditures under the Federal Election Act. Similarly, all states require some version of reporting. Nevertheless, the effectiveness of these disclosure requirements varies greatly. Although the Federal Election Commission does make an effort to report campaign finances in a timely fashion, its enforcement mechanisms are weak and ineffective. At the state level, enforcement activities are often nonexistent. Spending limits, on the other hand, were dealt a serious blow by the Supreme Court's conclusion that campaign spending constitutes a form of free expression protected by the First Amendment. The only spending limits constitutionally viable are those that are attached to voluntary or public funding programs.

Although the content of political campaigns in the media is largely unregulated, the use of media is regulated by all levels of government. The most extensive regulation occurs in the context of broadcasting. Broadcasters do not enjoy the same First Amendment protections accorded to print media. Nevertheless, the trend since the 1980s has been to loosen the broadcasting regulations. At the local level, media usage is often more dependent on the time-honored techniques of signs and placards. These are often highly regulated by local governments, and in some instances this vital form of communication is forbidden.

Endnotes

1. Quoted in Gary C. Jacobson, *The Politics of Congressional Elections*, 2nd ed. (Boston: Little, Brown, 1987), 77. The quote is originally in John W. Kingdon, *Candidates for Office: Beliefs and Strategies* (New York: Random House, 1968), 87.
2. Angus Campbell, "Surge and Decline: A Study of Electoral Change," *Public Opinion Quarterly* 24 (Fall, 1960): 397-418.
3. Gregory A. Caldeira and Samuel C. Patterson, "Getting Out the Vote: Participation in Gubernatorial Elections," *American Political Science Review* 77 (1983): 684-685.
4. Steven J. Rosenstone and John Mark Hansen, *Mobilization, Participation, and Democracy in America* (New York: MacMillan, 1993), 183.
5. Richard Boyd, "Election Calendars and Voter Turnout, *American Politics Quarterly* 14 (January 1986): 94-95.
6. For an excellent summary of the history of campaign finance reform from which much of this discussion is drawn, see Anthony Corrado, "A History of Federal Campaign Finance Law," in Anthony Corrado, Thomas E. Mann, Daniel R. Ortiz, Trevor Potter, and Frank J. Sorauf, eds., *Campaign Finance Reform: A Sourcebook* (Washington: Brookings, 1997), 27-35.
7. The reporting requirements for primaries were thrown into serious doubt by the U.S. Supreme Court decision in *Newberry v. United States*, 256 U.S. 232 (1921). In that case the Court ruled that Congress had no authority over the primary elections. Although the issue in question was the spending limits attached to the bill, Congress acceded to this check on its powers.
8. For a trenchant critique of the workings of the commission, see Thomas E. Mann, "The Federal Election Commission: Implementing and Enforcing Federal Campaign Finance Law," in Anthony Corrado, Thomas Mann, Daniel Ortiz, Trevor Potter, and Frank J. Sorauf, eds., *Campaign Finance Reform*, 277-280.
9. 256 U.S. 232 (1921). Interestingly, Justice Joseph McKenna provided the fifth vote necessary to the majority, but he reasoned that the law would have been constitutional if it had been passed after the adoption of the Seventeenth Amendment providing for the direct election of senators. Nevertheless, Congress accepted the Court's ruling and never attempted to take advantage of McKenna's opening. In 1941 the court overruled the *Newberry* decision in *United States v. Classic*, 313 U.S. 299 (1941).
10. Stephen J. Wayne, *The Road to the White House: 1992* (New York: St. Martins, 1992), 46.
11. 116 S.Ct. 2309 (1996).
12. Drew Linzer and David Menefee-Libey, "The 2000 California Twenty-seventh Congressional District Race," in David B. Magleby, ed., *Election Advocacy: Soft Money and Issue Advocacy in the 200 Congressional Elections* (Provo, Utah; Center for the Study of Elections and Democracy, Brigham Young University, 2001), 132-144.
13. For an excellent discussion of the funding options available to congressional candidates, see Paul S. Herrnson, *Congressional Elections: Campaigning at Home and in Washington* (Washington: Congressional Quarterly, 1998), 72-102.
14. Federal Election Commission, *Advisory Opinion 1991-22*.

15. Federal Election Commission, *Advisory Opinion 1989-25*.
16. Stephen A. Salmore and Barbara G. Salmore, *Cadidates, Parties, and Campaigns: Electoral Politics in America* (Washington: Congressional Quartely, 1985), 56.
17. For an excellent discussion of these kinds of activities and a provocative critique of the role played by the media in presidential elections, see Thomas E. Patterson, *Out of Order* (New York: Alfred A. Knopf, 1993).
18. For an excellent review of the uses of paid television advertising, see Darrell M. West, *Air Wars: Television Advertising in Election Campaigns. 1952-1992* (Washington: Congressional Quarterly Press, 1993).
19. Timothy E. Cook, *Governing with the News* (Chicago: University of Chicago Press, 1998), 19.
20. This language actually was carried over from the Federal Radio Commission which was the predecessor of the Federal Communications Commission.
21. Newton Minow, *Equal Time: The Private Broadcaster and the Public Interest* (New York: Atheneum, 1965), 8.
22. The almost identical rule for cable television is known as the "equal opportunities" rule and varies only slightly from the regulations covering over the air broadcasting.
23. *Red Lion Broadcasting Co. v. F.C.C.*, 395 U.S. 372, 390 (1969).
24. *Miami Herald Publishing Co. v. Tornillo*, 418 U.S. 241 (1974).
25. For an argument that newspaper endorsements are influential in presidential elections, see Robert S. Erikson "The Influence of Newspaper Endorsements in Presidential Elections: the Case of 1964," *American Journal of Political Science* 20 (May 1976): 207-233.
26. See Joel Lieske, "The Political Dynamics of Urban Voting Behavior," *American Journal of Political Science* 33 (February 1989): 150-174.
27. Cited in Kathleen Hall Jamieson and Karlyn Kohrs Campbell, *The Interplay of Influence: Mass Media & Their Publics in News, Advertising, Politics* (Belmont, CA: Wadsworth, 1983), 222.
28. This rule has also been extended to cover cable television systems.
29. Leslie Wayne, "Air Time Is at Premium as Election Draws Near," *The New York Times* (November 1, 2000): 30.
30. Stephen Ansolabehere, Roy Behr, and Shanto Iyengar, *the Media Game: American Politics in the Television Age* (New York: MacMillan, 1993), 29-32.
31. *McIntyre v. Ohio*, 514 U.S. 334 (1995).
32. Federal Election Commission, *Advisory Opinion 1978-24*
33. Federal Election Commission, *Advisory Opinion 1980-36*.
34. Federal Election Commission, *Advisory Opinion 1986-11*.
35. Federal Election Commission, *Advisory Opinion 1981-27*.
36. *Renne v. Geary*, 501 U.S. 312 (1991).
37. Daniel N. McPherson, "Note: Municipal Regulation of Political Signs: Balancing First Amendment Rights Against Aestetic Concerns," *Drake Law Review* 45 (1997): 769.
38. *Matthes v. Town of Needham*, 764 F. 2d 58 (1st Cir. 1985). See also *City of Ladue v. Gilleo*, 114 S. Ct. 2038 (1994).
39. See *Arlington County Republican Committee v. Arlington County*, 983 F.2d 587 (4th Cir. 1993) (striking down an ordinance restricting residents on two political signs on their property).
40. *Members of the City Council v. Taxpayers for Vincent*, 466 U.S. 789 (1984).
41. 376 U.S. 254 (1964).
42. Douglas Frantz, "Plenty of Dirty Jobs in Politics and a New Breed of Diggers," *The New York Times* (July 6, 1999): A-12.

Chapter 5
Casting and Counting the Ballots

The campaign is over and the voters troop to the polls (or in some states the campaign is still going on and they mail in their vote), but what they see there depends on their residence. The type of voting mechanism used, the number of candidates for each office, the number of offices to be voted on, the voting options open to the elector, and how the ballots are counted are all dictated by state laws and local government decisions. Because all elections in the United States are conducted by states and their local governments, there is little uniformity in the process. Even in presidential election years, voters in different states will have diverse experiences as they vote. Moreover, the standards for what constitutes a valid vote will differ from state to state even in presidential elections. The only thing that all elections have in common is the use of the Australian ballot.

The Australian Ballot

When it comes to actually casting the vote, no change has had more impact on American elections than the introduction of the Australian ballot. Throughout most of the nineteenth century elections were party affairs. Each political party printed its own ballot—called "strip" or "unofficial" ballots—listing only its candidates. These ballots were printed in distinctive colors and sizes so that they were easily identified. Party activists distributed their ballots to voters who marked them and dropped them into a ballot box. Of course, this system negated the possibility of a secret ballot, since the different ballots were easily identifiable by party workers, who could record how everyone voted.

This setup underwent drastic change at the end of the nineteenth century, however, when states reformed their electoral systems by taking responsibility for elections and introducing the Australian ballot. The Australian ballot is a state prepared and administered ballot that lists all of the candidates on a single ballot. Because there is only one consolidated ballot, voters can cast a secret vote.

The creation of a truly secret ballot undoubtably reduced incidents of some types of election fraud. As James Morone points out, "Straight-arm voting—in which floaters were lined up, paid and marched to the voting box with a colorful party ballot held out in the ward heeler's view—was rendered impossible."[1] Jerold Rusk has also convincingly demonstrated that the introduction of the Australian ballot significantly increased the incidence of split-ticket voting between

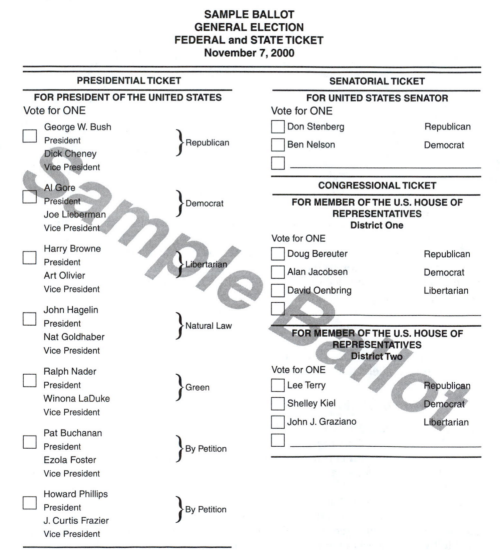

FIGURE 5.1

An Office Block Ballot with Party Labels (Nebraska)

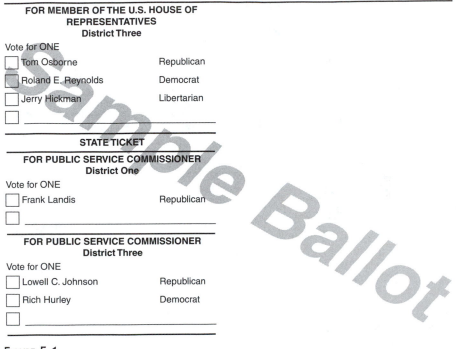

SAMPLE BALLOT
GENERAL ELECTION
FEDERAL and STATE TICKET
November 7, 2000

FOR MEMBER OF THE U.S. HOUSE OF REPRESENTATIVES
District Three

Vote for ONE

☐ Tom Osborne   Republican

☐ Roland E. Reynolds   Democrat

☐ Jerry Hickman   Libertarian

☐ _____

STATE TICKET

FOR PUBLIC SERVICE COMMISSIONER
District One

Vote for ONE

☐ Frank Landis   Republican

☐ _____

FOR PUBLIC SERVICE COMMISSIONER
District Three

Vote for ONE

☐ Lowell C. Johnson   Republican

☐ Rich Hurley   Democrat

☐ _____

FIGURE 5.1
Continued

1876 and 1908. Prior to the Australian ballot is was possible, but not easy, to vote a split ticket. Voters could scratch the name of one party's candidate off the ballot and write in the name of another party's candidate. Alternatively, a voter could take the ballots of different parties, marking each for certain offices and have the various ballots attached. After the introduction of the Australian ballot, split-ticket voting obviously became much easier. But as Rusk demonstrates, there was more to it than that. The internal formatting differences among Australian ballots also made a difference. Although all states have adopted the Australian ballot, certain details regarding the internal format of ballots differ. A few jurisdictions incorporate the style of the strip ballot by listing the candidates in party columns. This format, known as the "party column" or "Indiana party column" simply consolidates the strip format onto a single ballot. Initially a popular version of the Australian ballot, the party column has, in recent years, been displaced by the office block format. The office block, sometimes referred to as the Massachusetts office block, lists the candidates by office rather than party. (See Figure 5.1) In some states the party designation for the candidates is included on the office block ballot, in others it is not. Split-ticket voting in states adopting the party column format was in the first few years after reform only slightly higher than under the classic strip ballot. The office block, on the other hand, early on demonstrated a much stronger split-ticket pattern[2]

The office block format does not prevent straight party voting, but it makes it more difficult. Moreover, because the voter must mark or pull a lever for each office it is assumed that the voter will be less likely to follow party labels. In 1960, the authors of the classic voting study, *The American Voter*, promoted this assumption when they concluded:

> In 1956, of the Eisenhower voters in single choice [Party-Column] states, fifty-nine percent voted a straight ticket; in multiple choice [Office-Block] states, forty- eight; of the 1956 Stevenson voters in single-choice states, sixty-nine percent voted a straight ticket, in multiple-choice states, sixty per cent. Since the distribution of party identifiers in the two types of states did not differ we conclude that the sheer ease of voting a straight ticket facilitated this type of behavior.[3]

This is not a conclusion that surprises politicians. Political candidates have long suspected that the office block format discourages straight party voting. In 1949, Ohio Republicans spent over $85,000 in a successful campaign to replace the party column with the office block ballot, all in an effort to save Senator Robert Taft from defeat in the election of 1950. Later Taft claimed that the change "was responsible 'for something between 100,000 and 200,000' of his total majority of 430,000."[4] Figure 5.2 provides another example of a manipulated format. The figure shows a typical office block format that contains party labels and a straight party vote option. But look at it closely. You will notice that a straight party vote still needs to cast a presidential vote. This peculiar structure was created by conservative Democratic legislators in 1972. They wanted to deter Democratic voters from casting their ballots for the party's presidential nominee, Senator George McGovern, who they considered ultra-liberal. By separating the contests, Democrats could vote for McGovern's opponent Richard Nixon and then return to cast a straight party vote for the Democrats. More recently, the Illinois legislature under the control of Republicans eliminated the straight party option on the state's ballots on the presumption that it benefitted Democrats.

As an unintended consequence the office block format may well facilitate voter fatigue or what is sometimes called "voter roll-off." Voter roll-off occurs when voters make choices in the high visibility elections (e.g., presidency, Senate, and gubernatorial) but overlook the races for the less publicized offices and ballot issues. In the less noticeable offices, the voters simply do not make a choice. Roll-off has long been recognized as a problem endemic to the long ballot. Originally a Jacksonian reform, the long ballot was based on the belief that government could be made more democratic only by electing all officials, eliminating where possible appointed positions. The result was lengthy ballots (thus the name "long" ballot) with numerous voting choices. In the view of its critics, the long ballot asked voters to make too many choices. With so many offices on the ballot voters were incapable of making intelligent choices that held elected officials accountable. Indeed, Woodrow Wilson declared the elimination of the long ballot "the key to the whole problem of the restoration of popular democracy in this country."[6]

There is more to it than the length of the ballots, however. The office block format has also been shown to increase voter fatigue and roll-off. The complexity and difficulty of marking the office block ballot increases voter fatigue, especially among the less educated who are more easily confused by the format. The leading study on this subject estimated that states using the party

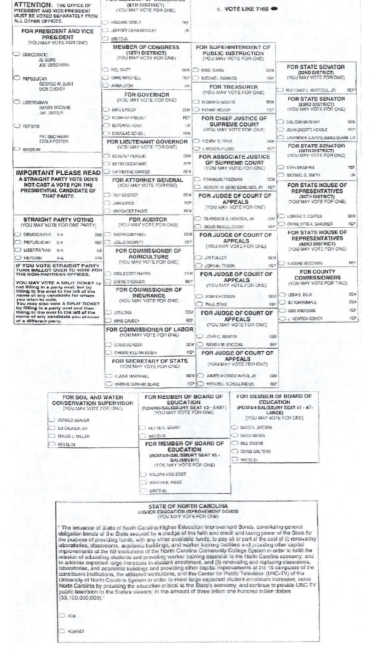

FIGURE 5.2
An Office Block Ballot with Party Labels and a Straight Party Option

113

column format experienced a mean of from .2 percent to 2.0 percent less voter fatigue than states using the office block ballot. To Jack Walker the point is clear, "The more complex the design of the ballot, the greater the tendency for voters to neglect races at the bottom of the ticket."[7]

Ballot complexity resurfaced as a major issue in the 2000 presidential elections, when one county in Florida (Palm Beach) utilized a format known as the "butterfly ballot." Although an example of the office block ballot, the butterfly staggered the candidate's names across two pages with the hole punches down the middle (see Figure 5.3). The butterfly ballot design was, in this case, used to accommodate ten presidential candidates in a typeface large enough to be easily read by Palm Beach County's sizeable elderly population. Unfortunately, as often happens, good intentions went amiss. Many voters complained that the design was confusing, making it difficult to cast their intended vote. Lending credence to the complaints is the fact that more than 19,000 voters in Palm Beach County cast a vote for more than one presidential candidate—thus invalidating their vote. Additionally, many voters believed that they unintentionally voted for the Reform Party candidate, Patrick Buchanan. Buchanan was the first candidate listed on the right-hand page, but the second hole to be punched in the middle. (Gore was the second candidate listed on the left-hand page, but the

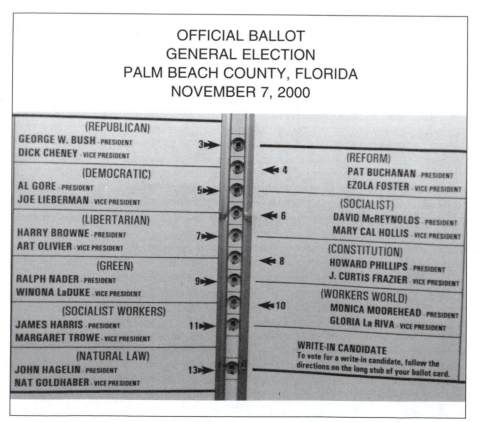

FIGURE 5.3
The Infamous Butterfly Ballot of 2000. © AP/World Wide Photos.

third hole to be punched.) Suspicions of voter confusion was heightened by the fact that Buchanan received an unexpectedly large number of votes from a county heavily populated by Democratic voters unlikely to support him. Even Buchanan speculated that it was doubtful that he received that many votes in a county in which he had never campaigned.

Ballot Position   Type of ballot aside, it is well established that position on the ballot—whatever the medium—does have consequences. In 1956 two enterprising political scientists demonstrated that no matter what type of ballot was used the candidates listed first were substantially advantaged.[8] More recent evidence substantiates this point, but notes that the advantage is even greater for contests at the end of the ballot.[9] As a result states use a variety of methods to deal with advantageous ballot position. Indiana, for instance, requires that the candidates of the party that received the most votes for secretary of state in the previous election be listed first. More commonly, states draw lots to determine the first position, others list candidates in alphabetical order, and still another option used is to list candidates in the order they filed for office. For the most part these procedures do not eliminate the bias; they just distribute it more fairly.

Opening and Closing the Polls   All elections involving federal offices are, according to federal laws,[10] required to be held on the first Tuesday after the first Monday in November. As discussed earlier purely state and local elections can be held on any day selected by state law.

Why are federal elections held on this particular day? The reasons are rooted in the nation's rural past. November was selected as the month because it was the month thought most likely to enable farmers and rural residents to travel to the polls. Any date in the spring would interfere with planting. Summer months would obviously conflict with the needs of farmers to tend their crops, and an early fall date would disrupt the harvest. November, especially early November, seemed to offer the least conflict with the demands of agricultural life, while still offering mild enough weather to permit travel to polling places.

Of course, this does not explain why the day selected was a Tuesday. Here the explanation gets a little blurry. We can figure out why Tuesday instead of Monday. Monday was considered unacceptable because the need to travel long distances over unimproved roads would have required many to leave the day before the election in order to arrive on election day. A Monday election would have meant traveling on Sunday. But why the first Tuesday after the first Monday? Congress wanted to assure that election day would be early in November, but not on the first day of November. November 1 is All Saints Day, a holy day for Roman Catholics. The first was also traditionally the day that merchants did their accounts for the previous month. Congress may have been worried that merchants would be overly influenced by the immediate balance sheet if the election occurred on the day they did the books.

Does it matter? In the end some day had to be chosen, and the first Tuesday after the first Monday in November may be as good as any. On the other hand, many analysts of voting statistics argue that the traditionally low voter turnout in the United States is in part the result of holding elections on a workday. Most of the world's democracies hold their elections on a holiday or a Sunday. Making election day a holiday might make it easier for people to vote and thereby increase turnout. Unfortunately, there is little evidence that holding elections on a holiday or on a Sunday would increase turnout in the United States and there is a great deal of public opposition to such schemes.

Creating a new holiday for elections would undoubtably encounter opposition from businesses unwilling or unable to close or pay employees extra for working the holiday. The closest existing holiday that could be used is November 11th, Veteran's Day. Most likely, however, veterans' groups would strongly object to the diversion of attention away from the nation's veterans and their sacrifices.[11] Moreover, Veteran's Day is not a holiday observed by the private sector.[12] If the point is to increase turnout by holding the election on a holiday, Veteran's Day would have to be made a legal holiday in the private as well as the public sector.

Sundays present a similar problem. Because Sunday is the traditional day of religious observance for Christians, it is reasonable to expect that opposition would arise over Sunday elections. Further complicating the issue is the fact that many jurisdictions around the country use churches as voting places.

Nevertheless, interest in making election day a holiday may be increased by the experiences of the 2000 election. In their last contract with the automakers, the United Auto Workers negotiated a clause that made election day a paid holiday for their members. Some analysts see this provision as aiding organized labor, particularly in Michigan, in their get-out-the-vote drive. If further analysis should prove the contract provision instrumental in encouraging worker turnout, it is likely that there will be increased attention to proposals to move election day.

Although federal election day is the same in all states, there is some variability in the hours of polling place operation. Nationally most states close their polling places at 8 P.M. local time, but several close at 7 P.M. Hawaii closes the earliest, at 6 P.M. Similarly most states mandate that the polls open at 6 A.M., but again there is some variability. Montana allows some jurisdictions, depending on size, to open as late as noon on election day. In several states the opening time is set by the local jurisdictions, with state law providing acceptable ranges. In New Hampshire, for instance, state law requires that the polling stations open no later than 11 A.M. Despite the differences in opening and closing times, almost half the states require that the polls be open at least thirteen hours on election day. The shortest period is Hawaii; their polls are open only eleven hours.

Although there is little empirical evidence linking the hours of operation with turnout, every election produces anecdotes of voters being turned away because the polls were closing. During the 2000 election some precincts in St. Louis had long lines waiting to vote as closing time approached. Because these voters could not be processed before the polls closed, the local Democratic party requested a local court order for the polls to stay open until all those in line had voted. The trial judge granted relief, but was quickly overturned by an appellate court. As a result the polls closed at 7 P.M. and those still in line were denied the ability to vote.

The St. Louis case illustrates one of the differences among the states and even among local jurisdictions within states. Most states provide little legal guidance on what to do if there are lines of voters when the polls close. As a result, local officials often exercise substantial discretion. In some jurisdictions, the policy is to let anyone in line when the polls close vote. In other jurisdictions, the polls are closed at the required hour and anyone standing in line is turned away. Because few states are explicit on this matter variability exists not just across states but within states and even within local jurisdictions.

Differing closing times, combined with time zone differences, have when combined with the media practice of calling presidential elections caused some critics to charge that the television networks alter election results in states that close late. The television networks have agreed not to call the election results in a state until its polls are closed. (In 2000, however, the networks called the results in Florida, for the first time, before the polls in the state's panhandle had closed. The panhandle jurisdictions closed later than the rest of the state.) Nevertheless, because of time zone differences network calls may well occur before western states have closed.

Some observers believe that these early calls lead those in states where the polls are still open to change their votes. This can occur in two ways. It may be that calling the election may lead some voters in states where the polls are still open to switch their vote to the asserted winner. This is the so-called "bandwagon effect." Other observers have argued, however, that upon hearing the election called for a candidate, some voters will move toward the apparent loser—the "underdog effect." Despite a number of studies designed to measure these effects, there is little evidence to suggest that either occurs to any significant degree.[15]

Still, differing closing hours and the media practice may have significant effects. Of greatest concern is the possibility that calls made while the polls in the West are still open may depress turnout in those states. Scholars who have looked at this problem have produced substantially different estimates of the effect.[14] Nevertheless there does seem to be a consensus pointing to a small effect of early calls on turnout, but even then only under certain conditions. Most importantly, for the calls to have much effect they must provide new information. An early call in a presidential race that was not assumed in doubt is not likely to change voter turnout. The early call is most likely to affect turnout when the race is close or was expected to be close. Thus the greatest effect is to be seen in an election like 1980. Polls prior to the election predicted a close race, but early exit polling showed a Reagan sweep. In this case, the early call was new information for West Coast voters, who were expecting a tight race. Whether true or not, many Democrats blamed the loss of some California House seats on the early network call. As the political wisdom has it, Carter supporters stayed home when they learned of Reagan's victory, resulting in a low Democratic turnout in some key House races.

Fear that media calls affect the election has prompted reform efforts that would either prohibit the announcement of a projected winner until the all polls are closed or require all polls to close at the same time. The first suggestions has serious First Amendment problems. It seems unlikely that the Congress can prohibit the networks from announcing their judgment without broaching freedom of press. The second reform, uniform closing times, has twice passed in the House, but has never succeeded in the Senate. Although uniform closing laws may seem an obvious solution, the geography of the United States makes this difficult. Are the eastern states to stay open later? Or do the western states close earlier? How do you achieve uniformity here? Of course, this becomes even more difficult when we recognize the time difference between the East Coast and Hawaii.

Ballot Medium

How voters physically cast their ballot varies greatly from state to state and within most states from one local jurisdiction to another. The highly decentralized nature of elections administration is rooted in the Constitution, which leaves the task to the states. The vast majority of the states in turn leave the implementation of elections to cities and counties, often with only general guidelines. Only eight states mandate a single ballot medium for use in all elections. The remaining states leave the choice of the mechanism up to the cities and counties. Most states do certify the equipment to be used, allowing local governments to use only those devices and models approved by the state. These states also specify that whatever medium used, it must make write-in votes possible. Nevertheless, the local governments generally have a wide array of devices and models from which to choose. The result, in most states, is a hodgepodge system based on what the cities and counties can afford. What kind of equipment and its state of repair or disrepair depends in most cases on what the local jurisdiction can afford.

Voting in Person   The oldest vehicle for voting is the paper ballot. Voters mark the choice next to their candidate or issue choice and drop the ballot into a sealed box. Used primarily in small communities and rural areas, just under 2 percent of registered voters used paper ballots in the 2000 election.

Another 20 percent of the electorate in 2000 cast their vote using a mechanical lever machine. These machines assign a lever to each candidate or issue. The voter casts a vote by pulling down the selected levers which activates a series of counterwheels that records the vote. These machines are being phased out and are no longer manufactured. Indeed it is becoming increasingly difficult to repair broken machines, as replacement parts are no longer available.

A third option is the punchcard system. Punchcard systems employ a card (or cards) and a small clipboard-sized device for recording votes. The voters, using a punch device supplied in the booth, punch holes in the cards opposite their choices. With one version of the punchcard system (the Votomatic), the locations for punching holes are indicated on the card by a number. This is the only information printed on the card. The list of candidates or issues to be voted on are printed in a separate booklet. With the Datavote system, the card contains the names of the candidates or a statement of the issues next to the location of the hole to be punched. Whether it's the Votoamatic or Datavote system the procedure is the same once the voter has completed the ballot, the card is placed in a ballot box. In 2000 over 37 percent of registered voters used one of these versions of the punchcard system.

Another quarter of registered voters in 2000 used a system known as Marksense. Familiar to all students, Marksense is simply an optically scanned voting system, frequently used to grade multiple-choice exams. Voters simply fill in a rectangle, circle, oval, or arrow next to the candidate's name or their choice on an issue. The completed ballot is then placed in a sealed box or fed into a computer (some version of an optical scanner) and then passed into a sealed box— providing a paper record for verification. Precincts that do not have the scanning devices transmit the sealed boxes to a central location where they are opened and scanned to produce the totals. If the ballots are scanned at the precinct level, the vote totals are transmitted by phone, modem, or by delivery of memory cartridges to a central location.

The newest procedure is a system known as direct recording electronic (DRE). Voters complete the ballot by use of a touch screen or push buttons, similar to the ubiquitous ATM machines. Touching the screen or the appropriate buttons enters the vote directly into electronic storage (diskette or smart card) where the vote is added to all others. Most of these machines have alphabetic keyboards to allow for the possibility of write-in votes.

Currently a few states are considering or experimenting with Internet voting. The Department of Defense is conducting a pilot project to allow overseas residents from selected states to vote by Internet. Alaska, Arizona, and California have also experimented with the technology.

Absentee Voting   Absentee voting in America began during the Civil War when several states adopted temporary measures allowing soldiers to vote absentee. At the turn of the century several states adopted some version of absentee voting although these laws often narrowly defined the categories of qualified absentee voters. Kansas first made absentee voting available only to railway workers. By 1938, however, forty-two states had some version of an absentee voting procedure. During World War II Congress created a system of absentee voting for the uniformed services. But after the war, several states, fearing election fraud, returned to or instituted restrictive provisions to discourage the practice.[15]

Traditionally states have allowed individuals to qualify as absentee voters if they met certain criteria. Individuals physically unable to go the polls have commonly been eligible to receive absentee ballots. Those absent from the state on election day and those who, for religious reasons, are prevented from going to the polling place have also often been deemed eligible. Over the last couple of decades numerous states have liberalized these laws. Moreover, Congress, in amendments to the Voting Rights Act, requires all states to permit absentee voting in presidential elections if the voter requests the ballot within seven days of the election and returns the ballot before the polls close. In the process these reforms have, as J. Eric Oliver says, "quietly transformed the nature of electoral politics in the United States."[16] According to his estimate more than 7 percent of Americans cast their vote in 1992 without going to the polls—that is more than twice as many as did so in 1972. In many areas where turnout is low, absentee ballots have become the focal point of competition.[17]

Even though the trend has been toward liberalization of the laws, there is still great variability across the states in access to absentee ballots. Several states still apply the traditional standards, while others have expanded the eligibility requirements. Texas, for instance, allows for automatic eligibility for anyone over age sixty-five. Still other states allow anyone to vote absentee—this is sometimes referred to as "no-fault" absentee balloting. That the extent of liberalization makes a difference in how many people vote absentee is hardly surprising. The more permissive state law is on the matter, the more citizens take advantage of the process.[18] But this does not mean that more liberalized absentee eligibility laws increase turnout. After all many absentee voters may well go to the polls if that is what is required, they simply vote absentee because it is more convenient. The best evidence on absentee voting and turnout indicates that more liberalized laws do increase voter turnout, but only when they are combined with political party efforts to mobilize absentee voters. Without party mobilization efforts, increased absentee voter eligibility does little to elevate turnout. Moreover, absentee liberalization combined with party activity increases turnout among those already most likely to vote. "Removing absentee restrictions and mobilization activity greatly reduces the 'costs' of voting for those individuals who are more likely to vote, thus enlarging their representation in the electorate."[19] Even the most liberal absentee ballot laws do little to increase the turnout of those least likely to vote.

Additionally, the liberalization of absentee balloting alters the way candidates conduct their campaigns. Candidates in the most permissive states must aggressively target the absentee vote. It is becoming standard practice for candidates to send out thousands of absentee applications along with their campaign literature. This, of course, costs money, further escalating campaign costs. Indeed a cottage industry of experts in mail balloting has grown up around the practice as candidates in many states reach out for the absentee vote.

Mailing in the Vote   A natural extension of the liberalized absentee voting requirements is the universal mail-in ballot. Several states have begun experimenting with mail-ballots. Typically all voters receive a ballot through the mail two or three weeks before the election. In most states the voters can fill it out and mail it in, return it to the polling place on election day, or simply ignore it and cast their vote at a polling place on election day. Sixteen states have adopted some version of the mail-ballot, usually for referenda issues. Recently, however, Oregon has moved to implement mail-ballots across all elections. In 1995, Oregon held the first all mail-ballot party primaries, and in 1996, the state held an all mail-ballot special election to fill the seat of a retiring U.S. Senator. Then in 1998 Oregon voters approved a measure to conduct all elections exclusively by mail. Although several states are watching the Oregon experience closely, the mail-in election has it critics. Oregon's law is being challenged in court as a violation of federal law which requires that congressional and presidential elections occur on the same day in November.

Do these differences affect voter turnout? There is little evidence that the medium used to cast the ballot impacts the likelihood of persons voting. A handful of studies have suggested that the introduction of the mechanical lever machines did, at least in the early stages, decrease the voters' propensity to vote on referendum questions, but these studies have not been replicated for more modern elections.[20] On the other hand, some studies have suggested that all-mail elections increase turnout.[21] The only study that looked at all-mail elections involving candidates for office—as opposed to elections involving only ballot measures—concludes that in Oregon the all-mail elections increased registered voter turnout between 1960 and 1996 by 10 percent.[22] Still, the selection of voting systems is not without its controversies. To the contrary, these issues have substantial impact on the outcomes of elections.

Election Night and Beyond

Once the ballots have been cast, election officials in the local precincts go to work counting and tallying the results. It is these tallies that are then certified by the responsible officials as the results. But just which votes count, how the tallies are arrived at, and when the vote count is complete depends, even in presidential elections, on the decisions of the local officials who run the elections. Just which votes count varies from jurisdiction to jurisdiction.

Counting the Votes

Most of us give little thought to the actual counting of ballots. We have heard stories of corruption and the occasional missing ballot box, but these seem to be historical oddities from an earlier time. Counting the votes seems automatic. The reality is that the final vote tallies are approximate. In every election there are uncounted votes and some votes that should not have counted. Sometimes the ballots are intentionally miscounted or the totals intentionally misreported, but more often the tallies simply reflect the errors that humans make. We seldom hear about such problems because most elections are not close enough for the mistakes to matter.

What complicates this task is the decentralized nature of ballot counting. Just as there is no single ballot or medium for casting the vote, there is no central authority on how votes are to be counted. As Roy Schotland has said, "Congress leaves it to the states, states leave it to the cities and counties, and the cities and counties leave it to, let's face it, fairly low level political patronage employees with very weak budgets."[23] To make matters worse, all of these diverse authorities must depend upon volunteers to not only get the job done, but to get it done quickly. Although technology may be helpful here, the fact is that a highly decentralized process that often requires even minimal human intervention will, at times, fail. The search for the technological fix is elusive, but ongoing.

When the mechanical lever machines were first introduced they were touted as an effective means of providing a quick count, free of vote fraud. Without all those paper ballots to count or miscount the machines were widely acclaimed as the quick and accurate way to tally the votes. Similarly, the punchcard systems were introduced to great fanfare. The automatic computing of the punched cards was presumed to not only speed up the process but increase the reliability of the counts. The new generation of electronic systems, the Marksense and DRE, promises even faster and more accurate counts.

Unfortunately, none of these systems can guarantee exact counts. As many Americans learned for the first time in 2000, all voting systems are subject to problems. Paper ballots, for instance, have obvious shortcomings. Honest counting mistakes are easily made as officials pour through hundreds and even thousands of votes. Errors of addition, mistakenly transposed numbers, and poor handwriting are obvious, and not infrequent, sources of miscount. Intentional miscounts and fraud are also sometimes alleged. Additionally, counting the votes often requires judgment. If, for instance, the instructions require the voter to place an X in the box next to the candidate, do you count a check mark in the box? What if the mark is outside the box? Does the vote count if the candidate's name is circled? State laws are often ambiguous on these issues. Most states require that those counting the votes make every effort to determine the elector's choice, but those counting the ballots may not assume a voter's choice. These potentially contradictory charges are seldom clarified by state law. Few states provide much clarity on exactly what counts as a valid vote. Much discretion and often little guidance is given to those doing the counting.

As the 2000 election in some Florida counties demonstrated, the punchcard system is also fraught with problems. Indeed, the 2000 election introduced for many citizens a new word—chad. The chad (no one seems to know where the name comes from) is the little piece of cardboard that is supposed to be punched out when the voter pushes the stylus through the hole next to the candidate's name. Once the voting has been completed, the cards are fed into a mechanical card reader that detects which holes have been punched (where the chad is missing) and records the vote. A vote is recorded if the machine can detect light shining through the punched out hole.

The problem is that the chad may not be punched out entirely. In this case the machine does not register a vote. It may be that the voter fails to push hard enough with the stylus. Alternatively, if the card is not placed in the holder (a clipboard-like device) correctly, even a punched hole will not be recorded because it does not push out the chad. If, for instance, the card is even a quarter of an inch off in the holder, the stylus will not push out the chad, even if the voter punches a hole in the card. In this case the hole may go through a part of the chad but will not dislodge it. Additionally, repeated use of the same holder creates a build-up of chad (the word is both singular and plural) making it potentially difficult, even with substantial pressure, to punch out the chad. These problems make even machine counts of punchcards problematic. The machines will not record a vote unless the chad is dislodged. This creates what is called an "undercount"—fewer votes recorded than cast.

To confuse the issue further, repeated machine counting of the ballots often dislodges some of the chad while pushing others back in, producing different totals with each count. Illustrative of this are the three machine counts of the ballot in Palm Beach County during the 2000 election. Each count produced different results in the presidential race.

Failure to punch out the chad completely then creates questions as to what should be counted. Unfortunately, few states have legislated extensively on this issue. California is one of the exceptions. Under California law, a vote may be counted if it contains what is called a "hanging chad"—one attached to the ballot by a single corner. Swinging chad (two corners attached) and "tri-chad" (three attached corners) cannot be counted. Washington State, on the other hand, requires local election officials to inspect the cards, removing any hanging chad before putting the cards into the counting machine. Ironically, given the 2000 election, Texas has established one of the more liberal interpretations of a valid vote. Texas law requires that, during a handcount, a vote is usable if "at least two corners of the chad are detached." Furthermore, Texas Election Code provides that the so-called "pregnant" or "dimpled" ballots (chad is punched or dimpled, but all corners are attached) may be counted. A pregnant chad may be recorded as a vote if election officials decide that "an indentation on the chad from the stylus or other object is present and indicates a clearly ascertainable intent of the voter to vote."[24]

Mechanical lever machines obviously avoid the problem of the hanging chad, but these machines are no longer produced and repair parts are difficult to find. Indeed, many of the existing machines are cobbled together with salvaged parts from decommissioned machines. Not surprisingly the machines are subject to frequent breakdowns. Moreover, the mechanical lever machines have entered the political folklore as sources of voting fraud. Anecdotes describing instances of machines recording hundreds of votes prior to the polls opening have long been standards tales of American politics.

Like the mechanical lever machines, optical reading equipment avoids the problem of interpreting the chad and yet provides for a speedy count. Moreover, in those jurisdictions that immediately scan the ballot, the systems offer the advantage of identifying overvotes (votes cast for more than one person for the same office) instantly. This instant identification makes it possible for the voter to request another ballot and cast a valid vote. The optical readers also provide a paper record that, in the case of contested elections, can be checked against the machine tabulations. Nevertheless, the systems are not without their problems. As all students know, even the most sophisticated optical reading equipment makes mistakes. The accuracy of the systems depends on adequate maintenance of the readers and the use of ballots printed on the appropriate paper. Even then, however, the technology may fail. In 2000, Volusia County, Florida, initially lost 16,000 votes because of faulty memory cards in some machines. (The lost votes were recovered and counted, but the experience demonstrates the dangers of assuming that technology can solve the counting problem.) To complicate matters, although the voter need only fill in a box, a circle, oval, or arrow, many voters circle the candidate's name or punch holes in the ballot and others press so lightly that their shading is too light to be read by the scanner. In short, many of the problems encountered by paper ballots appear on the optically scanned ballots. Should these votes be counted? In the end that decision is left to local officials, because few states provide any real statutory guidance on these questions. Even in states that do provide guidance, it is not clear that well-meaning election officials always follow the rule. Oklahoma, for example, instructs poll workers not to count votes that are improperly filled out. Nevertheless, as Lance Ward, Oklahoma's election board secretary, said, "We give them instructions not to try to determine the voter's intent, but they'll do it [anyway]."[25]

Finally, the newer electronic systems, direct recording electronic systems and Internet voting, have attracted a great deal of attention and some concern. Because these methods can provide almost immediate tabulation and feedback they have attracted a large number of advocates. The electronic systems are also attractive because they can be easily programmed to block overvoting. It is an easy task to program the systems so that they will not accept two votes for the same office.

Still these methods have their detractors. Many fear that the these systems are vulnerable to fraud and manipulation. Howard Strauss, a computer scientist at Princeton University, warns that as the electronic systems centralize vote-counting they increase the opportunity for manipulation. According to Strauss, the security protecting electronic voting is "not a door without locks, it's a house without doors."[26] This may be hyperbole, but it is important to remember that no software can be certified as virus free. As anyone involved in computer security knows, firewalls can be breached. But the suspicion of electronic systems is not limited to intentional fraud. The tabulation process is only as good as the software. If the software has bugs, the votes may not be counted accurately. Indeed, in 1998 Dallas County, Texas, discovered the dangers of faulty software when its new high-technology DRE system failed to count 40,000 votes. These problems are compounded by the fact that most electronic systems leave no paper trail; the only thing that the voter sees is an electronic screen. Lacking a paper trail, it is difficult to impossible to audit election returns. Fraudulent or faulty software cannot be checked when there is no record other than what the software creates. This can be changed, however, because some of the newer DRE systems do produce a paper printout of the vote, similar to the ATM receipt, that lists the votes cast. These printouts could be deposited in a sealed box and thus be available for comparison with the electronically generated tabulations.

The option of providing a paper trail is, of course, not available for Internet voting which is done off site. Additionally, Internet voting raises serious questions regarding the possible corrosion of the secret ballot. Even with passwords and voter identification procedures, Internet voting cannot guarantee that the vote is actually being cast by the voter. Nor can it guarantee that the voter is free of pressure. What critics ask, prevents, for example, employers from monitoring the Internet votes of employees? Similarly, Internet voting could encourage vote buying. The greatest impediment to vote buying is the secrecy entailed in casting the Australian ballot. Because Internet voting makes it possible to look over the voter's shoulder, buying votes seems more viable. So far the experiments with Internet voting have required voters to use publicly provided machines with voting officials standing by to monitor the activities. If Internet voting is to fulfill its promise it must be made more convenient and yet secure.

Liberalized absentee voting and mail ballots raise many of these same questions. Voters may in these instances use paper ballots, sometimes punchcards, and increasingly optically scanned ballots. In addition, however, absentee and mail-in ballots create problems not encountered by votes cast at the polling both. When, for instance, does an absentee or mail-in ballot have to be received for it to be counted? Generally, states require that the ballot must be postmarked no later than election day, but the number of days after the election that it may be received and still count varies from state to state. California, for instance, requires that all absentee ballots arrive by the time the polls close on election day. On the other hand, as the whole country learned in 2000, Florida counts all overseas ballots, postmarked by election day, and delivered within ten days of the election. What if the ballot arrives within the allowable period but lacks a clearly discernable postmark? As is so often the case on these issues, state laws are seldom very specific. Instead, they tend to leave the counting to the discretion of local election officials.

Similarly, what are election officials to do with damaged ballots—badly mangled or water soaked in the delivery process? Almost all states require election officials, where possible, to prepare an exact duplicate of the damaged ballot and enter the properly marked duplicate as a valid vote. Of course, there is a great deal of discretion in determining whether or not the original ballot can be properly deciphered and thus a duplicate prepared. What may be readable to one election official may be illegible to another.

Absentee and mail-in ballots also produce slow counts. Even if the jurisdiction uses a punchcard or optically scanned ballot, the process of verifying that the ballot is from a properly registered and eligible voter can be painstakingly slow and tedious. In the 2000 election, the state of Washington took over two weeks to produce a first count in its tight Senate race in part because almost half the ballots were mailed in. Finally, like Internet voting, liberalized absentee balloting and mail-in elections raise serious questions about the integrity of the process. It is impossible to know if these votes are in fact secretly cast.

These issues came to a head in 2000 when the United States Supreme Court in *Bush v. Gore* overruled the Florida Supreme Court's order to recount votes in selected counties. A seven-member majority of the Court ruled that the court ordered recount violated the equal protection clause of the Fourteenth Amendment because there was no uniform way of counting votes. (Two members of the majority agreed that the recount violated the Fourteenth Amendment, but dissented because they believed that criteria could be established and the votes recounted in time to appoint electors.) Based as it was on the equal protection clause, the Court's decision raises serious questions about the conduct of future elections. That differences across jurisdictions would emerge in a Florida recount is hardly news to those involved in counting and tallying votes. Nor is this a problem limited to Florida. As we have seen, few states have detailed laws on how to count votes. Local discretion is the rule, not the exception. Florida's law requiring voting officials to determine the intent of the voter without instructions on how this is to be done is typical. Even the Texas statute which allows, under some circumstances, for the counting of dimpled chad, lacks specificity to prevent votes from being counted differently across jurisdictions.

Moreover, the Court's opinion opens up the question of whether equal protection can ever be guaranteed in a process that uses varying methods of casting the vote. If some methods are more prone to problems than others, is equal protection provided? Does equal protection require uniform methods of voting? Chief Justice Rehnquist in a concurring opinion joined by Justices Scalia and Thomas argued that the Fourteenth Amendment did not require uniform voting mechanisms. According to the Chief Justice, the Fourteenth Amendment only required that all votes cast by the same medium be counted by the same rules. The Chief Justice's concurrence also stressed that the standards are different in presidential elections. But Rehnquist did not speak for the majority here. There are no indications as to how the majority felt on these issues. Just how encompassing this nationalization of the electoral process is remains to be seen. Given that the least reliable methods of voting tend to be concentrated in the poorest jurisdictions, further challenges are sure to follow. Future cases will clearly test just how far the Court is willing to go in nationalizing vote counting.

Given all of these problems, why not institute a national system of voting with one medium and one set of decisions regarding how to count votes? This would seem to satisfy any equal protection claims. Part of the answer lies in federalism. With regard to elections for national office, the U.S. Constitution clearly assigns the majority of power over the electoral process to the states. Uniform rules in the conduct of elections would be seen by states as a serious infringement on their powers.

Still, in the wake of the 2000 election several critics of the electoral processes, inside and outside of Congress, have called for reform. A December 2000 *Washington Post*-ABC poll reported that 87 percent of the public would support a federal law, requiring all states and counties to use one kind of voting machine. Similarly, the poll reported that 88 percent would support a federal law requiring the same design and layout for all election ballots.[27]

The most popular version of reform and the one least threatening to state power involves a standardization of the ballot medium. Many commentators of the current practices have called for the updating and standardization of the equipment in all jurisdictions. Generally those favoring such a reform effort favor the use of some type of electronic system.

Attractive as this idea seems, it runs into a simple but substantial obstacle— cost. Because the administration of elections is generally relegated by the states to local governments, the cost of more sophisticated techniques would in many cases be borne by jurisdictions already hard pressed to meet their citizens' needs for basic services. For example, that the punchcard system presents problems comes as no surprise to experienced election officials. The problems are legendary. Nevertheless, punchcards have stayed a vital part of election systems because they are economical. A punchcard booth costs only about $300. The counting machine costs a few thousand, but you do not need one at each location. Thus the cost for the counting machine can be spread across several polling places. On the other hand, upgrading to a DRE system can get very expensive quickly. Each DRE voting booth can cost anywhere from $3,500 to $5,500. The equipment to tabulate the votes is even more costly.

Are Americans ready and willing to bear that kind of cost? Will the national government and the states provide financial help for jurisdictions unable to afford the changes? Perhaps the turmoil surrounding the 2000 election will create the support necessary to institute real change. Nevertheless, because the problems only become apparent in very close elections, the 2000 experiences may fade and with them the demand for change. As William Galvin, the Massachusetts secretary of state, said, "It's like people who have a number of mild winters, forget about it, have a bad one and then start screaming about the snowplows."

That enhanced technology can improve the counting of ballots is undeniable, but even the best equipment leaves the vote tallies as approximates. Improved technology without, for instance, better training for election workers may prove hollow. Election workers ill trained in the new technology may proffer bad instruction to voters, misread machine counts, or mistreat sensitive computer technology. (It is worth noting that one of the problems with punchcard machines—chad build-up—has a low-tech solution, simply shake the machines of their chad occasionally. Most election workers seem not to know this, however.) More importantly, technology cannot save Americans from razor-thin elections. If one takes the best estimates of the systems' reliability, those provided by the manufactures of voting equipment, you are still left with doubts in very close elections. Most manufacturers of the more advanced voting systems claim that their machines are, when operated at optimal conditions, 99.99 percent accurate. Simple math demonstrates that even this highly optimistic estimate would have allowed for the miscount of 600 Florida votes in 2000. If the systems are only 99.9 percent accurate, the Florida vote could have been off by over 6,000 votes.

The fact is, counting votes is not as automatic or precise as Americans may wish. Marie Garber, an elections consultant, expressed it best when she said, "When I was a political activist, I used to go to bed and say, 'Please God, let my candidate win tomorrow.' When I became an elections official, after a couple of elections, I went to bed and said, 'Please God, whoever wins, let them win big.'"[28] Many election officials across the country share that prayer.

Recounting the Votes

The ballots have been counted and the race is razor close. What happens next depends on state law. In seventeen states automatic recounts are mandated when the margin of difference between the candidates is very small. Connecticut, Delaware, and New York, on the other hand, prohibit recounts. The remaining thirty states provide for recounts under varying conditions; many allow the recount on the basis of a request from the losing candidate. Vermont, for instance, specifies that if the difference between the number of votes cast for a winning candidate and the losing candidate is less than 5 percent of the total votes cast for all the candidates, the loser shall have the right to have the votes for that office recounted. Illinois, Louisiana, Minnesota, and Mississippi allow for recounts only as the result of a court order.[29]

Not surprisingly, given the decentralized nature of elections, the methods of conducting recounts also varies across the states. Twenty-seven states allow for hand recounts, while the remaining states that allow recounts provide that they can only be done by machine. Florida, for instance, has a law requiring mandatory recounts in very close elections, with a hand recount optional. Virginia, on the other hand, allows for a recount with the method of counting to be decided by a three-judge panel. Washington has one of the more detailed provisions regarding recounts. Under Washington law, if the margin of victory after the original count is 0.5 percent of the total vote cast, the statute requires a machine recount. If, however, the difference is 0.25 percent or within 150 votes, the law requires a hand recount.

What standards are to be used for these recounts? As with the original counts there is often little guidance from the states. Some states prohibit trying to determine the voter's intent, and some require poll workers to do just that. In short, the laws are no more specific on how to recount than count. Indeed in some cases they are even less specific. South Dakota, for example, simply requires that "the recount shall proceed as expeditiously as reasonably possible until completed."[30]

Breaking Ties   But what happens if after the count and a recount, the candidates are tied? As unlikely as this seems, ties do occur in American elections—usually in races for local office. In 1996, for instance, the election of a local judgeship in New Mexico resulted in a dead heat. New Mexico law provides that the winner can be decided by any means that would determine the winner by lot. (Dueling is specifically prohibited, however.) In this case the two candidates played a single hand of five-card draw poker. The best hand won the judgeship. As strange as this seems, most states have similar solutions to the problem.

California law is quite detailed on this issue, in that it provides that if at any election, except those for governor or lieutenant governor, "two or more persons receive an equal and the highest number of votes for an office to be voted for in more than one county, the Secretary of state shall . . . determine the tie by lot." The statute further provides that tied elections for offices contained within a single jurisdiction (i.e., county, city, or special district) may be decided by lot or by a special election called by the jurisdiction's legislative body. If the race for governor or lieutenant governor should end in a tie, California law provides that the winner shall be determined by a joint vote of both houses of the state legislature. Michigan laws are similar, but they even specify that the method of determination shall be a drawing. According to state statute, if two or more persons receive the same number of votes for one office, the county clerk shall prepare a number of slips of paper equal to the number of tied candidates and write the word "elected" on as many of them as there are offices to be filled and the words "not elected" on the remaining slips. The slips are then placed in a box from which the candidates shall each draw one slip. Any person drawing a slip on which is written "elected" is deemed to be legally elected to the office. Thus in the 2000 contest Mary Hanson won the office of Onota Township (Michigan) clerk when, after the voters produced a tie, her opponent Janelle Snyder reached into a genuine fox fur hat and drew the slip that said "not elected." Months of campaigning then may and on occasion does come down to a simple turn of chance.

Conclusions

Nothing better illustrates the patchwork nature of American elections than the multiple ways in which votes are cast and counted. Although all states use some form of the Australian ballot, there are a variety of versions in use. The states decide whether to use the office block or the party column format and whether or not to facilitate straight party voting. These may seem like small differences but they do have consequences for vote totals and voter turnout. The office block format encourages split-ticket voting, providing greater opportunities for candidates of the minority party. This is especially true if the ballot does not provide a straight party vote option. On the other hand, the office block seems to encourage voter roll-off, and thus for the less visible offices lower turnout. Similarly, states allocate positions on the ballots in different ways. While this may appear to be a trivial matter, for low visibility offices position on the ballot is worth votes. Several studies have indicated that under these conditions being listed first is advantageous. Again, while these differences may seem to be simply the minutia of elections they do have consequences.

The medium used by voters to cast their ballot also varies greatly across the country. Because states generally delegate the administration and the cost of elections to counties and local governments, there is substantial variability even within states. Most states use a variety of devices, based on county and local government decisions. Although the consequences of the different voting technologies are seldom recognized, the 2000 presidential election demonstrates amply how important this issue can be. To simply note that in 2000 the presidential election hinged on a simple thing like a chad, is to recognize that the differences in voting technology can and do make a difference. In this sense, the 2000 election only highlighted the reality of all elections.

Likewise, although most Americans assume that counting votes is straightforward and at least reasonably precise, the rules for vote counting look more like a patchwork quilt of vague or often contradictory mandates. Most states provide very little guidance to local officials, and as a result, the rules for election counting and recounting vary not just across states but across jurisdictions within states. Despite the Supreme Court's ruling in *Bush v. Gore*, it is not the case that votes are, even within a single state, counted the same way. Local election officials exercise a great deal of discretion here. Again this is not unique to the 2000 election or presidential elections, but a common reality in American elections. Candidates often win or lose elections based on how the votes are counted and what standards are used.

Endnotes

1. James A. Morone, *The Democratic Wish: Popular Participation and the Limits of American Government* (New Haven: Yale University, 1990), 110.
2. Jerold G. Rusk, "The Effect of the Australian Ballot Reform on Split ticket Voting: 1876-1908," *The American Political Science Review* 64 (December 1970): 1220-1238.
3. Angus Campbell, et al., *The American Voter* (New York: John Wile, 1960), 276.
4. V. O. Key, *Politics, Parties, and Pressure Groups*, 4th ed. (New York: Thomas Y. Crowell, 1958), 694.

5. Dirk Johnson, "Straight-Ticket Voting Losing Its Ease in Illinois," *The New York Times* (October 29, 1998): A-22.

6. Quoted in Richard Hofstadter, *The Age of Reform* (New York: Vintage Books, 1955), 266.

7. Jack L. Walker, "Ballot Forms and Voter Fatigue: An Analysis of the Office Block and Part Column Ballots," *Midwest Journal of Political Science* 10 (November 1966): 462.

8. D.S. Hecock and H. M. Bain, Jr., *The Arrangement of Names on the Ballot and Its Effect on the Voter's Choice* (Detroit: Wayne University Press, 1956).

9. Delbert A. Taebel, "The Effect of Ballot Position on Electoral Success," *American Journal of Political Science* 19 (August 1975): 519-526.

10. The reliance on the first Tuesday after the first Monday in November came in three steps. This formula for establishing election day was initially set in 1854 as the date for the appointment of presidential electors every fourth year. In 1875 Congress extended the practice by requiring that elections for members of the House be held on this date, every even numbered year. Then in 1914, the first Tuesday after the first Monday in November was fixed as the date for electing U.S. senators.

11. On this point, see Stephen J. Wayne, *Is This Any Way to Run a Democratic Election?* (Boston: Houghton Mifflin, 2000): 28-30.

12. At present twelve states make election day a holiday, but none of them require that the private sector observe the day. These twelve states, as well as many others that do not make the day a holiday, do require that private employers provide from one to three hours of paid leave for those who want to vote.

13. Nelson Polsby and Aaron Wildavsky, *Presidential Elections: Contemporary Strategies of American Electoral Politics* (New York: Free Press, 1991), 268-270.

14. See Laurily Epstein and Gerald Strom, "Election Night Projections and West Coast Turnout," *American Politics Quarterly* 19 (October 1981): 486; John Jackson, "Election Reporting and Voter Turnout," *American Journal of Political Science* 27 (November 1983): 633; Seymour Sudman, "Do Exit Polls Influence Voting Behavior?" *Public Opinion Quarterly* 50 (Fall 1986): 338; and Michael X. Carpini, "Scooping the Voters? The Consequences of the Networks' Early Call of the 1980 Presidential Race," *Journal of Politics* 46 (August 1984): 890.

15. For a fuller account of the history of absentee voting, from which this sketch was drawn, see Samuel C. Patterson and Gregory A. Caldeira, "Mailing in the Vote: Correlates of Absentee Voting," *American Journal of Political Science* 29 (November 1985): 766-788.

16. J. Eric Oliver, "The Effects of Eligibility Restriction and Party Activity on Absentee Voting and Overall Turnout, *American Journal of Political Science* 40 (May, 1996): 498.

17. Randy Hamilton, "American All-mail Balloting: A Decade's Experience," *Public Administration Review* 48 (1988): 860-866.

18. Oliver, "The Effects of Eligibility Restriction," 498-513.

19. Oliver, "The Effects of Eligibility Restriction," 510.

20. Jack L. Walker, "Ballot Forms and Voter Fatigue: An Analysis of the Office Block and Party Column Ballots," *Midwest Journal of Political Science* 10 (November 1996): 451 cites two studies making this point; John P. White, *Voting Machines and the 1958 Defeat of Constitutional Revision in Michigan* (Institute of Public Administration, University of Michigan, 1960); and George B. Mather, *Effects of the Use of Voting Machines on Total Votes Cast: Iowa 1920-1960* (Institute of Public Affairs, University of Iowa, 1964).

21. Hamilton, "American All-Mail Balloting," 860–868: and David Magleby, "Participation in Mail-ballot Elections," *Western Political Quarterly* 40 (1987): 79-93.

22. Priscilla L. Southwell and Justin I. Burchett, "The Effect of All-Mail Elections on Voter Turnout," *American Politics Quarterly* 28 (January 2000): 72-79.

23. Robin Toner, "The Elections Officials: Behind the Scenes, Its Old News that Elections are Not an Exact Science," *The New York Times* (November 17, 2000): 29.

24. John Mintz, "Most States Don't Count Dimples," *Washington Post* (November 24, 2000): A36.

25. Siobhan Gorman, "Florida times 50," *National Journal* 49 (December 2, 2000): 3724.

26. Quoted in Glenn H. Utter and Ruth Ann Strickland, *Campaign and Election Reform* (Santa Barbara, CA: ABC-CLIO, 1997): 9.

27. Richard Morin and Claudia Deane, "Public Backs Uniform U.S. Voting Rules," *The Washington Post* (December 18, 2000): A13.

28. Quoted in Gorman, "Florida Times 50," 3720.

29. Ibid., Gorman, "Florida Times 50," 3723.

30. Ibid., 3730.

Chapter 6
A Special Case Study: The Electoral College

We end this review of the rules of the game with a discussion of the electoral college and presidential elections. This uniquely American selection system is often vilified and a perennial target of political reformers. It has been variously described as archaic, an anachronism, a ticking time bomb, and a loaded pistol pointed at the head of the American people. One of its sharpest critics, Lawrence Longley, undoubtably spoke for many when he said:

> The American electoral college is a deplorable political institution. . . . If the electoral college were only a neutral and sure means of counting and aggregating votes, it would be the subject of little controversy. The electoral college, however, is neither certain in its operations nor neutral in its effects. . . . In short the electoral college is a flawed means of determining the president. Its workings at best are neither smooth nor fair, and at worst contain the potential for constitutional crisis.[1]

Whether Longley's judgment of the folly of maintaining the electoral college is warranted or unwarranted is debatable. All the more so after the 2000 elections. At the very least, defenders of the electoral college cannot respond to the critics with the retort, "If it ain't broke, don't fix it." Nevertheless, there are those who defend the institution.[2] What is particularly engaging about the electoral college, however, is that it embodies and highlights the importance of the rules. No one can doubt that presidential elections are profoundly affected by the workings of the electoral college. Moreover, the workings of the electoral college personify many of the characteristics of the American electoral system writ large. It is true, for instance, that presidential elections are held before an increasingly nationalized electorate, but it is also true that this electorate is filtered through the various states. While the qualifications for voting have been broadened with nationalization, presidential votes are still aggregated at the state level and those eligible to vote are defined by the states. It is the states, not a national majority, that presidential candidates must win and presidential campaigns must be structured to accommodate that fact. Wise or not, the electoral college illustrates the workings of a federal electoral system. Additionally, the electoral college draws in sharp relief the impact of a single-member, first-past-the-post electoral system. Discussion of the seats-to-vote ratio is particularly relevant to the electoral college.

An Overview of the Electoral College

Like all other aspects of American elections, the workings of the electoral college are dictated by a combination of U.S. Constitutional provisions, federal law, and state laws. Under Article II, Section 1 of the U.S. Constitution, each state is allocated a number of electors equal to its number of Senators and Representatives. (Since the ratification of the Twenty-third Amendment, in 1961, the District of Columbia has also had three electors.[3])

Article II further specifies that the electors shall be chosen in such manner as dictated by the individual states. Once selected the electors are required by the Constitution to meet in their respective states at a date and time dictated by Congress wherein they cast their ballots. Electors are further required to make a list of all persons voted for, itemizing the number of votes received by each person. This list is then certified and signed by the electors and transmitted to the president of the Senate (vice-president of the United States).

In the presence of both the House and the Senate, the certified ballots are opened and counted. The winner is the candidate with the most votes, providing that the total constitutes a majority of the electoral votes cast. If no candidate receives a majority of the electoral votes, the selection of the president is made by the House of Representatives, with each state having a single vote. The vice-president in these circumstances is selected by the Senate. This thumbnail sketch of the process does not portray the complexities of the rules, however.

The Electors

Article II of the U.S. Constitution gives the individual state legislatures the authority to select electors as they see fit, by specifying that, "Each State shall appoint, in such Manner as the Legislature thereof may direct, a Number of Electors, equal to the whole Number of Senators and Representatives to which the State may be entitled in the Congress. . . . " The only constitutional limitation is that " . . . no Senator or Representative, or Person holding an Office of Trust or Profit under the United States, shall be appointed an Elector."[4]

Not surprisingly this broad delegation of authority to the states produced diverse methods across states and time. Reviewing the various practices used by the states up to 1892, U.S. Supreme Court Chief Justice Fuller noted:

> that various modes of choosing the electors were pursued, as, by the legislature itself on joint ballot; by the legislature through a concurrent vote of the two houses; by vote of the people for a general ticket; by vote of the people

in districts; by choice partly by the people voting in districts and partly by the legislature; by choice by the legislature from candidates voted for by the people in districts; and in other ways, as, notably, by North Carolina in 1792, and Tennessee in 1796 and 1800.[5]

As Edward S. Corwin has pointed out, about the only method not tried is the selection of electors by lot, although the delegates to the Constitutional convention briefly contemplated a scheme that would have staffed the electoral college with members of Congress, selected by lot.[6] For the first three presidential elections, appointment by the legislature was the usual mode of selection, but by 1824 electors were chosen by popular vote either in districts or statewide in all but six states. Since 1832 the states, with few exceptions, have chosen electors by popular vote.[7]

Still, constitutionally it appears that state legislatures may use any method they choose to select electors; they may appoint them or delegate that authority to the executive, or even to private bodies.[8] It is highly unlikely that any state legislature would eliminate the popular election of electors. Nevertheless, this power was much discussed in 2000, when the Florida legislature, in the wake of the disputed presidential election, considered a special session to appoint a slate of electors. The call for legislative action ended when the U.S. Supreme Court intervened in the dispute and issued an order disallowing the Florida recount, thus removing a possible dispute over competing slates of electors.[9]

Nominating Electors   Before the presidential election takes place every state must certify a list of electors for each candidate. Of course, the procedures for doing so vary among the states. Twenty-nine states require that the political parties nominate their slates by party conventions. Six states and the District of Columbia call for the nomination by the central committees of the parties. Additionally, twelve states leave it up to the political parties to decide on the method. (Most of these states use the party conventions.[10])

Additionally, three other states make unique provisions for the nomination of electors. Pennsylvania, for example, provides that the presidential nominees shall name their party's electors. In Wisconsin, state law mandates that electors shall be nominated by a convention composed of the candidates for senate and assembly nominated by each political party at the primary, the state officers, and the holdover state senators of each political party. The members of this convention are required to nominate one presidential elector from each congressional district in the state and two at-large electors.

California, on the other hand, provides detailed and different procedures for the each party. With regard to Republican electors, state law provides that:

> the Republican nominee for Governor, Lieutenant Governor, Treasurer, Controller, Attorney General, and Secretary of State, the Republican nominees for United States Senator at the last two United States senatorial elections, the Assembly Republican leader, the Senate Republican leader, all elected officers of the Republican State Central Committee, the National Committeeman and National Committeewoman, the President of the Republican County Central Committee Chairmen's Association, and the chairperson or President of each Republican volunteer organization officially recognized by the Republican State Central Committee shall act as presidential electors, except that Senators, Representatives, and persons holding an office of trust or profit of the United States shall not act as electors.[11]

Any remaining vacancies are to be filled by appointment of the chairperson of the Republican State Central Committee.

On the Democratic side, California law provides that each congressional nominee of the party shall chose one presidential elector. Furthermore, each U.S. senatorial nominee, determined by the last two U.S. senatorial elections, shall designate one elector. If no senatorial or congressional nominee exists, the nomination is made by the state party chair. California law further specifies that electors of the American Independent Party are to be nominated by state convention.[12]

Provisions for nominating electors of third parties and independent candidates vary across the states. Generally, however, the states allow independent and minor party candidates to name their slate of electors at the time they file their petitions to appear on the ballot.

However the electors are selected, the result is much the same. Electors are individuals known for their commitment to the political party, their support of the nominee, or as is often the case, their generous financial contributions. Service as an elector is an honor used to reward the faithful, not a position of power.

The People Vote

With the nomination of electors in place, the voters get their turn at the selection process. On the first Tuesday after the first Monday in November, every four years the voters cast their ballot for president and vice-president. But, of course, what the voters are really voting for are the electors pledged to the candidates, not the candidates themselves. What makes this a mystery to many is that most states do not list the electors, only the presidential and vice-presidential candidates. Forty-three states and the District of Columbia use what is called the "presidential short ballot." This form of the ballot lists each pair of presidential and vice-presidential candidates and instructs the voter to select one pair.[13] Some states that use the short ballot do inform voters that they are voting for unseen electors. In the 2000 election, for instance, a voter in Virgina wishing to vote for George W. Bush and Dick Cheney would have seen a box identified as,

REPUBLICAN PARTY
Electors for
George W. Bush, President
Dick Cheney, Vice President

This same format was then repeated for the other five parties with candidates on the ballot.

The seven states not using the presidential short ballot list the electors and identify the candidate they support.[14] Voters are instructed to vote for the electors, usually as a block.[15]

Whether the electors are listed or not, in forty-eight states the vote for electors is statewide. The ticket receiving the plurality of votes picks up all the state's electoral votes. This so-called "unit rule" is simply an application of the winner-take-all, first-past-the-post practice discussed in Chapter 1. As such the unit rule illustrates, in sharp relief, the problem of the seats-to-votes ratio. Winning one of these forty-eight states, even by a single vote, earns all the electoral votes. Coming close in the state vote nets no seats (electors).

Two states, Maine and Nebraska, use what is called a "district plan." In Maine, for instance, each of the two congressional districts chooses an elector and the two remaining electoral votes are awarded to the ticket that receives the plurality of statewide votes. Thus a ticket may receive four electoral votes or one ticket may pick up three electoral votes, while the other ticket is awarded one elector. The Nebraska plan is the same, except that the state has three congressional districts. Of course, the district plan does not eliminate the seat-to-votes ratio problem, since it is still based on the winner-take-all, first-past-the-post principle. It does, however, lessen the impact of the winner-take-all formula because a candidate who loses statewide may still receive some electoral representation by winning a congressional district.

The Electors Vote

Federal law requires that as soon after the November election as is practicable the governor of each state is to send to the archivist of the United States a list of all electors and the number of votes they received. (An example of this list, called the "certificate of ascertainment" is presented in Figure 6.1) Thus shortly after the election, the archivist has available a complete list of candidates for elector, both successful and unsuccessful.

Title 3, Chapter 1 of the U.S. Code further specifies that the electors will meet in their respective states to cast their votes on the first Monday after the second Wednesday in December following the election.[16] On this day the electors gather in their states to cast their vote for president and vice-president. Originally Article II specified that the electors were to vote for two persons for the office of the presidency, at least one of whom was not an inhabitant of their state. The candidate receiving the most votes, so long as this number constituted a majority of the electoral votes cast, was elected president and the runner-up was proclaimed the vice-president. This practice of voting for two persons created problems as early as 1796. In that election some Federalist electors purposefully withheld votes from Adams' vice-presidential running mate, Thomas Pinckney, in order to prevent a tie between Adams and Pinckney (a tie would have thrown the election into the House of Representatives). Unfortunately for the Federalists, they withheld too many votes, giving the vice-presidency to Thomas Jefferson.[17] Then in 1800, perhaps having learned the lesson of 1796 too well, the electors of the Democrat-Republican party cast all of their votes for Thomas Jefferson and his intended vice-president Aaron Burr. The tie between Jefferson and Burr threw the election into the Federalist-dominated lame-duck Congress. Although it was well understood that Jefferson was the party's candidate for the presidency, the Federalist-dominated Congress attempted to sow discord among their opposition by casting several votes for Burr. (Many Federalists also saw Burr as a less formidable opponent than Jefferson.) As a result, the House deadlocked on the selection, with no candidate receiving a majority. On the thirty-sixth round Jefferson was finally selected when Alexander Hamilton announced that, "If there be a man in the world I ought to hate, it is Jefferson. With Burr I have always been personally well. But the public good must be paramount to every private consideration."[18] Hamilton's influence led many Federalists to abstain, giving ten states to Jefferson and four to Burr. Jefferson was thus elected president and Burr vice-president.

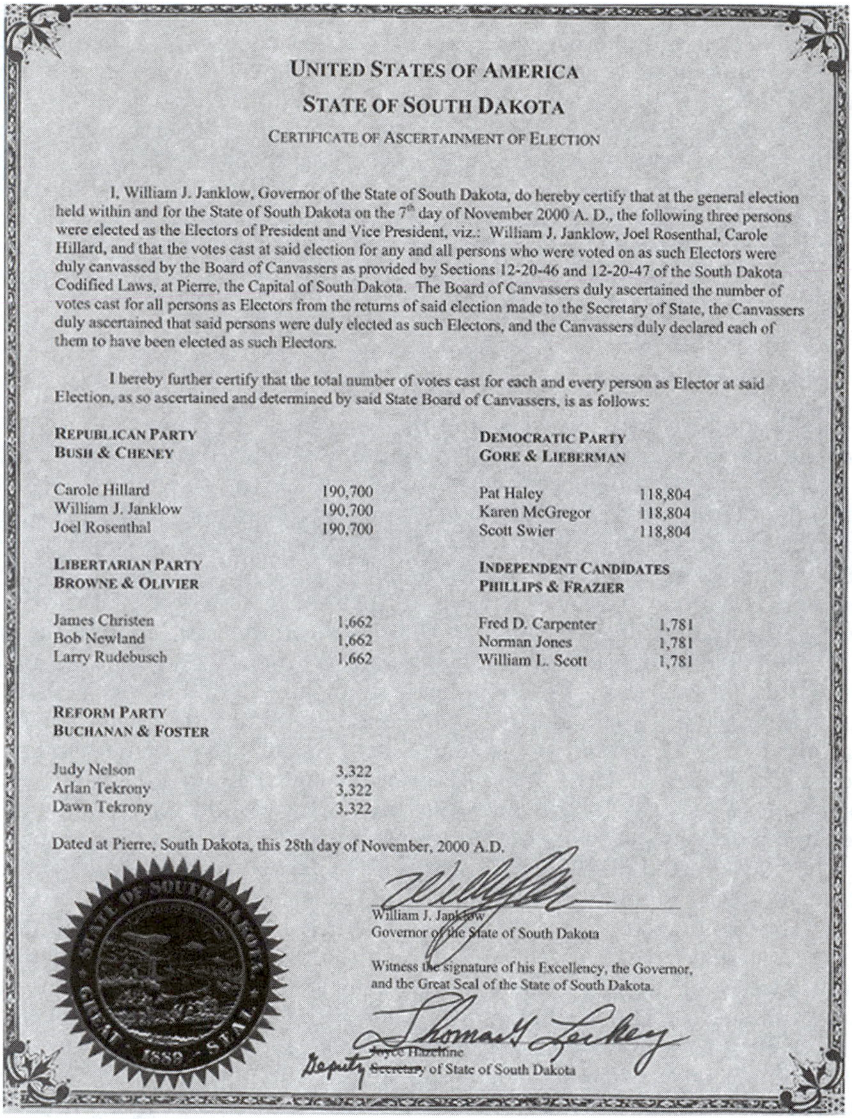

UNITED STATES OF AMERICA

STATE OF SOUTH DAKOTA

CERTIFICATE OF ASCERTAINMENT OF ELECTION

I, William J. Janklow, Governor of the State of South Dakota, do hereby certify that at the general election held within and for the State of South Dakota on the 7th day of November 2000 A. D., the following three persons were elected as the Electors of President and Vice President, viz.: William J. Janklow, Joel Rosenthal, Carole Hillard, and that the votes cast at said election for any and all persons who were voted on as such Electors were duly canvassed by the Board of Canvassers as provided by Sections 12-20-46 and 12-20-47 of the South Dakota Codified Laws, at Pierre, the Capital of South Dakota. The Board of Canvassers duly ascertained the number of votes cast for all persons as Electors from the returns of said election made to the Secretary of State, the Canvassers duly ascertained that said persons were duly elected as such Electors, and the Canvassers duly declared each of them to have been elected as such Electors.

I hereby further certify that the total number of votes cast for each and every person as Elector at said Election, as so ascertained and determined by said State Board of Canvassers, is as follows:

REPUBLICAN PARTY
BUSH & CHENEY

Carole Hillard	190,700
William J. Janklow	190,700
Joel Rosenthal	190,700

DEMOCRATIC PARTY
GORE & LIEBERMAN

Pat Haley	118,804
Karen McGregor	118,804
Scott Swier	118,804

LIBERTARIAN PARTY
BROWNE & OLIVIER

James Christen	1,662
Bob Newland	1,662
Larry Rudebusch	1,662

INDEPENDENT CANDIDATES
PHILLIPS & FRAZIER

Fred D. Carpenter	1,781
Norman Jones	1,781
William L. Scott	1,781

REFORM PARTY
BUCHANAN & FOSTER

Judy Nelson	3,322
Arlan Tekrony	3,322
Dawn Tekrony	3,322

Dated at Pierre, South Dakota, this 28th day of November, 2000 A.D.

STATE OF SOUTH DAKOTA GREAT SEAL 1889

William J. Janklow
Governor of the State of South Dakota

Witness the signature of his Excellency, the Governor, and the Great Seal of the State of South Dakota.

Thomas G. Leckey
~~Joyce Hazeltine~~
Deputy ~~Secretary~~ of State of South Dakota

FIGURE 6.1
Certificate of Ascertainment—South Dakota 2000 election

As a result of the election of 1800 the practice of voting for two persons for president was eliminated by the Twelfth Amendment which specifies that the electors are to:

> . . . vote by ballot for President and Vice-President, one of whom, at least, shall not be an inhabitant of the same state with themselves; they shall name in their ballots the person voted for as President, and in distinct ballots the person voted for as Vice-President, and they shall make distinct lists of all

persons voted for as President, and of all persons voted for as Vice-President, and of the number of votes for each, which lists they shall sign and certify, and transmit sealed to the seat of the government of the United States, directed to the President of the Senate. . . .

Since 1804 then, the electors have been directed to cast separate ballots for president and vice-president.

There is in the Twelfth Amendment a limitation carried over from Article II. Electors must cast at least one vote for a candidate not from their state. This does not mean that a president and vice-president must be from different states, only that electors may not vote for two candidates from their own state. Thus the Constitution encourages the practice long followed by the parties of nominating a presidential candidate from one state and a vice-presidential candidate from another. But, in an era of multiple residencies and easy mobility, this provision constitutes a minimal restraint on the electors. Illustrative of this is the litigation accompanying the 2000 election, where three Texas voters sought an injunction preventing the Texas electors from voting for both George W. Bush and Richard B. Cheney. Their suit alleged that Cheney was an inhabitant of the state of Texas. In denying the request for an injunction the U.S. District Court for the Northern District of Texas held that although Cheney had resided in Texas for some time, he had through a series of actions in July of 2000 demonstrated an intent to make Wyoming his place of habitation.[19]

When on the appointed day the electors cast their ballots, they complete the action by forwarding to the president of the Senate and the archivist of the United States a document called the "Certificate of Votes"[20] (see Figure 6.2). Although there is no specific form for the "Certificate of Votes," it must list all persons who received electoral votes for the president and the number of electors who voted for each person. The certificate must also list all persons who received votes for the vice-president and the number of electors who voted for each person. Finally, the certificate must be signed by all of the electors. It is the "Certificate of Votes" from each state that is read and counted before both houses of Congress that constitutes the official vote for president and vice-president.[21]

Faithless Electors

One of the anomalies of the electoral college is that although we assume that the electors will cast votes consistent with their state's election results, some electors have fallen short of expectations. This is often referred to as the faithless elector problem. The first faithless elector, one Samuel Miles, cast his 1796 vote for Thomas Jefferson rather than his fellow partisan John Adams. An outraged Federalist on learning of Miles' betrayal uttered the famous response: "Do I chuse Samuel Miles to determine for me whether John Adams or Thomas Jefferson shall be President? No! I chuse him to act, not think."[22] The early appearance of a faithless elector should not mislead us into believing that this is a frequent problem. To the contrary, only fourteen electors have cast their votes for president other than in accordance with the popular vote in their state.[23] (That is 14 faithless votes out of almost 20,000 electoral votes cast during the period.) Moreover, none of these votes have altered an election.

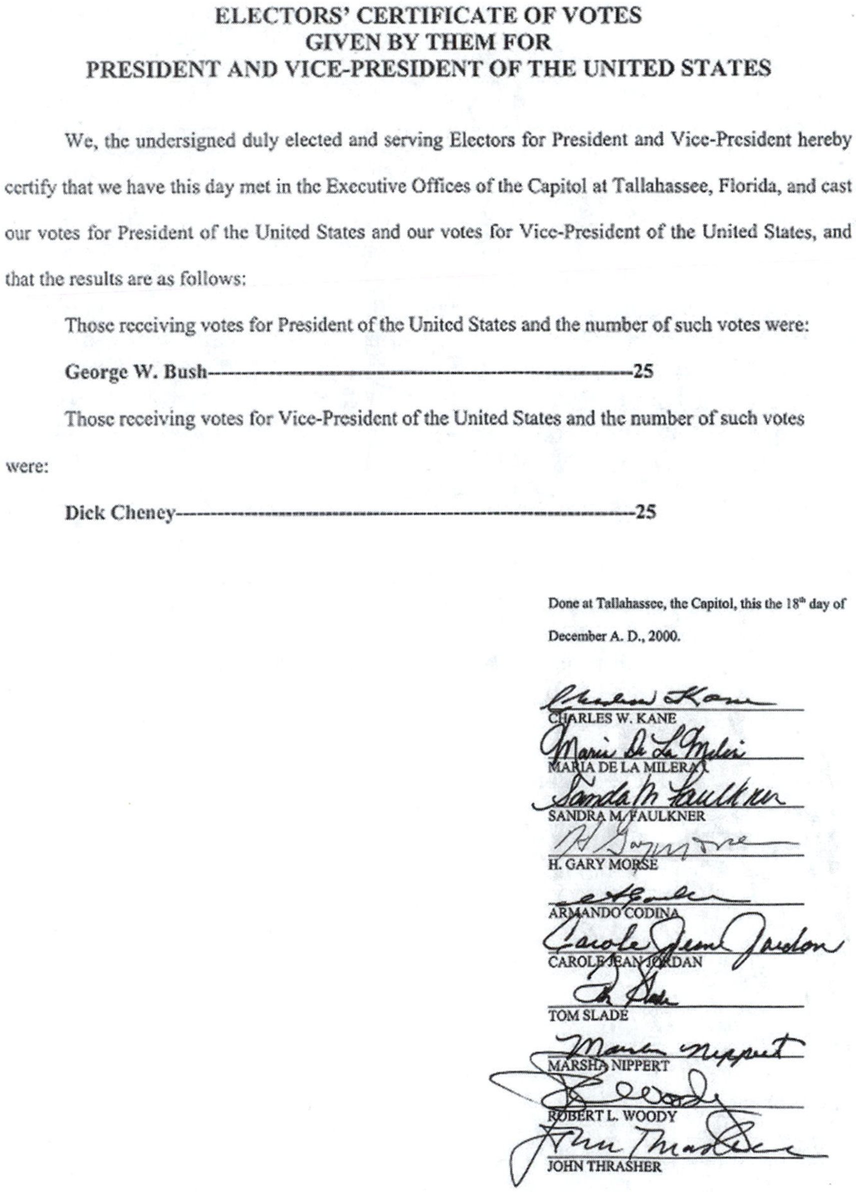

ELECTORS' CERTIFICATE OF VOTES
GIVEN BY THEM FOR
PRESIDENT AND VICE-PRESIDENT OF THE UNITED STATES

We, the undersigned duly elected and serving Electors for President and Vice-President hereby

certify that we have this day met in the Executive Offices of the Capitol at Tallahassee, Florida, and cast

our votes for President of the United States and our votes for Vice-President of the United States, and

that the results are as follows:

Those receiving votes for President of the United States and the number of such votes were:

George W. Bush--25

Those receiving votes for Vice-President of the United States and the number of such votes

were:

Dick Cheney---25

Done at Tallahassee, the Capitol, this the 18ᵗʰ day of

December A. D., 2000.

CHARLES W. KANE

MARIA DE LA MILERA

SANDRA M. FAULKNER

H. GARY MORSE

ARMANDO CODINA

CAROLE JEAN JORDAN

TOM SLADE

MARSHA NIPPERT

ROBERT L. WOODY

JOHN THRASHER

FIGURE 6.2
Certificate of Votes—Florida 2000 Election

MEL MARTINEZ

FELICIANO M. FOYO

AL HOFFMAN

ALFRED S. AUSTIN

THOMAS C. FEENEY, III

JOHN M. MCKAY

CYNTHIA M. HANDLEY

DARRYL K. SHARPTON

DR. ADAM W. HERBERT

BERTA J. MORALEJO

JEANNE BARBER GODWIN

DEBORAH L. BROOKS

DR. DORSEY C. MILLER

GLENDA E. HOOD

DAWN GUZZETTA

ATTEST:

SECRETARY OF STATE   _GOVERNOR_

FIGURE 6.2
Continued

Infrequent though the practice may be, the possibility of electors voting in opposition to their state's electorate excites great controversy. Twenty-seven states and the District of Columbia have some type of requirement binding electors to abide by the popular vote, but these statutes take varying forms. The most common provision is one that simply dictates that an elector shall vote for the party that nominated him or her. A second type of law requires that electors take an oath to vote for the party's candidates. Finally, some state statutes authorize the political parties to obtain a pledge of support from their electors.

Violations of these statutes seldom carry serious punishment. Indeed only five states even provide specific penalties for violating the obligation. (The largest fine permissible in any of these states is $1,000.) On the other hand, North Carolina, Michigan, and Utah stipulate that failure to vote for the party's candidates constitutes an immediate resignation as a matter of law. It is not clear whether these laws are constitutional, however. Several legal scholars claim that the Constitution intended electors to exercise independent judgment, but there is little consensus on this point.[24] The only U.S. Supreme Court decision even touching on the issue upheld the right of political parties to demand that electors take an oath to support the party, but the decision did not speak to the power to enforce such pledges, let alone state laws demanding compliance.[25]

The Role of Congress

With the electoral votes cast and the Certificate of Votes transmitted to the president of the Senate, the final step in the process belongs to Congress. On January 6th, the date set by federal law, the Certificates of Votes are opened, counted, and announced one state at a time in alphabetical order. The January 6th date in combination with the Twentieth Amendment ensures that the new Congress, not a lame-duck Congress, does the counting. Under the provisions of the Twentieth Amendment (ratified in 1933), the seating of the new Congress was moved from March 20 to January 3.

If at the conclusion of the count one person has the highest number of votes for president and that number constitutes a majority of the electoral votes (270), that person is duly elected president. The Twelfth Amendment specifies the same standards for the candidates for vice-president.

What If There Is No Majority?

Should no candidate receive a majority, the election is thrown into Congress. At this point the Senate would withdraw from the House, the Senate being charged with the selection of the vice-president, and the two houses are to immediately go about selecting the president and vice-president. Again the Twelfth Amendment is consequential in that it specifies that if no candidate receives a majority, the House shall choose from among a list of the top voter-getters, that list not to exceed three candidates. The Senate is similarly charged with selecting the vice-president, but it must choose from the "two highest numbers on the list."

At this point the selection process is determined by House and Senate rules and precedents. The rules that would most likely be followed are those laid down to decide the election of 1824—the last time that the Congress was required to settle an electoral college deadlock. Under these rules, the members of the House are to be seated together by state, and each state delegation is to be provided with its own ballot box. For the purpose of electing the president a quorum of the House exists when at least one representative from two-thirds of the states is present.

One particularly important aspect of the House rules is that the individual states must cast a majority of votes for a candidate. If no candidate receives a majority of a state's vote, the state is recorded as divided and casts no vote.[26] Under the Twelfth Amendment, no candidate may be elected without a majority of the states.[27] If no candidate receives a majority, the rules specify that the House is to continue balloting, without the interruption of other business, until a president is selected.

Over in the Senate, the process for choosing the vice-president is similar, except that the Senate chooses from the two top candidates and Senators vote individually, not as part of a state delegation. The Twelfth Amendment also prescribes that a quorum shall consist of two-thirds of the whole Senate. Conceivably then, a minority party holding at least thirty-five seats could block the selection of the vice-president by simply boycotting the proceedings.

If by noon of January 20th the House has not selected a president, the vice-president, if one has been elected, assumes the duties of the president until the House has made its choice. Should the Senate be unable to select the vice-president by that date, the Presidential Selection Act of 1948 dictates that the next in line for the presidency is the Speaker of the House, followed by the president pro tempore of the Senate. These officers could serve as acting president until the House or Senate had completed the election [28]

What If the Electoral College Votes Are in Dispute?

Disputes regarding the validity of electoral college votes cast were relatively frequent in the nineteenth century. Controversies arose over whether states were officially admitted to the Union before their votes were cast.[29] The procedures for readmission of the southern states after the Civil War also created clashes in the counting of electoral votes. These disputes tended to be handled by Congress in an ad hoc fashion.

Finally, in 1877 Congress provided a legal framework for dealing with disputed electoral college votes. The 1877 act places the burden of straightening out contested votes on the states. According to the statute, if a state uses a procedure for reaching a final determination resolving disputed votes that was established by state law passed prior to the date established for the appointment of electors, and the resolution occurred at least six days prior to the meeting of electors, that determination shall be conclusive. This is the so-called "safe harbor" provision that the U.S. Supreme Court invoked to end the Florida recount in the 2000 election.

Congress may overturn the state resolution, but only if both houses agree. As each state's electoral vote is read, the president of the Senate asks if there are any objections. A valid objection must be in writing, specifying the reasons for the objections, and it must be signed by at least one Representative and one Senator. If a valid objection is raised, the Senate withdraws to its own chamber and the two bodies separately debate and vote on the objection. The houses have two hours to resolve the issue. Unless both houses decide that the contested electoral vote or votes were not regularly given, the decision of the state prevails. Once the contested issue is resolved, the count of the states resumes.

This procedure was unsuccessfully invoked in 2001, when written objections to the Florida electoral vote were entered. These objections did not, however, have the signature of even one Senator. Lacking a senatorial signature, Vice-President Gore, the president of the Senate at the time, ruled each of the objections out of order and the count of the states continued.

If a state should forward more than one set of electors without a valid resolution according to state law, the Congress may decide which slate to count. If the two houses do not agree, the list of electors signed by the governor of the state will be counted.

Who Benefits from the Electoral College?

The distribution of electoral votes varies greatly among the states. Seven states and the District of Columbia each possess just 3 of the 538 votes. California, on the other hand, cast in 2000 54 votes, just over 10 percent of the electoral college vote. Theoretically, a candidate need only win the electoral votes of the eleven largest states (California, New York, Texas, Florida, Pennsylvania, Illinois, Ohio, Michigan, New Jersey, North Carolina, and Georgia) to win the election. To many observers then it is obvious that the largest states are benefitted the most by the system. On the other hand, these eleven largest states contained in 2000 57 percent of the nation's population, but they selected only 50.1 percent of the electors. The twenty-two smallest states made up 13 percent of the population, but chose 19 percent of the electors. The difference is due to the fact that each state, no matter what its population, is guaranteed a minimum of three seats—two Senators and one Representative. Looked at from this perspective, the small states seem overrepresented and thus benefit by the electoral college.

An alternative way of looking at the disparities is to compare voter power across the states. To what extent does the relative power of a vote cast depend on where it is cast? Several studies, using different methodologies, have attempted to estimate the relative power of citizens to affect the outcome.[30] Although the various studies have produced somewhat disparate results, there is a general consensus that voters in California have the most voting power. For example, Longley and Peirce estimate that the voters of California have over 2.5 times the relative voting power of those in Montana, the state they estimate having the least voting power.[31] George Rabinowitz and Stuart Elaine MacDonald reached a similar conclusion with regard to the relative advantage accruing to California voters, but their results, which take into account the electoral competitiveness of the states, indicates that Rhode Islanders have the least voting power.[32] The power rankings produced by the various studies differ in other particulars, but there is general agreement on the overall effect of the electoral college on voter strength. The system advantages residents of the largest states (so long as they are politically competitive) and, to a lesser extent, those in the smallest states. (Remember, as discussed in Chapter 1, the small states are also slightly advantaged by the Huntingdon apportionment system.) It is the residents of the medium-sized states that experience the least relative voting power through the electoral college.

The importance of the large, politically competitive states also works to advantage groups that are geographically concentrated within those states, as long as they demonstrate a degree of political cohesiveness. Thus urban and suburban residents in the large, politically competitive states have high relative

voting power. Given their concentration in some of the largest and most politically competitive states Hispanics enjoy considerable advantage in relative voting power. Their considerable numbers in Texas, California, and Florida suggest
that, if they vote as a group, they may have considerable influence on presidential elections. On the other hand, African Americans suffer relatively low voting
power under the electoral college. African Americans do benefit from urban and
suburban residency in some large, politically competitive states, but they are
also concentrated in states with low voting power (e.g., some southern states)
and in rural areas.

An even clearer example of beneficiaries of the electoral college are the two
major parties. Conversely, minor or third parties and independent candidates
are severely disadvantaged by the electoral college. Because the unit rule, as
applied in forty-eight states, makes the contest for electors a winner-take-all
proposition, it is very difficult for third parties and independent candidates to
garner sufficient votes to even make an appearance in the electoral college. In
1992, for instance, Ross Perot attracted an astonishing 19 percent of the popular vote, but he received no electoral college vote. Despite his strong national
showing, Perot was shut out of the electoral college because he did not win a
single state. Of course, third-party candidates have won electors, but the conditions under which they have are instructive. In 1948 Strom Thurmond and the
States' Rights party (also known as the Dixiecrats) won just 2.4 percent of the
popular vote nationally. Nevertheless, Thurmond received thirty-nine electoral
votes, just over 7 percent of the electoral college votes that year. What made the
difference is that Thurmond and the States' Rights party was a regionally based
coalition. Appealing to southern voters, Thurmond managed to win four
states—Louisiana, Mississippi, Alabama, and South Carolina. This illustrates the
dilemma for third parties and independents. They can win electoral votes, but
generally that requires that their appeal be geographically concentrated. If, on
the other hand, they seek to appeal nationally, they run the risk of ending up
like Perot—a good run in several states, but nothing to show for it.

This problem is further confounded by the difficulty that third parties and
independents face just getting on the ballot. Because this is a state-by-state task,
third parties and independent candidates need to exert substantial resources to
get on enough ballots to be competitive in the electoral college. Moreover, as
the Reform Party learned, getting on the state ballots in one election does not
guarantee a place at the next election. Although the Reform Party made it on all
fifty state ballots in 1996, it automatically qualified to appear on only seventeen
state ballots in 2000.

None of this is to suggest that third parties cannot be important participants
in the election of presidents under the electoral college. To the contrary, third
parties may play a momentous role as a spoiler. By drawing votes away from one
of the major party candidates in a few key states, it is possible that a third party
can alter the election. Theodore Roosevelt's run for the presidency in 1912 as a
Bull Moose split the Republican party and deprived its nominee, William
Howard Taft, of the election. In 2000 many Democrats attributed Al Gore's loss
in a few key states, particularly Florida, to Ralph Nader's presence in the election. Most preelection polls predicted that more than half of Nader's supporters
would have, if he were not on the ballot, voted for Gore. Obviously, if true that
would have made a difference in Florida. But the spoiler role is not one that nur-
tures a party. A third party limited to the spoiler role cannot last. Indeed the

accusation that major party candidates throw at third parties is that they cannot win, and that a vote for a third party is a wasted vote. The idea that a vote for a third party is a wasted vote is often tough to counter. For one thing, it has a self-fulfilling quality to it. If a third party does not win in one election, it often finds it harder to rally the forces for another run. Few financial contributors are willing to donate to parties that have slim chances of winning. Unable to shake the image of a wasted vote, third parties also find it difficult to recruit quality candidates. As William Riker pointed out, " . . . a potential leader buys a career. And as a rational purchase he has no interest in a party that may lose throughout his lifetime."[33]

From 1968 through 1988 Republican presidential candidates won five of the six elections. Furthermore, they won with some very impressive electoral college totals. So consistently did the Republicans win some states that many analysts began to talk about the "Republican lock on the electoral college." Indeed, as the 1988 election approached it became common wisdom among journalists and pundits that the Republican party advantage in the electoral college was all but unbeatable.[34] The argument was that the Republicans began the election cycle with so many small states firmly committed to them, the Democrats could win only if they took almost every state not firmly in the Republican column. This is, of course, a version of the seats-to-vote ratio problem discussed in Chapter 1. There was assumed to be a substantial pro-Republican bias in the seats-to-vote ratio; one so considerable that even large increases in the Democrat's popular vote could not assure electoral victory. One estimate suggested that the Democrat would need a minimum of 52 percent of the popular vote to capture a majority of the electoral vote. Not everyone has accepted the theory of the Republican lock, however. In fact, James C. Garand and T. Wayne Parent have argued that rather than favoring the Republicans, the seats-to-vote calculations for the electoral college manifest a decidedly Democrat advantage.[35] More recent analysis of the 1996 election results suggests that if there is a bias it is very small.[36] Nevertheless, the 2000 results will surely reopen this question.

Campaigning under the Electoral College

As even a cursory examination of the electoral college makes clear, presidential elections are the amalgamation of fifty-one separate elections, one in each state and the District of Columbia. Although presidential candidates strive to do well in the popular vote, it is the electoral college vote that they must win. Campaign strategists fashion messages and approaches that have national appeal. Indeed, given the attention paid by the national media they could hardly do otherwise. Nevertheless, campaign planners are always mindful that a winning strategy is built state by state. Set against the national appeal for voters are issues and presentations designed to appeal to specific states and regions. In the end, winning states, not a national electorate, is still the priority.

Choosing the Candidates

Because it is the electoral vote that counts, common wisdom has it that it is always advantageous to start with a candidate from a large swing state. The assumption is that candidates possess a "home state advantage"—a natural edge over an out-of-state rival. Logically, it follows that if voters in presidential elections tend to favor the home state candidate, the best candidates are those coming from large swing states where the most electoral votes are to be found. As it turns out this bit of political wisdom seems to be true. Even though candidates do not always win their home state (e.g., Al Gore in 2000), they do benefit from a home state advantage. After examining all presidential elections from 1884 to 1980, Michael Lewis-Beck and Tom Rice concluded that presidential candidates can count on an increase of about 4 percent in the home state over what would otherwise be expected. This advantage is greater in small states, but candidates from large states also benefit from the phenomenon.[37]

A 4 percent increase is not large. Still, in a close race it can make the difference between winning and losing. Consider the case of the 1968 election. Richard Nixon narrowly defeated Hubert Humphrey in a three-way race that also included George Wallace as a third-party candidate. As California's native son, Nixon received a home state advantage of 3.6 percentage points, enough to give him a slim victory in this electoral rich state. If Nixon had lost California no candidate would have had a majority of the electoral college vote and the election would have been thrown into the House of Representative where the Democrats controlled a majority of state delegations.[38] Even small advantages when strategically placed can have momentous consequences.

A similar logic is often applied to the selection of vice-presidential running mates. Political strategists have generally accepted the notion that to win a ticket needs to be balanced. Although balance can mean many things (e.g., ideology, religion, government experience) the dominant factor historically has been region. Between 1952 and 1980, for example, fifteen of the sixteen major party tickets showed regional balance. Only six demonstrated an ideological balance, five a religious balance, and seven balanced candidate experience (legislative vs. executive).[39] Similarly in the elections between 1884 and 1984, only 5 of the 52 major party tickets (Republicans in 1936 and 1976 and Democrats in 1900, 1908, and 1948) were not regionally balanced—and in four of these the party lacking regional balance lost. The emphasis on regional balance is based on the assumption that vice-presidential candidates, like presidential candidates, receive a home state advantage. This perception of a home state advantage explains why vice-presidential candidates have, like presidential candidates, been so likely to come from the electorally rich large states.[40]

Unlike presidential candidates, vice-presidential candidates are not the beneficiaries of a home state advantage, however. It is true that from 1884 to 1984, presidential candidates carried their running mate's state almost two-thirds of the time, but according to Robert Dudley and Ronald Rapoport, the vice-presidential candidate's home state advantage averaged only 0.3 percent. In only three elections (Muskie in 1968, Stevenson in 1892, and Mondale in 1980) did the vice-presidential candidate's presence on the ticket make the difference.[41] Despite the common wisdom, vice-presidential candidates increase on average neither the two-party vote nor their ability to carry their home state. It is the presidential candidates, not their running mates, who dominate electoral politics. Given the success enjoyed by tickets not regionally balanced in the last three elections, it may be that this bit of political folklore has been abandoned.

Designing the Campaign

When asked why he robbed banks, the notorious bandit Willy Sutton is reported to have replied simply, "That's where the money is." Why do presidential candidates campaign where they do? Because that's where the electoral votes are. As Nelson Polsby and Aaron Wildavsky have pointed out, the first rule must be, "campaign in states with large numbers of electoral votes."[42] Operating with finite resources, campaigns must allocate them effectively, and that means that they must be ever mindful that it is the electoral college that must be won. In general this means that the campaigns deploy their resources disproportionately in the largest states. Steven Brams and Morton Davis have offered as a rule of thumb for campaign allocation: the 3/2's rule. According to their analysis, campaign resources should be allocated in proportion to the "3/2's power" of the electoral vote for each state. The 3/2's power is calculated by taking the square root of a state's electoral votes and cubing it. The result is that " . . . candidates . . . should not simply allocate [their resources] on the basis of the electoral votes of each state but rather should allocate decidedly more proportionately to large states than to small states. For example, if one state has four electoral votes, and another state has sixteen electoral votes, even though they differ in size only by a factor of four, the candidates should allocate eight times as much in resources to the larger state. . . . "[43]

While there is some empirical evidence suggesting that presidential campaigns do in fact allocate resources roughly approximating the 3/2's rule, other strategic considerations are also important. No candidate since Richard Nixon in 1960 has campaigned in every state, including Richard Nixon in 1968 and 1972. Nor have candidates always campaigned heavily in every large state.

If the first rule of a presidential race is, "campaign in states with large numbers of electoral votes," a corollary to the rule is: never expend great resources in states that are not going to be close. Because, under the unit rule, there is no reward for second place in a state, candidates must decide where their efforts will make the most difference. It makes little sense to spend a lot of time and effort in even a very large state if the history of the state and the candidate's polling indicate that it is not winnable. There is no extra penalty for losing a state by a big margin, close or not, all the electoral college votes go to the plurality winner. Al Gore demonstrated the corollary in 2000 by paying little attention to Texas. With little chance of beating the Texas governor, Gore largely ignored this very rich electoral vote state. Similarly George W. Bush, although at times predicting he would take California, spent proportionally little time and resources in the state, because his campaign did not feel that they could overcome Gore's lead. He spent even less time in New York, another state firmly in the Gore camp. The corollary also works the other way. Candidates do not want to campaign heavily in states where they have a big lead. Thus in 1996 when Dole became convinced that he could not win in Illinois he withdrew his ads and redirected his money elsewhere. In response, Clinton also withdrew his Illinois ads. Adding extra votes to the margin in a state does not increase electoral votes.

The task for campaign strategists then is to pare down the fifty states to a smaller list of contested states and allocate resources to those where the campaign can make a difference. But this list will vary from election to election and candidate to candidate. In close elections, states that might otherwise be ignored may become prime targets of one or both candidates. During the 2000 election, for instance, both candidates paid a great deal of attention to Arkansas, even though it only had six electoral votes. Because neither candidate had a lock on the electorally rich states, both spent considerable time and effort wooing voters in some states, like Arkansas, that are traditionally given only cursory attention.[44]

But even this simplifies the problem. Candidates may campaign in states for reasons other than the electoral vote. Robert Dole, late in the 1996 race, expended a great deal of effort in California even though his polls showed Clinton with a substantial lead. Dole's efforts were probably aimed at helping the Republicans maintain control of the U.S. House of Representatives.[45]

In the end the electoral college, and particularly the unit rule, has a powerful pull on the shaping of presidential campaigns. But it should not be viewed in a vacuum. Campaigns are exercises in uncertainty. No campaign organization is so skillful that it can pinpoint a few selected states. As Richard Scammon and Ben Wattenberg caution:

> It is extremely difficult, and probably impossible, to move 32,000 votes in a New Jersey Presidential election without moving thousands and ten of thousands of votes in each of the other forty-nine states. The day of the pinpoint sectional or statewide campaign is gone—if it ever existed—and the fact that voters cannot be gathered in bushels on specific street corners is of crucial significance when one looks at the arithmetic of the future.[46]

The point is well taken. American elections and presidential elections in particular have, in the last few decades, experienced significant nationalizing forces. Nevertheless, if the electoral college is not the sole source of presidential campaign imperatives, it is still a powerful influence.

Reforming the Presidential Election System

Calls for reform of the presidential electoral system have become common in American politics. In the wake of the 2000 election, however, the calls have become intense. Indeed on the eve of the general election in 2000, two members introduced a constitutional amendment to abolish the electoral college. Of course, this was not the first such proposal, nor is abolition the only suggested alternative. Over the course of American history some version of four different plans have been repeatedly offered for congressional consideration. The most attention has been paid to what is generally called the direct election plan, a plan that would abolish the electoral college and make the winner the candidate receiving the most popular votes. Another proposal presenting something of a compromise between retention of the electoral college and its abolishment is the proportional plan. Under this scheme the electoral votes would be retained, but candidates would receive a proportion of each state's vote based on the percent of the popular vote in the state. A third alternative, the district plan, would also keep the electoral votes for each state but apportion them according to the plurality winner in each congressional district, plus two votes for winning the state. (In other words, the district plan currently used by Maine and Nebraska.) The final proposal, the bonus plan would keep the electoral college system intact, but award an extra 102 (two for each state and the District of Columbia) votes to the candidate who won the national vote.

Clearly the most popular method of reform is the direct election plan. Under this system, the electoral college would be abolished and the winner of the presidential election would be the candidate receiving a plurality of the popular vote nationwide. In many ways this is the simplest plan. It also appeals to a great number of Americans because it is seen as the most democratic system. Most certainly the direct election plan eliminates the possibility of a candidate winning without a plurality of the national vote. Under this plan there would be no possibility of a repeat of the elections of 1824, 1876, 1888, and 2000—all elections in which the winner of the popular vote lost the election in the electoral college.

As simple as the direct election plan seems, it does raise a couple of implementation questions that must be answered. First of all, anyone advocating the direct election plan needs to address the question of how large a popular vote would be necessary in order to win the presidency. Of course, this is not at issue in a two-candidate race, but with more candidates comes the real possibility that the plurality winner receives far below a majority. How far is acceptable? Most proposals for direct election incorporate the American Bar Association's recommendation that a successful candidate receive at least 40 percent of the vote. If no candidate receives this minimum vote, a run-off election between the two top vote getters would take place. Usually the plans specify a run-off two weeks after the general election. Some supporters of direct election have suggested that the plan incorporate an instant run-off feature. An instant run-off requires the voters to rank the candidates, but only the first-place votes are counted. If after the first tally of votes no candidate has met the threshold (say 40 percent), the candidate with the smallest number of first-place votes is eliminated and the top choice on each ballot is tallied again. Thus for those who ranked the eliminated candidate first, their second-place vote is counted. This procedure is repeated until one candidate receives enough votes to meet the minimum percent required to be elected. Instant run-offs have the advantage of eliminating the need for a second campaign, but this comes at some cost. Obviously, the voters' decisions are more complicated under an instant run-off system and that may discourage voting. More importantly, however, by encouraging voters to think strategically, instant run-offs may distort the voters' true preferences.[47]

A proposed constitutional amendment to implement the direct election system passed the House of Representatives in 1969. Over the next ten years the Senate held a variety of hearings on the plan, finally culminating in passage by a 51 to 48 vote, well short of the two-thirds needed to put it to the states.

The proportional plan keeps the electoral college in place, but it apportions the votes to the candidates based on the percent of vote they received in the statewide election. There are two different versions of this plan. One would divide the electoral votes to the nearest whole, while the other would divide them to the nearest tenth. Although more complicated than the direct election, the proportional plan appears to many a natural compromise between the current system and its abolition. Assigning electoral votes proportionally lessens the seats-to-vote ratio problem inherent in the unit rule, and allows every vote to count. It does not prevent electoral college deadlock, however. Neither version of this plan would have produced a majority vote in the electoral college in 1968, throwing the election into the House of Representatives. Similarly, dividing electoral votes to the nearest tenth would have produced a deadlock in 1960.

A third option, the district plan, would give one electoral vote to the candidate who won each congressional district within a state. The two extra votes in each state would go to the candidate winning a plurality of the statewide vote. In other words, the district plan would eliminate the unit rule used by forty-eight states. Because the unit rule is dictated by state laws, this plan could be easily implemented by the individual states. It seems unlikely, however, that the states would voluntarily abandon the unit rule. Most states believe that their power is maximized by casting their votes as a block, especially if other states retain the unit rule. Although Maine and Nebraska use this system, convincing most states to reduce their voting power in the electoral college is bound to be difficult.

Moreover, the district plan dramatically increases the significance of redistricting and further rewards creative gerrymandering. Cracking and packing congressional districts (see Chapter 1) takes on added importance when presidential electors are at stake.

In the final analysis, however, the weakest element of the district plan may well be that it does not guarantee the election of a popular vote winner. Indeed it is entirely plausible under this system that in a close election the runner-up wins.

Finally, the bonus plan first proposed by the 20th Century Fund (now called the Century Fund) would leave the electoral college in place. In addition to the 538 votes awarded by the electoral college, the bonus plan would automatically award another 102 electoral votes to the candidate receiving a plurality of the national vote, two for each state plus the District of Columbia. (These votes would be awarded to the plurality winner providing the plurality was at least 40 percent of the vote.) Structured this way, presidential candidates would be encouraged to seek as many votes as possible, even in states that they could not win. Similarly, voters would, even in states where their candidate could not win, have a reason to vote. Moreover, unlike the current system, it would be virtually impossible for the runner-up in the popular vote to be elected. It is highly unlikely that any runner-up in the popular vote could put together a coalition of states strong enough to overcome the 102 votes awarded the popular vote winner.

Election Outcomes under the Various Plans

To compare these plans, Table 6.1 presents the outcomes of seven modern elections. The first point to note regarding the electoral college is its tendency to magnify the winner's margin of victory. In 1996, for instance, Clinton's 8 percent margin over Dole translated into 72 percent of the electoral vote. Of course, in 2000 the electoral college elevated the runner-up in the popular vote to the presidency. Bush lost the popular vote by some 500,000 votes but won 271 electoral votes. Obviously, under the direct election plan Gore would have won the election. As would be expected, Gore would have also won if the bonus plan had been in effect. Indeed, under the bonus plan, Gore would have translated his narrow popular vote lead into over 57 percent of the electoral vote. In all other instances the bonus plan simply magnifies the margin of victory produced by the electoral college.

Table 6.1 also shows that given the popular vote returns for these elections, the proportional plan would have produced six elections without a clear winner.

TABLE 6.1 Presidential Election Outcomes under Alternative Plans

Election	Electoral College	Direct Election	Proportional Plan*	District Plan†	Bonus Plan
2000	**Bush wins** Bush 271 Gore 266 One blank vote	**Gore wins** Gore 48.4% Bush 47.9% Others 3.7%	**No one wins a majority** Bush 259.4 Gore 258.4 Others 20.3	**Bush wins†** Bush 271 Gore 266 One blank vote	**Gore wins** Gore 368 Bush 271 One blank vote
1996	**Clinton wins** Clinton 379 Dole 159 Perot 0	**Clinton wins** Clinton 49.2% Dole 40.7% Perot 8.4%	**No one wins a majority** Clinton 262.1 Dole 222.0 Perot 45.2	**Clinton wins** Clinton 345 Dole 193 Perot 0	**Clinton wins** Clinton 481 Dole 159 Perot 0
1992	**Clinton wins** Clinton 370 Bush 168 Perot 0	**Clinton wins** Clinton 43.0% Bush 37.4% Perot 13.9%	**No one wins a majority** Clinton 231.1 Bush 202.2 Perot 101.8	**Clinton wins** Clinton 324 Bush 214 Perot 0	**Clinton wins** Clinton 472 Bush 168 Perot 0
1988	**Bush wins** Bush 496 Dukakis 111 Others 1	**Bush wins** Bush 53.4% Dukakis 45.6% Others 1.0%	**Bush wins** Bush 288.1 Dukakis 245.1 Others 4.5	**Bush wins** Bush 377 Dukakis 159 Others 0	**Bush wins** Bush 528 Dukakis 111 Others 1
1976	**Carter wins** Carter 297 Ford 240 Others 1	**Carter wins** Carter 50.1% Ford 48.0% Others 1.9%	**Unclear‡** Carter 269.5 Ford 258 Others 10.5	**No one wins a majority** Carter 269 Ford 269 Other 0	**Carter wins** Carter 401 Ford 240 Others 1

TABLE 6.1 (Continued)

Election	Electoral College	Direct Election	Proportional Plan*	District Plan	Bonus Plan
1968	**Nixon wins** Nixon 301 Humphrey 191 Wallace 46	**Nixon wins** Nixon 43.4% Humphrey 42.7% Wallace 13.5%	**No one wins a majority** Nixon 233.8 Humphrey 223.2 Wallace 78.8	**Nixon wins** Nixon 289 Humphrey 192 Wallace 57	**Nixon wins** Nixon 403 Humphrey 191 Wallace 46
1960	**Kennedy wins** Kennedy 303 Nixon 219 Others 15	**Kennedy wins** Kennedy 49.7% Nixon 49.6% Others 0.7%	**No one wins a majority** Kennedy 264.8 Nixon 263.5 Others 7.7	**Nixon wins** Nixon 278 Kennedy 245 Others 15	**Kennedy wins** Kennedy 405 Nixon 219 Others 15

This is an updated version of a table constructed by Nelson W. Polsby and Aaron Wildavsky, *Presidential Elections: Strategies and Structures of American Politics* (New York: Chatham House, 2000), 251.

*Divided to the nearest tenth.

†These are preliminary results based on unofficial aggregation of counties to congressional districts. See Tom Squitieri, "Changes to Electoral College Would Not Alter Outcomes," *USA Today* (December 15, 2000): 8A.

‡Whether there is a winner or not depends on the definition of a majority. If a majority is defined as any number higher than 269.1, then Carter wins; otherwise the race remains undecided.

No candidate in these six elections earned a majority of the electoral votes. The district plan would have left the 1996 election uncertain, and on two occasions, 1960 and 2000, it would have elevated the runner-up to the presidency.

As instructive as comparisons like those presented in Table 6.1 are, it is important to recognize that they distort the political reality in a least three ways. First, by using the results of an election to predict how the candidates would have fared under a different system, such comparisons assume that the candidates would have campaigned the same way and that the voters would have responded the same way, no matter which system was in place. This is an assumption that simply cannot be supported. Candidates clearly design campaigns to maximize their advantages under whatever system is in place. Like Willy Sutton, candidates will go to wherever the votes are. Change the electoral system and candidates will alter their campaign strategy. Voters are also affected by the electoral system in place. Different systems may, for instance, motivate some voters and discourage others. Secondly, a comparison of expected outcomes from different presidential electoral systems tends to treat presidential elections in isolation from the larger electoral process. Finally, finite comparisons like this assume that there are no unintended consequences attached to change. As many a reformer has learned, there are always unanticipated and unintended consequences to political change.

Implementing the direct election system, for instance, shifts the electoral advantage away from the large states. By putting a premium on the popular vote margin, not the electoral votes, the importance of the large, politically competitive states is diminished. Because no candidate can be expected to carry these states by wide margins, medium-sized, one-party states, where political organizations can deliver a large turnout, are likely to be advantaged. Moreover, direct election of the president is unlikely to advantage small states, even if dominated by a single party, because there are too few votes available. Shifting the advantages enjoyed by the states means that campaign strategies will adjust to the new realities. Presidential candidates will allocate their resources to take account of the new rules.[48]

One change that is likely under the direct election system is a greater emphasis on television advertising and less reliance on personal appearances. The way in which TV time is purchased would also undergo change. Under the electoral college system, the candidates target particular states and concentrate much of their TV spending on local stations. These local ad buys, called spot ads, constitute almost all of the television advertising purchased by candidates. Network buys are few because they are expensive and largely wasteful because the candidate spends a great deal of money on voters in states that are not competitive. The need to reach a national audience under the direct election system would necessitate shifting advertising to the more expensive networks buys. This additional expense would place new pressure on the nation's campaign finance laws. The pressure may well grow disproportionally because the direct election plan also affects interest groups. With less emphasis placed on targeting particular states, interest group "issue advocacy" activities would need to take a more national scale and the race for contributions would become even more intense.

This issue of campaign finance is also relevant because the direct election system requires a run-off election if no candidate receives a threshold percentage (usually 40 percent). Currently, the campaign finance laws make no provision for a presidential run-off. Obviously this omission can be corrected, but the need to address the issue demonstrates the interrelationship of all aspects of American elections.

Of greater concern to many observers of American elections is the prospect that the direct election would encourage the growth of third party and independent candidates. Some believe that the direct election would encourage the multiplicity of parties and candidates all hoping to send the election into a run-off, where they could negotiate with the major candidates, extracting some advantage for their support. Visions of numerous groups and candidates running in the first election, only to recombine during the run-off may or may not be realistic. It is true, however, that the electoral college system (at least when combined with the unit rule) discourages third parties and splinter groups from contesting the election.[49]

It is unlikely that the direct election system would have much impact on the nominating process of the political parties. All things considered, candidates from large states would probably still be advantaged in the nomination process. Presidential hopefuls might approach the primaries differently, however. Because the direct election removes some of the barriers to running as an independent, it is conceivable that a presidential hopeful who did well in the party's primaries, but not well enough to win nomination, might be encouraged to leave the party and run as an independent. John McCain's 2000 bid offers an illustration of this scenario. McCain won some primaries, but mostly in states with open primaries, his greatest strength was in attracting Democrats and Independents. Despite his popularity, McCain would have had little chance of succeeding as an independent candidate under the electoral college. But a direct election system might have encouraged him to run as an independent, hoping that a multicandidate field might allow him to slip into a run-off.[50] At the very least the prospect of such an undertaking may encourage candidates to stay in the race for the nomination longer. The longer they stay in the race the better able they are to gauge their chances at the general election.

Direct elections of president may also have an effect on voter turnout, but analysts disagree on the nature of that effect. Many argue that voter turnout for presidential elections would increase under the direct system. Because all votes would be counted, regardless of where they were cast, voters would feel empowered by the change. Additionally, if the direct election produced more candidates (third parties and independents) voters might well be energized by a wider array of choices. On the other hand, some students of voting believe that the direct election would reduce voter turnout. Defenders of the current system argue that the direct election system would reduce turnout because a national campaign would devalue grassroots campaigns designed to energize groups of voters. A national campaign conducted largely on TV would, they charge, generate less voter interest. In the final analysis it is unclear just what effect the direct plan would have on voter turnout, but the probability is high that it would alter the makeup of the electorate in presidential election years. No matter what direction this alteration took, other candidates on the ballot would also feels its effect.

The direct election plan's promise of counting every vote equally is a powerful force in a democratic nation, but it is important to keep in mind that the promise cannot be fulfilled by simply abolishing the electoral college. A direct election plan that leaves in place the substantial variability among the states on other crucial questions of election laws does not produce a national election, only a national tally of votes. As we have seen, the states decide who is on the ballot, what the ballot looks like, who may vote, and how the votes are to be counted. If the goal is a national presidential election, reform needs to proceed well beyond abolishing the electoral college.

Because the proportional plan keeps the electoral college it probably has less effect on the current practice of electoral politics than the direct plan. Nevertheless, because the proportional plan weakens the role of the large states, candidates would of necessity change their campaign strategies. Inasmuch as the large states tend to be politically competitive, the proportional system would lessen their power within the electoral college. The large states would present fractured electoral counts, while many smaller one-party states would present unified electoral slates, not drastically different than those presented under the unit rule. Presidential campaigning would certainly become more difficult. Moreover, third parties and independent candidates would again have a real incentive, because even small fractions of votes translate into electoral votes. The district plan seems even more problematic. It would fall heaviest on the large competitive states, but more importantly it would put a real premium on the drawing of districts. With votes being awarded on the basis of congressional district, the distortions present in the seats-to-vote ratio take center stage in presidential elections. The electoral power of one party states, or those most ingenuously designed to maximize the strength of one party, are clearly advantaged under this system.

Conclusions

Clearly the electoral college is not a neutral institution. The rules of the presidential election under the electoral college advantage certain groups and disadvantage others. Voters in large states and to a lesser extent those in the small states enjoy significantly more voter power than those in the medium-sized states. Certain groups within those states may also possess voting power greater than their numbers would predict. The clearest winners, of course, are the two major political parties. So long as the unit rule is the norm for selecting electors, third parties and independents will find the electoral college hostile to their political fortunes. Furthermore, there is no question that the electoral college defines how American presidential campaigns are conducted. Presidential campaign activities are carried out in the shadow of the electoral college. Desiring victory candidates shape their activities and expend their resources in ways dictated by the mathematics of the electoral college. Moreover, voter responses are shaped by the way the electoral college affects campaigning. Because candidates target states, the voters receive different levels of exposure to the candidates and even different messages. The simple fact is that what a voter sees of a presidential campaign depends mostly on where the voter lives. The state-by-state campaign follows the federal nature of American politics. The presidency may be a national office, but it is won one state at a time, and not in a national referendum.

Suggestions for reforming the presidential election system lay bare a simple fact of elections. There is no such thing as a neutral selection system. Each of the proposed alternatives favors some interests and disfavors others. This shifting of advantages among states, groups, and parties would alter the way campaigns are conducted and the incentives for voters to participate. Some of these

changes can be predicted, but because every reform has unanticipated consequences it is impossible to predict all of the ramifications of the reform proposals. Candidates and would-be candidates will always play to the rules given them
and voters can only respond to the choices presented to them.

An examination of the electoral college also reveals the intricacy and interre-
latedness of electoral rules. Changes in the electoral college transform many
other aspects of American elections. The tendency to see presidential elections
as national elections understates the role of the federal system in the electoral
process. Although shifting to the direct election of the president may contain
considerable merit, it will not create a national election. At least, it will not do
so alone. So long as the states define the voters and the candidates, and the
means of casting and counting votes, presidential elections will still be state
affairs. American elections have over the course of history become more nationalized activities, but there is still substantial state variation that cannot be erased
by changing only part of the process.

Endnotes

1. Quoted in Judith Best, *The Choice of the People? Debating the Electoral College*
   (Lanham, MD: Rowman and Littlefield, 1966).
2. See particularly, Judith Best, *The Case Against Direct Election of the President: A
   Defense of the Electoral Collage* (Ithaca: Cornell University Press, 1971); and Martin Diamond, *The Electoral College and the American Idea of Democracy* (Washington: American Enterprise Institute for Public Policy Research, 1977).
3. The amendment provides that the District of Columbia shall have the number of
   electors equal to the number of Senators and Representatives it would have if it
   were a state. The amendment goes on, however, to provide that this number shall
   never exceed the number of electors allocated to the least populous state.
4. This provision is open to some interpretation, because it is not clear whether
   the prohibition extends to all federal officials. Does it, for instance, apply to anyone who is employed, at any level, by the national government? In the election
   of 1876 this provision became an issue when Oregon appointed as one of its
   electors a local postmaster. Fearing that his positions as postmaster and elector
   conflicted with the Constitution, the appointee resigned as an elector and then
   resigned as postmaster. Using the Oregon law providing for the filling of vacancies among the electors, the remaining Republican electors promptly reap-
   pointed him. This particular electoral vote was contested before the Electoral
   Commission, but the issue was limited to whether the vacancy to which the former postmaster was appointed ever existed. The commission did not take up
   the issue of whether serving as a postmaster disabled one from serving as an
   elector.

   Because this issue has never been tested, the National Archives and Records
   Administration, the agency charged by Congress with administering the electoral
   college, advises the states that the restriction "could disqualify any person who
   holds a Federal government job from serving as an elector." National Archives and
   Records Administration, "Responsibilities of the States in the Presidential election." Posted on the National Archives web site, www.nara.gov.
5. *McPherson v. Blacker*, 146 U.S. 1, 29 (1892).
6. See Edward S. Corwin, *The President: Office and Powers 1787-1957*, 4th ed.
   (New York: New York University Press, 1957), 38-39.

7. The few exceptions to popular election after 1832 included South Carolina until 1860, Florida in 1868, and Colorado in 1876.

8. This position was announced in *McPherson v. Blacker*, 146 U.S. 1 (1892), but see also *Burroughs v. United States*, 29 U.S. 534 (1934). Only Justice William O. Douglas has even hinted that the power may not be absolute. In *Williams v. Rhodes*, 393 U.S. at 38 Justice Douglas said, "It is unnecessary in this case to decide . . . whether states may select [electors] through appointment rather than by popular vote, or whether there is a constitutional right to vote for them."

9. *Bush v. Gore*, 531 U.S. 98 (2000).

10. For a discussion of these procedures and a table categorizing the method used in each state, see Walter Berns, ed., *After the People Vote: A Guide to the Electoral College* (Washington, DC: American Enterprise Institute, 1992), 10–11 and Appendix C.

11. California Election Code, Section 7300.

12. California Election Code, Sections 7100 and 7578, respectively.

13. The constitutionality of the presidential short ballot was upheld by a federal court in *State ex. rel. Hawke v. Myers*, 4 N.E. 2d 387 (Ohio, 1936). The court held that the voter did not have a constitutional right (under Article II, Section 1 of the U.S. Constitution) to have the names of the electors listed.

14. The seven states not using the presidential short ballot are: Arizona, Idaho, Kansas, North Dakota, Oklahoma, South Dakota, and Tennessee.

15. Although no write-in candidate for the presidency has received enough votes to qualify for electoral votes, the states do provide for such a contingency. State laws provide that the candidate selects the slate following the election.

16. Federal law allows the states to decide where in the state the meeting is to take place, but it does not permit the states to choose an alternate date for the meeting.

17. This is discussed in Richard J. Ellis, *Founding the American Presidency* (Lanham, MD: Rowman and Littlefield, 1999), 114.

18. Quoted in Norman J. Ornstein, "Three Disputed Elections," in Berns, ed. *After the People Vote*, 360.

19. The court took into consideration several actions taken by Cheney. The court noted for instance that he had changed his voter registration from Texas to Wyoming, that he had acquired a Wyoming driver's license, and that he had informed the Secret Service that his primary residence was to be his home in Jackson, Wyoming. *Jones v. Bush*, 122 F. Supp. 2d 713. On appeal to the U.S. Supreme Court, certiorari denied, January 5, 2001.

20. Although the Constitution's reference to ballot might be assumed to mean a secret vote, this is seldom the case among electors. Indeed, states require an oral vote from their electors. On this point, see Lawrence D. Longley and Neil R. Peirce, *The Electoral College Primer* (New Haven: Yale University Press, 1999), 113–14.

21. To further safeguard against loss of the original certificate federal law requires that two copies of the certificate be kept by the secretary of state of the state and one copy is to be sent to the Chief Judge of the U.S. District Court where the electors meet.

22. Quoted in Best, *The Case Against Direct Election of the President*, 39.

23. This total includes the blank vote cast by an elector from the District of Columbia in the 2000 election. The blank ballot was in protest of the lack of congressional representation for the District of Columbia.

24. For a complete discussion of this problem, summarizing both sides, see James C. Kirby, Jr., "Limitations on the Power of State Legislatures Over Presidential Elections," *Law and Contemporary Problems*, 27 (1962); 495; and Beverly J. Ross and William Josephson, "The electoral College and the Popular Vote," *Journal of Law*

and Politics 12 (Fall, 1996): 665. The last article discusses the use of the Fourteenth Amendment as an enforcing mechanism to be used against "faithless electors." The authors conclude that the Fourteenth is not an adequate authority authorizing enforcement of state laws binding electors. In light of the U.S. Supreme Court's invocation of the Fourteenth Amendment to end the Florida recount in the 2000 election, this argument may be renewed. See *Bush v. Gore* (2001).

25.   *Ray v. Blair,* 343 U.S. 154 (1952).

26.   As Walter Berns points out, this could be changed because it is only a House rule and not a constitutional requirement. See Berns, *After the People Vote,* 21.

27.   Interestingly, although the District of Columbia is granted three Electoral College votes by the Twenty-third Amendment, its delegates, not being representatives, would have no vote in the process.

28.   Of course, it is conceivable that neither the speaker of the House nor the president pro tempore of the Senate would accept the job. Article I of the Constitution prohibits members of Congress from holding both a legislative and executive office—this is known as the incompatibility clause. In order for the speaker of the House or the president pro tempore of the Senate to accept the role as acting president that person would have to resign from Congress. If both declined to resign from Congress, the acting president would be selected from the cabinet of the outgoing administration in an order dictated by law. Because cabinet officers remain in office until they resign or are discharged by the president, the succession would be limited to those already serving. This provocative possibility is discussed, at length, by Berns, *After the People Vote,* 23-24.

29.   The elections of 1817, 1821, and 1837 produced extended congressional wrangling over this issue. These controversies involved the votes cast by Indiana, Missouri, and Michigan, respectively.

30.   Longley and Peirce, *The Electoral College Primer;* John F. Banzhaf, "One Man 3.312 Votes: A Mathematical Analysis of the Electoral College," *Villanova Law Review* 12 (1968): 304-332; Howard Margolis, "Probability of a Tie Vote," *Public Choice* 31 (1977): 15-138; Howard Margolis, "The Banzhaf Fallacy," *American Journal of Political Science* 27 (1983): 321-326; Guillermo Owen, "Evaluation of a Presidential Election Game," *American Political Science Review* 69 (1975): 947-953; and George Rabinowitz and Stuart Elaine MacDonald, "The Power of the States in U.S. Presidential Elections," *The American Political Science Review* 80 (March 1986): 65-87.

31.   Longley and Peirce, *The Electoral College Primer,* 141-146.

32.   George Rabinowitz and Stuart Elaine MacDonald, "The Power of the States in U.S. Presidential Elections," *The American Political Science Review* 80 (March, 1986): 65-87.

33.   William H. Riker, "Duverger's Law Revisited," in Bernard Grofman and Arend Lijphart, eds., *Electoral Laws and Their Political Consequences* (New York: Agaton Press, 1986), 40.

34.   For one of the better accounts of the Republican lock, see William Schneider, "An Insider's View of the Election," *Atlantic Monthly* (1988): 29-57.

35.   James C. Garand and T. Wayne Parent, "Representation, Swing, and Bias in U.S. Presidential Elections, 1982-1988, *American Journal of Political Science* 35 (November 1991): 1011-1031.

36.   Paul R. Abramson, John Aldrich, and David W. Rohde, *Change and Continuity in the 1996 and 1998 Elections* (Washington: Congressional Quarterly Press, 1999), 57-59.

37. Michael S. Lewis-Beck and Tom Rice, "Localism in Presidential Elections: The Home State Advantage," *American Journal of Political Science* 27 (August 1983): 548–556.
38. Lewis-Beck and Rice, "Localism in Presidential Elections," 551.
39. Joel K. Goldstein, *The Modern American Vice Presidency* (Princeton: Princeton University Press, 1982), 69.
40. Danny M. Adkison, "The Electoral Significance of the Vice Presidency," *Presidential Studies Quarterly* 12 (1982): 334.
41. Robert L. Dudley and Ronald B. Rapoport, "Vice Presidential Candidates and the Home State Advantage: Playing Second Banana at Home and on the Road," *American Journal of Political Science* 33 (May, 1989): 537–540.
42. Nelson W. Polsby and Aaron Wildavsky, *Presidential Elections: Contemporary Strategies of American Electoral Politics* (New York: Free Press, 1991), 227.
43. Steven J. Brams and Morton D. Davis, "The 3/2's Rule in Presidential Campaigning," *The American Political Science Review* 68 (March 1974): 121–122.
44. George W. Bush, for example, made eight personal appearances in Arkansas during the campaign. This was a substantial commitment to a state with only six electoral votes, but then the election was extremely close.
45. Paul R. Abramson, John H. Aldrich, and David W. Rohde, *Change and Continuity in the 1996 and 1998 Elections,* (Washington: Congressional Quarterly Press, 1992), 51.
46. Richard M. Scammon and Ben J. Wattenberg, *The Real Majority: An Extraordinary Examination of the American Electorate* (New York: Coward McCann, 1970), 213.
47. Under certain conditions, for instance, ranking the most preferred candidate first may hurt that candidate's chances of winning.
48. See Polsby and Wildavsky, *Presidential Elections,* 247.
49. For a concise summary of this view, see John F. Bibby, *Politics, Parties, and Elections in America* (Chicago: Nelson-Hall Publishers, 1996), 229.
50. Alexis Simendinger, James A. Barnes, and Carl M. Cannon, "Pondering a Popular Vote," *National Journal* (November 18, 2000): 3656.

Index

Note: Page numbers followed by "t" refer to tables.